.NET Gotchas

Other Microsoft .NET resources from O'Reilly

Related titles

Programming C#
C# Cookbook
Learning C#
C# in a Nutshell
Learning Visual Basic .NET

Programming Visual Basic
.NET
VB.NET Language in a
Nutshell
Visual Studio Hacks

.NET Books Resource Center

dotnet.oreilly.com is a complete catalog of O'Reilly's books on .NET and related technologies, including sample chapters and code examples.

ONDotnet.com provides independent coverage of fundamental, interoperable, and emerging Microsoft .NET programming and web services technologies.

Conferences

O'Reilly & Associates bring diverse innovators together to nurture the ideas that spark revolutionary industries. We specialize in documenting the latest tools and systems, translating the innovator's knowledge into useful skills for those in the trenches. Visit *conferences.oreilly.com* for our upcoming events.

Safari Bookshelf (*safari.oreilly.com*) is the premier online reference library for programmers and IT professionals. Conduct searches across more than 1,000 books. Subscribers can zero in on answers to time-critical questions in a matter of seconds. Read the books on your Bookshelf from cover to cover or simply flip to the page you need. Try it today with a free trial.

.NET Gotchas

*75 Ways to Improve Your C#
and VB.NET Programs*

Venkat Subramaniam

O'REILLY®

Beijing · Cambridge · Farnham · Köln · Paris · Sebastopol · Taipei · Tokyo

.NET Gotchas
by Venkat Subramaniam

Copyright © 2005 O'Reilly Media, Inc. All rights reserved.
Printed in the United States of America.

Published by O'Reilly Media, Inc., 1005 Gravenstein Highway North, Sebastopol, CA 95472.

O'Reilly books may be purchased for educational, business, or sales promotional use. Online editions are also available for most titles (*safari.oreilly.com*). For more information, contact our corporate/institutional sales department: (800) 998-9938 or *corporate@oreilly.com*.

Editor:	John Osborn
Development Editor:	Ralph Davis
Production Editor:	Philip Dangler
Cover Designer:	Ellie Volckhausen
Interior Designer:	Marcia Friedman

Printing History:

May 2005:	First Edition.

 This book uses RepKover™, a durable and flexible lay-flat binding.

ISBN: 0-596-00909-7

[M]

To my teachers: Mr. J. Govindaswamy, Dr. Dayalan, Mrs. Kranti Ramakrishnan, and Professor N. Venkateswaran, who spent countless hours to motivate, inspire, and turn me around. I dedicate achievements in my professional life to you.

—Venkat Subramaniam

Table of Contents

Preface

If you've picked up this book, you're probably among the many programmers who have come to appreciate how powerful the Microsoft .NET Framework can be as a platform for development. But you've also learned that, as with any platform, .NET has quirks that can trip up even the savviest programmer. Have you been surprised by feature behavior in the .NET language or the .NET Framework—including the CLR and Framework Class Library—or in Visual Studio .NET? If you've worked with .NET for any length of time, I suspect you are nodding your head with a sigh of agreement. Experience teaches us what to do and what to avoid, but in programming, we commonly acquire our knowledge the hard way: by making costly, hard-to-debug and time-consuming mistakes. My goal in writing this book is to save my fellow developers from some of that pain, by sharing the experiences (and bad code) that brought the pitfalls of .NET to light for me, and showing you how to avoid them (and write code that works).

I started working with .NET when it was in pre-release Beta 2. The following years have been a lot of fun. However, there have been days (and nights) when things were not so obvious, when the code would behave, shall I say, strangely, given my expectations as an experienced developer.

The gotchas and guidelines presented in this book have come from three sources: First, the insights I have gained from developing .NET applications. Second, the questions raised by the hundreds of inquisitive software developers I've had the privilege of training. Third, the thought-provoking articles and discussions I have come across at symposiums, user-group meetings, the Internet, as well as the MSDN documentation itself.

What's a *gotcha*? According to Merriam-Webster, gotcha is defined as follows:

```
"Main Entry: got·cha
Pronunciation: 'gä-ch&
Function: noun
Etymology: alteration of got you
: an unexpected usually disconcerting challenge, revelation, or catch."
```

For me, *.NET gotchas* are those things that pop up unexpectedly when you're programming in .NET. Things that are buried, just waiting for you! It is as if the environment is there, aware of its own idiosyncrasies, watching you as you work, but unable (or unwilling) to warn you as you fall into one of its traps.

I'm not talking about those little annoying quirks in Visual Studio that make it misbehave occasionally, nor the transient flaws you see while working with the debugger or editor. In this book, I focus on the .NET Framework and language features that have consistently exhibited behavior that was not obvious to me. Why should you be interested in learning about these? Because knowing these little gotchas will help you avoid mistakes. You'll develop applications more quickly. Some solutions will improve the performance of your applications. Others will help you stay clear of problems that will make your code incorrect. Yet others will help you with hidden problems such as proper garbage collection.

Most books on .NET start by assuming that the reader knows little about it. Those books are intended to bring readers up to speed with .NET or one of its associated languages. As more and more people learn to use any technology, a need arises not just to learn how use it, but how to use it well, and do things *right*. Because experience is our best teacher, it always takes a few years for books that address those needs to appear.

Consider my own case, some years ago. I had taken the time to learn the C# language and was a serious developer (or so I thought), working hard to put the features and facilities of the language to prudent use. One day in the early '90s, I walked into my colleague's office and found a book entitled *C++ FAQs* by Marshal Cline on her table. Picking it up, I asked "Why would anyone who *knows* C++ read a book that lists questions and answers?" She smiled. I flipped through a few pages, and before I knew it, I found I had been standing there for several minutes reading the book, page after page. She finally interrupted and said, "Why would anyone who *knows* C++ be reading that book for so long?" I found it to be invaluable and bought a copy for myself (and I still have that book and its next edition in my library!) Other great books that I have enjoyed reading are *Effective C++* and *More Effective C++* by Scott Meyers, *Essential COM* by Don Box et al., and *Effective Java* by Joshua Bloch.

Programming in .NET has entered a stage where a large number of developers have learnt how to program what was a brand new platform only a few years ago. The time has arrived for books that teach good practices. I hope this book will serve, like the classics on COM and C++ that have preceded it, to educate software developers on the dos and don'ts of programming the .NET platform.

Who This Book Is For

This book is intended for the .NET programmer in the trenches. This includes both C# and VB.NET programmers. I assume that you are fairly familiar with .NET programming using either C# or VB.NET. I also assume that you are acquainted with the terms and vocabulary used by Microsoft in describing the .NET platform. In addition to programmers, project leads and senior programmers may find this book helpful in setting standards and guidelines for their development teams.

How This Book Is Organized

.NET Gotchas is organized into eight chapters, each focusing on a different area of interest in .NET. Each item has a name, title, and includes code examples, discussions, and guidelines "In a Nutshell." The items are grouped into the area that I find to be the most appropriate. At the end of each item, related gotchas are referenced for your convenience. The examples are presented in both C# and VB.NET (clearly marked so you can easily identify these without having to examine the code). The code is labeled with the directory where you can find the example when you download the source code from the online resource. The output shown is from the C# code, unless the output from C# differs from the VB.NET output, as is the case in a few gotchas. Where they are different, both the C# output and the VB.NET output are shown and discussed.

CLR/FRAMEWORK GOTCHAS

The Common Language Runtime (CLR) and the .NET framework provide programmers with a high level of abstraction and ease of use. They pave the way for writing code, more or less consistently, in any of the different languages supported by .NET. However, there are aspects of both that are confusing, misleading, or prone to misuse. Also, certain features and choices can impact the behavior or performance of your code. In this chapter I focus on those issues.

VISUAL STUDIO AND COMPILER GOTCHAS

The translation of your source code into Microsoft Intermediate Language (MSIL) is the job of the C# and VB.NET compilers. However, there are things that are "lost in the translation." While .NET allows you to develop code in the language of your choice, there are things that certain compilers do not look out for. In this chapter I discuss issues that will surprise you in the area of program compilation and the use of Visual Studio for development. Also, you will learn about the inconsistencies between the different language compilers.

LANGUAGE AND API GOTCHAS

.NET languages support object-oriented development, while avoiding some of the perils of powerful (but treacherous) languages like C++. Unfortunately, the .NET languages have introduced features that lead to poor object-oriented practices. Furthermore, while your experience with other languages may lead you to expect that certain features will behave in familiar ways, with .NET you will learn that this is not always so.

LANGUAGE INTEROPERABILITY GOTCHAS

The MSIL is the core language of .NET. Code written in different .NET supported languages is translated into MSIL. This provides you the ability to interoperate with code written in different languages in a powerful and useful way. You can use the .NET language of your choice—the one that you are most comfortable with. Your team can mix different languages in developing your system. While all this sounds terrific, are there any issues that will get in the way? In this chapter you will learn the issues that can affect your efforts to interoperate between .NET languages.

GARBAGE COLLECTION GOTCHAS

.NET provides automatic garbage collection. There is nothing we have to do or worry about in terms of object lifetime. Just sit back and relax, we're told. Does that sound too good to be true? While garbage collection is automatic, it may not do its work on the schedule you might prefer. As long as you are dealing with only managed resources this is not a problem. However, the reality is that you must often contend with unmanaged resources, which the CLR won't know how or when to clean up. In this chapter you will learn about the various issues related to garbage collection and how to write code that works correctly.

INHERITANCE AND POLYMORPHISM GOTCHAS

Inheritance and polymorphism are core features in object-oriented programming. Compared to other object-oriented languages, .NET has introduced keywords and facilities that are either new or different. While these were provided with good intent, some are misleading. Not understanding these features can affect the extensibility of your code and make it harder to derive from your classes. In this chapter you will learn what to avoid and how to use other features related to inheritance and polymorphism.

MULTITHREADING GOTCHAS

Creating a thread is easy; managing it is another story. How do you take care of thread safety? Should you create your own thread or use a thread from the thread pool? How are exceptions handled in multithreaded applications? What other issues do you need to think about when creating a .NET multithreaded application? This chapter will help you understand the fundamental issues that can make a difference between the success or failure of a multithreaded application.

COM-INTEROP AND ENTERPRISE SERVICES GOTCHAS

If you have to work with legacy code, .NET and COM interoperability is of interest to you. The COM-Interop facilities provided in .NET make this task almost seamless, and putting it to use appears pretty simple. However, to use COM-Interop correctly, you need some forethought and planning. If you think using a COM component from .NET is simple, think again. You need to fully understand issues related to the apartment of the thread, the resource cleanup, and the layering of your application. How do you expose your .NET components for COM interoperability? Should you just turn on the Visual Studio settings to register the type library? What do you need to do to make this effective? In this chapter you will learn how to effectively interoperate between .NET and COM.

What You Need to Use This Book

I developed the gotchas in this book through my explorations of .NET Framework 1.1 and the language versions, tools, and compilers that accompany it, all of which are available in any edition (beyond the Standard Edition) of Visual Studio 2003. You will need Visual Studio 2003 and .NET Framework 1.1 to run my examples. I have also tested each of the gotchas with .NET 2.0 Beta 1 (a.k.a. Whidbey) and have noted any changes in behavior. If you are using a later .NET 2.0 Beta, your experience may differ from mine, depending on the build version you are using. Comments on .NET 2.0 are based on Beta 1, which is subject to change. I think it is inappropriate to comment on the behavior of a product while it is in Beta 1, so I have not added any new gotchas spotted when working with .NET 2.0 Beta 1.

Measure of Performance

Occasionally, I compare the speed of execution of a code example with the speed of execution of an alternative way of implementing the same logic. The performance comparison is simply empirical and has been done on a Dell Latitude C640 with a 2 GHZ Pentium 4 processor, 512 MB of RAM, and a 40GB hard drive running Windows Server 2003 Standard Edition. In running these comparisons, I used Visual Studio .NET 2003 with .NET 1.1. Nothing else intensive was being executed while measuring the performance.

Conventions Used in This Book

The following typographical conventions are used in this book:

Plain text
> Indicates menu titles, menu options, menu buttons, and keyboard accelerators (such as Alt and Ctrl).

Italic
> Indicates new terms, URLs, email addresses, filenames, file extensions, pathnames, directories, and Unix utilities.

Constant width
> Indicates commands, options, switches, variables, attributes, keys, functions, types, classes, namespaces, methods, modules, properties, parameters, values, objects, events, event handlers, XML tags, HTML tags, macros, the contents of files, or the output from commands.

Constant width bold

> Shows commands or other text that should be typed literally by the user.

Constant width italic

> Shows text that should be replaced with user-supplied values.

 This icon signifies a tip, suggestion, or general note.

 This icon indicates a warning or caution.

Several code examples used in this book illustrate errors or problems, and are not intended to be used as-is. To remind readers of this, I have marked those "gotcha" code examples with a ✗ in the code heading. Usable, gotcha-free code is marked with a ✓.

I've also provided several bibliographic resources in the Appendix. When referring to these sources in the main text, I have bracketed the author names as a citation. See the Appendix for full bibliographic information.

Using Code Examples

This book is here to help you get your job done. In general, you may use the code in this book in your programs and documentation. You do not need to contact us for permission unless you're reproducing a significant portion of the code. For example, writing a program that uses several chunks of code from this book does not require permission. Selling or distributing a CD-ROM of examples from O'Reilly books *does* require permission. Answering a question by citing this book and quoting example code does not require permission. Incorporating a significant amount of example code from this book into your product's documentation *does* require permission.

We appreciate, but do not require, attribution. An attribution usually includes the title, author, publisher, and ISBN. For example: ".*NET Gotchas* by Venkat Subramaniam. Copyright 2005 O'Reilly Media, Inc., 0-596-00909-7."

If you feel your use of code examples falls outside fair use or the permission given above, feel free to contact us at *permissions@oreilly.com*.

Comments and Questions

Please address comments and questions concerning this book to the publisher:

O'Reilly Media, Inc.
1005 Gravenstein Highway North
Sebastopol, CA 95472
(800) 998-9938 (in the United States or Canada)
(707) 829-0515 (international or local)
(707) 829-0104 (fax)

We have a web page for this book, where we list errata, examples, and any additional information. You can access this page at:

http://www.oreilly.com/catalog/netgotchas

To comment or ask technical questions about this book, send email to:

bookquestions@oreilly.com

For more information about our books, conferences, Resource Centers, and the O'Reilly Network, see our web site at:

http://www.oreilly.com

Safari® Enabled

 When you see a Safari® Enabled icon on the cover of your favorite technology book, that means the book is available online through the O'Reilly Network Safari Bookshelf.

Safari offers a solution that's better than e-books. It's a virtual library that lets you easily search thousands of top tech books, cut and paste code samples, download chapters, and find quick answers when you need the most accurate, current information. Try it for free at *http://safari.oreilly.com*.

Acknowledgments

When I read single-authored books, I usually visualize the author talking to me. Since I started working on this book, that image has changed; I visualize not just the author, but a team. I realize now that a great deal of teamwork goes into it! Some bright people from France, California, Massachusetts, Tennessee, Texas, and Virginia contributed to this book.

I am amazed to see how things have progressed since the thought of writing this book got into my head one hot summer afternoon last year. I would first like to thank Bruce Tate and Michael Loukides for connecting the dots and putting me in touch with O'Reilly. Thanks to John Osborn of O'Reilly for his encouragement and spearheading the development of this book. I like his high expectations for quality and emphasis on coverage to meet the needs of Java and C++ programmers.

This book would have been hard to read and taken a lot more time to get out if not for the incredible effort of Ralph P. Davis as the development editor. Ralph is diligent, technical, so pleasant to work with, and has a great sense of humor. I am amazed at how he managed all the edits and versions without missing a beat at any time. Thanks Ralph. I was also very fortunate to have the expert opinions of Christophe Nassare as the technical editor. A number of gotchas and examples are better due to him. *Merci beaucoup*, Christophe.

Thanks to Anthony Mason for reviewing the book and offering to help in any way possible when he heard I was writing. Naresh Chaudhary was one of the early reviewers of the book. Naresh, thanks for the important role you played in making this a better book. Thanks to Chau Nguyen and John A. Fuqua for taking time from their very busy schedule and providing valuable input. Special thanks to Surendra Bhat for not only reviewing the book, but for recommending other good reviewers as well. I admire your quality. I consider Ted Neward a perfect example of a great software developer. I am very privileged to have had him as one of the early reviewers of this book. Thanks Ted!

I would like to express my special thanks to Brad Abrams, lead program manager of the CLR team at Microsoft, for being kind enough to spend and hour discussing the book with me at the end of a very long day. The comments he provided after reviewing parts of the book have been very valuable.

Thanks to my friend Siva Thiagarajan who gave me the wings to get into training and mentoring, and paved the way for me to experiment and learn. I would like to thank Jay Zimmerman for providing me an opportunity to speak at the No Fluff Just Stuff software symposium series, and for encouraging me to write. You are a good friend and mentor.

I've learnt a great deal from my students in the industry and at the University. I'd like to thank those who have taken my courses and asked those excellent questions to further their understanding and mine.

Most of what I do has been influenced by the hard work of my parents, Padmavathy and Ramamurthy. Thank you both. Thanks to Professor PSK (uncle P. S. Krishnamoorthy) for getting me excited about computers. You have had more far-reaching influence on others than you realize. Thanks to my dear aunt and uncle, Mythili and Balu, for shaping me.

None of this would've been possible but for the sacrifice of my family. Thanks to my sons, Karthik and Krupakar, for being so patient when I had to hide in the office several nights and weekends. I am blessed with incredible support and encouragement from my wife Kavitha. Thank you for your love without gotchas!

CHAPTER 1

CLR/Framework Gotchas

The Common Language Runtime (CLR) provides a common platform for the execution of programs in .NET. The code written in a .NET language is first translated into the Microsoft Intermediate Language (MSIL). The CLR then executes the MSIL. The .NET Framework exposes a rich class library to give your applications access to its underlying capabilities.

In this chapter I discuss the features in the CLR and the Framework that can impact the behavior and performance of your application. I will also discuss items that are somewhat confusing, misleading, or prone to misuse.

Developers coming into .NET knowing other languages expect behavior similar to what they're used to. C++ and Java programmers expect C# to act almost the same, since it looks almost the same. VB6 programmers have like expectations of VB.NET.

However, when it comes to the aliases for data types, and the behavior of value types versus reference types, .NET has a few surprises. Furthermore, some features may be convenient to use, but may not provide the best performance. Suffice it to say that when dealing with a rich but new API, you need to clearly understand its behavior. Idiosyncrasies often cost you precious time.

GOTCHA

#1 Type alias size doesn't match what you're familiar with

The Common Language Specification (CLS) provides rules to enable interoperation of types written in different languages. The Common Type System (CTS) enables cross-language integration, type safety, and high-performance execution of managed code. However, not all types supported in the .NET Framework are interoperable or CLS-compliant. When developing your class library, make sure the types you write and expose are CLS-compliant. Run your code through FxCop to make sure it complies with the Microsoft "Design Guidelines for Class Library Developers" (see "On the Web" in the Appendix).

As a convenience to C++, Java, and VB6 programmers, .NET languages provide aliases for the CTS data types, like int and long in C# and Integer and Long in VB.NET [Albahari02, Drayton03, Evjen04, Hamilton03, Robinson04, Thai03]. The aliases appear to match data types in those other languages, but some of the most important do not.

If you're a C++ programmer, you might assume that a long in C# corresponds to a long in C++. If you're coming from VB6, you might think that Integer and Long in VB.NET are equivalent to the Integer and Long you're used to in VB6. But in both cases, you'd be wrong.

Let's look at an example. How do I make an application beep? One possibility is to use PInvoke to call the Win32 Beep() method. PInvoke is a .NET facility that allows managed code to call unmanaged functions in DLLs. In VB6, Beep() has this declaration:

```
Beep(dwFreq as Long, dwDuration as Long) as Boolean
```

The Long type in VB6 is a 32-bit integer.

The underlying Win32 prototype is:

```
Beep(dwFreq as DWORD, dwDuration as DWORD) as Boolean
```

Now, let's use Beep() in .NET. The code to do this is shown in Example 1-1:

Example 1-1. Producing Beeps

✗ C# (Aliases)

```
using System;
using System.Runtime.InteropServices;

namespace InvokeBeep
{
    class Test
    {
        [DllImport("kernel32")]
        public static extern bool Beep(long dwFreq,
            long dwDuration);

        [STAThread]
        static void Main(string[] args)
        {
            Beep(1000, 1000);
        }
    }
}
```

Example 1-1. Producing Beeps (continued)

✗ VB.NET# (Aliases)

```
Imports System.Runtime.InteropServices

Module Module1

    Public Declare Function Beep Lib "Kernel32" ( _
        ByVal dwFreq As Long, ByVal dwDuration As Long) As Boolean

    Sub Main()
        Beep(1000, 1000)
    End Sub

End Module
```

When you compile and run this example, it fails to produce the desired result. On my system, I don't hear any beeps. What went wrong?

While the CTS defines the data types available to all .NET languages, such as System.Int32 and System.Double, each .NET language defines its own aliases for these types. For instance, C# uses int as an alias for System.Int32 and VB.NET uses Integer. These aliases appear to correspond to the types C++ developers (in the case of C#) and VB6 developers (in the case of VB.NET) are familiar with.

Table 1-1 shows the CTS types and the size differences between C# and C++. Table 1-2 shows the CTS types and the size differences between VB.NET and VB6.

Table 1-1. Some CTS types and aliases in C#

CTS type	Size	C# alias	Type equivalent in C++
System.Int32	4 bytes	int	int or long
System.Int64	8 bytes	long	__int64
System.Char	2 bytes	char	WCHAR
System.Double	8 bytes	double	double

Table 1-2. Some CTS types and aliases in VB.NET

CTS type	Size	VB.NET alias	Type equivalent in VB
System.Int32	4 bytes	Integer	Long
System.Int64	8 bytes	Long	N/A
System.Char	2 bytes	Char	String * 1
System.Double	8 bytes	Double	Double

As you can see from these tables, a long in C++ is not the same size as a long in C#. Nor is a Long in VB6 the same size as a Long in VB.NET. Long in VB6 corresponds to Integer in VB.NET. In the code of Example 1-1, you were actually passing 64-bit arguments to a function that expected 32 bits due to the improper declaration of the Beep( ) method. The code change in Example 1-2 fixes the problem.

Technically, sending an Integer in VB.NET is not a completely accurate mapping. Beep( ) expects two *unsigned* 32-bit (DWORD) arguments. A VB.NET Integer is a *signed* 32-bit integer. There is no VB.NET alias for System.UInt32 (which is not CLS-compliant). You may use System.UInt32 as the parameter type in the Beep method.

You can take a trial-and-error approach to figuring out the PInvoke signature in C#/VB.NET. Or you can quickly look up the signature for most Win32 and other APIs at *http://www.pinvoke.net*.

Example 1-2. Proper declaration for the Beep method

 C# (Aliases)

```
[DllImport("kernel32")]
public static extern bool Beep(uint dwFreq,
    uint dwDuration);
```

 VB.NET (Aliases)

```
Public Declare Function Beep Lib "Kernel32" ( _
    ByVal dwFreq As Integer, ByVal dwDuration As Integer) _
As Boolean
```

 IN A NUTSHELL

Be mindful of the sizes of the aliases used in .NET languages. If in doubt, use the fully qualified name from the CTS, as in System.Integer. For PInvoke signatures, look up the correct type mapping at *http://www.pinvoke.net*.

SEE ALSO

Gotcha #2, "struct and class differ in behavior."

GOTCHA
#2 struct and class differ in behavior

In C++, you can create an object on the stack or on the heap. When you use the new keyword, you create the object on the heap. In Java, you can only create objects on the heap; primitive built-in types are created on the stack, unless they are embedded within an object. Also, you can't use the new keyword on primitive built-in types.

.NET behaves more like Java than C++. An object is created on the heap if it is a reference type. If it is a value type, it is created on the stack, unless it is embedded within an object. Whether an object is a value type or reference type depends on how it is defined. If it is defined using the class keyword, it is a reference type. If it is defined with the struct keyword in C# or Structure in VB.NET, it's a value type. Even though you are using the same new keyword in the syntax, an instance of a reference type is created on the managed heap but an instance of a value type is created on the stack. This leads to some confusion when looking at code. Specifically, the effect of an assignment statement varies between structures (value types) and classes (reference types). This is illustrated in Example 1-3. The potentially troublesome assignment statements are highlighted.

Example 1-3. Assignment of reference type

✔ C# (ValueReferenceTypes)

```
//AType.cs
using System;

namespace ValTypeRefTypeAssignment
{
    public class AType
    {
        private int aField;

        public int TheValue
        {
            get { return aField; }
            set { aField = value; }
        }
    }
}

//Test.cs
using System;

namespace ValTypeRefTypeAssignment
{
    class Test
    {
        [STAThread]
        static void Main(string[] args)
        {
            AType firstInstance = new AType();

            firstInstance.TheValue = 2;

            AType secondInstance = new AType();
            secondInstance.TheValue = 3;

            Console.WriteLine("The values are {0} and {1}",
                firstInstance.TheValue,
```

Example 1-3. Assignment of reference type (continued)

```
            secondInstance.TheValue);

    firstInstance = secondInstance; // Line A

    Console.Write("Values after assignment ");
    Console.WriteLine("are {0} and {1}",
        firstInstance.TheValue,
        secondInstance.TheValue);

    secondInstance.TheValue = 4;

    Console.Write("Values after modifying TheValue ");
    Console.Write("in secondInstance are ");
    Console.WriteLine("{0} and {1}",
        firstInstance.TheValue,
        secondInstance.TheValue);
    }
  }
}
```

✔ VB.NET (ValueReferenceTypes)

```vbnet
'AType.vb
Public Class AType
    Private aField As Integer

    Public Property TheValue() As Integer
        Get
            Return aField
        End Get
        Set(ByVal Value As Integer)
            aField = Value
        End Set
    End Property
End Class

'Test.vb
Public Class Test
    Public Shared Sub Main()
        Dim firstInstance As New AType

        firstInstance.TheValue = 2

        Dim secondInstance As New AType
        secondInstance.TheValue = 3

        Console.WriteLine("The values are {0} and {1}", _
            firstInstance.TheValue, _
            secondInstance.TheValue)
```

Example 1-3. Assignment of reference type (continued)

```
firstInstance = secondInstance ' Line A

Console.Write("Values after assignment ")
Console.WriteLine("are {0} and {1}", _
    firstInstance.TheValue, _
    secondInstance.TheValue)

secondInstance.TheValue = 4

Console.Write("Values after modifying TheValue ")
Console.Write("in secondInstance are ")

Console.WriteLine("{0} and {1}", _
    firstInstance.TheValue, _
    secondInstance.TheValue)
    End Sub
End Class
```

The output produced by the above code is shown in Figure 1-1.

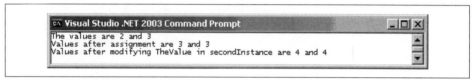

Figure 1-1. Output from Example 1-3

In the assignment statement:

```
firstInstance = secondInstance
```

you are modifying the reference firstInstance. The effect of that statement is shown in Figure 1-2.

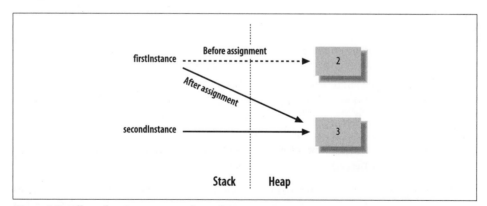

Figure 1-2. Effect of assignment on reference type

Therefore, when you change secondInstance.TheValue, you also change firstInstance.TheValue, since firstInstance and secondInstance now refer to the same object.

Let's make just one change. Let's modify AType from a class to a struct (Structure in VB.NET). This is the only change. There is no other change to the Test class or its Main( ) method. The output produced by the program now is shown in Figure 1-3.

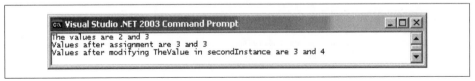

Figure 1-3. Output after modification of class to struct/Structure in Example 1-3

This time, the assignment statement at Line A (firstInstance = secondInstance) changes the value stored in the firstInstance structure. The effect of that statement is shown in Figure 1-4.

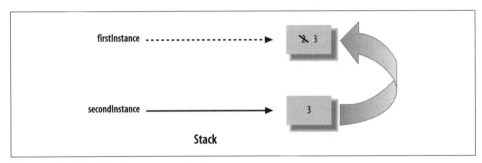

Figure 1-4. Effect of assignment on value type

Therefore, changing secondInstance.TheValue has no effect on firstInstance.TheValue, since in this case they are still different objects. The assignment made a bit-wise copy.

The effect of an assignment statement differs for the two types of object. In the case of the reference type (where AType is declared as a class), firstInstance refers to the object on the heap. Therefore, after the assignment statement, firstInstance and secondInstance end up referring to the same instance on the heap. This is very similar to pointer manipulation in C++. However, when AType is declared as a struct/ Structure, the firstInstance becomes a variable local to the stack representing an instance of the value type. Therefore, the assignment statement copies the memory content from secondInstance to firstInstance.

Given this confusion, is it worth using a value type? Well, since the core CLS types (such as System.Int32, System.Char, and System.Double), are value types, they must have their uses and benefits. What are they?

Value types are allocated on the stack. They are passed by value as method parameters (unless tagged as ref/ByRef), so the called method cannot change them inadvertently. This argues for keeping value types small: by-value parameters are copied, and copying large objects can be expensive.

Another good candidate for value types is objects used to represent the internal state of a larger object (and not exposed to users of that object).

You need to exercise caution when using value types with collections in .NET 1.1 (non-generic collections). See Gotcha #9, "Typeless ArrayList isn't type-safe."

I recommend that you use a class unless you have a specific need for a struct/Structure, such as when:

- The object is really small and you want to eliminate the overhead of a reference
- You intend to create a large array of these types and do not want the overhead of constructor calls for each object in the array

 IN A NUTSHELL

Assignment may lead to confusion because you can't quite figure out if you are using a value type or a reference type merely by looking at the code. Do not make any assumptions when you see an assignment statement—explore the object further to make sure you understand how the assignment will behave. Also, limit the use of value types, as much as possible, to small objects.

SEE ALSO

Gotcha #1, "Type alias size doesn't match what you're familiar with," Gotcha #3, "Returning value types from a method/property is risky," Gotcha #4, "You can't force calls to your value-type constructors," and Gotcha #9, "Typeless ArrayList isn't type-safe."

GOTCHA
#3 Returning value types from a method/property is risky

Value types are either stored on the stack or embedded within objects on the heap. What happens when a property or a method of a class returns a member which is a struct/Structure (i.e., a value type)? It makes a copy of the object. While value types may be passed by reference as method parameters, C# and VB.NET (unlike C++) do not provide any mechanism to return them by reference. Consider Example 1-4.

Example 1-4. Example of returning a value type

```
using System;

namespace ValTypeProp
{
    struct A
    {
        public int val;
    }

    class Test
    {
        private A theA;

        public Test()
        {
            theA = new A();
        }

        public A MyValue
        {
            get { return theA; }
            set { theA = value; }
        }

        [STAThread]
        static void Main(string[] args)
        {
            Test obj = new Test();

            A myValue = obj.MyValue;
            myValue.val = 4;

            Console.WriteLine(obj.MyValue.val);
        }
    }
}
```

```
Structure A
    Public val As Integer
End Structure

Class Test
    Private theA As A
```

Example 1-4. Example of returning a value type (continued)

```
Public Sub New( )
    theA = New A
End Sub

Public Property MyValue( ) As A
    Get
        Return theA
    End Get
    Set(ByVal Value As A)
        theA = Value
    End Set
End Property

Public Shared Sub Main( )
    Dim obj As New Test

    Dim myValue As A = obj.MyValue

    myValue.val = 4

    Console.WriteLine(obj.MyValue.val)
End Sub
End Class
```

In the above example, the MyValue property of the Test class returns the object theA of type A. In Main, you get this property and set its val field to 4. Then you again fetch the property from the Test object (obj) and print its val field.

The output from the above program is 0 and not 4. Why? Well, when the property MyValue returns theA, it returns a copy of the structure, not a reference to it. The assignment statement myValue.val = 4 has no effect on obj.MyValue.val. In fact, you will get an error if you try to modify the obj.MyValue property directly.

Consider this small change shown in Example 1-5.

Example 1-5. Modifying value type returned from a property

✗ C# (ReturningValueType)

```
//...
[STAThread]
static void Main(string[] args)
{
    Test obj = new Test( );

    obj.MyValue.val = 4;

    Console.WriteLine(obj.MyValue.val);
}
```

Example 1-5. Modifying value type returned from a property (continued)

✗ VB.NET (ReturningValueType)

```
' ...
Public Shared Sub Main( )
    Dim obj As New Test

    obj.MyValue.val = 4

    Console.WriteLine(obj.MyValue.val)
End Sub
```

Now you get a compilation error. In C#, you get the message:

```
error CS1612: Cannot modify the return value of 'ValTypeProp.Test.MyValue' because it
is not a variable.
```

In VB.NET, you get:

```
error BC30068: Expression is a value and therefore cannot be the target of an
assignment.
```

 If you replace struct/structure with class you get the intuitive result of 4 instead of 0.

 IN A NUTSHELL

If you call a method or access a property that returns a value-type object, do not modify it or call *mutators* (methods that modify its state or data) on it. You are dealing with a copy and any change you make does not affect the real instance.

SEE ALSO

Gotcha #2, "struct and class differ in behavior, Gotcha #4, "You can't force calls to your value-type constructors," and Gotcha #9, "Typeless ArrayList isn't type-safe."

GOTCHA
#4 You can't force calls to your value-type constructors

Among other differences between reference types and value types, one of the most surprising is that you are not allowed to define your own no-parameter constructor (one that takes no parameter) for a value type. If you try, you get the following error:

```
error CS0568: Structs cannot contain explicit parameterless constructors.
```

C# and VB.NET provide a no-parameter constructor and won't let you write an alternate implementation.

The consequence of this is that you have no control over how your value-type object is created by a user. For instance, in the case of a reference type (class), you can dictate what parameters are necessary to create an object by writing different constructors. The compiler makes sure that a user calls one of these constructors when creating the object. In the case of a value type, you can't define a no-parameter constructor. So you can't force developers to enter some specific values before using a value type. They can create an instance of your value type with no parameters. Take a look at Example 1-6.

Example 1-6. Example of using no-parameter constructor of value type

✔ **C# (ValueTypeConstructor)**

```
//MyType.cs
using System;

namespace ValueTypeInstantiation
{
    public struct MyType
    {
        private int val;

        public override string ToString()
        {
            return "The value is " + val;
        }

        //public MyType() {} // Can't be provided

        public MyType(int initialValue)
        {
            val = initialValue;
        }
    }
}



using System;

namespace ValueTypeInstantiation
{
    class Test
    {
        [STAThread]
        static void Main(string[] args)
        {
            MyType instance1 = new MyType(10);
            Console.WriteLine("instance1: " + instance1);
```

Example 1-6. Example of using no-parameter constructor of value type (continued)

```
        MyType instance2 = new MyType( );
        Console.WriteLine("instance2: " + instance2);
    }
  }
}
```

✔ VB.NET (ValueTypeConstructor)

```
'MyType.vb

Public Structure MyType
    Private val As Integer

    Public Overrides Function ToString( ) As String
        Return "The value is " & val
    End Function

    'Public Sub New( ) ' Can't be provided
    'End Sub

    Public Sub New(ByVal initialValue As Integer)
        val = initialValue
    End Sub
End Structure


'Test.vb

Public Class Test
    Public Shared Sub Main( )
            Dim instance1 as new MyType(10)
            Console.WriteLine("instance1: " & instance1)

            Dim instance2  as new MyType
            Console.WriteLine("instance2: " & instance2)
    End Sub
End Class
```

Note that the value type MyType has one constructor which takes an integer. However, in Main of the Test class you are able to create an instance of MyType not only using the constructor provided, but also using the no-parameter constructor. What if you want to enforce a rule that MyType.val must be set to the value given in the constructor or to a value of, say, 10? Unfortunately that is not possible. Each field of a value type is initialized to its default value. For instance, int/Integer fields will be initialized to 0 and bool/Boolean types to false. The output from Example 1-6 is shown in Figure 1-5.

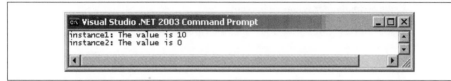

Figure 1-5. Output from Example 1-6

 IN A NUTSHELL

Be aware that for value types, no matter how many constructors you write, you are not allowed to write your own no-parameter constructor. A user of your type may create an object using the no-parameter constructor and there is no guarantee that any of the constructors you write is ever used.

SEE ALSO

Gotcha #2, "struct and class differ in behavior," Gotcha #3, "Returning value types from a method/property is risky," and Gotcha #9, "Typeless ArrayList isn't type-safe."

GOTCHA
#5 String concatenation is expensive

Objects of the String class in .NET are *immutable*. An immutable object is one that can't be modified once created. What is the effect of using the + operator (or & in VB.NET) to append a String? Each call creates a new String object. This can cause object-allocation overhead and put pressure on the garbage collector. What alternative do you have?

System.Text.StringBuilder provides a means for appending almost anything to a StringBuilder object. The benefits of using StringBuilder over String's +/& is illustrated in Example 1-7.

Example 1-7. Using StringBuilder versus +/ &

✔ **C# (StringAppend)**

```csharp
using System;

namespace StringAppendPerformance
{
    class Test
    {
        [STAThread]
        static void Main(string[] args)
        {
```

Example 1-7. Using StringBuilder versus +/ & (continued)

```
            Console.Write("Enter number of strings to append:");
            int count = Convert.ToInt32(Console.ReadLine());

            string str = null;
            int startTick = Environment.TickCount;
            for (int i = 0; i < count; i++)
            {
                str = str + ".";
            }
            int endTick = Environment.TickCount;

            double timeTakenByPlus =
                (endTick - startTick) / 1000.0;

            System.Text.StringBuilder bldr =
                new System.Text.StringBuilder();

            startTick = Environment.TickCount;
            for (int i = 0; i < count; i++)
            {
                bldr.Append(".");
            }
            endTick = Environment.TickCount;

            double timeTakenByStringBuilder =
                (endTick - startTick) / 1000.0;

            Console.Write("+ and StringBuilder took ");
            Console.WriteLine("{0} and {1} seconds",
                    timeTakenByPlus,
                    timeTakenByStringBuilder);
        }
    }
}
```

✔ **VB.NET (StringAppend)**

```
Module Test

    Sub Main()
        Console.Write("Enter number of strings to append:")
        Dim count As Integer = Convert.ToInt32(Console.ReadLine())

        Dim str As String = Nothing
        Dim startTick As Integer = Environment.TickCount
        Dim i As Integer

        For i = 0 To count - 1
            str = str & "."
```

Example 1-7. Using StringBuilder versus +/& (continued)

```
        Next
        Dim endTick As Integer = Environment.TickCount

        Dim timeTakenByPlus As Double = _
            (endTick - startTick) / 1000.0

        Dim bldr As New System.Text.StringBuilder

        startTick = Environment.TickCount

        For i = 0 To count - 1
            bldr.Append(".")
        Next
        endTick = Environment.TickCount

        Dim timeTakenByStringBuilder As Double = _
            (endTick - startTick) / 1000.0

        Console.Write("& and StringBuilder took ")
        Console.WriteLine("{0} and {1} seconds", _
          timeTakenByPlus, _
          timeTakenByStringBuilder)
    End Sub
End Module
```

Executing the above program with different values for the number of strings to append produces the results shown in Table 1-3.

Table 1-3. Performance, in seconds, of concatenation versus StringBuilder

# of appends	+	StringBuilder
10	0.000	0.00
100	0.000	0.00
1,000	0.000	0.00
2,500	0.000	0.00
5,000	0.020	0.00
7,500	0.050	0.00
10,000	0.090	0.00
15,000	0.250	0.00
25,000	1.052	0.00
35,000	2.373	0.00
50,000	5.699	0.00
65,000	10.625	0.00
75,000	14.831	0.01
85,000	19.418	0.01

Table 1-3. Performance, in seconds, of concatenation versus StringBuilder (continued)

# of appends	+	StringBuilder
100,000	27.159	0.01
150,000	65.374	0.01
250,000	209.221	0.02
350,000	441.615	0.02
500,000	910.129	0.04
650,000	1521.708	0.06
750,000	1999.305	0.06
850,000	2576.575	0.06
1,000,000	3562.933	0.07

The timing using the ampersand (&) in VB.NET is comparable to that of the concatenation operator (+) in C#. As the above example shows, StringBuilder is much less expensive than using + (or &) to build up a string. Furthermore, if you use StringBuilder you create fewer objects than using the +/&. This can be seen using the CLR Profiler (see "On the Web" in the Appendix). For instance, if you run 10,000 appends, the number of String instances created using +/& is 10,039. However, if you replace the +/& with StringBuilder.Append( ), the number of String instances drops to 51.

For an interactive client application with a few concatenations here and there, it may not make a big difference. For a server-side application, however, the difference may be significant and the use of StringBuilder is probably better. It must be noted that the instance members of a StringBuilder are not thread-safe, so you may have to take care to appropriately synchronize access to them.

 IN A NUTSHELL

If you find yourself appending a large number of strings, you will improve performance by using StringBuilder.Append( ) instead of the concatenation operators (+/&). This is especially important in server-side/backend applications.

SEE ALSO

Gotcha #9, "Typeless ArrayList isn't type-safe" and Gotcha #21, "Default performance of Data.ReadXML is poor."

GOTCHA
#6 Exceptions may go unhandled

No one likes an application to crash. It's embarrassing if your application presents the user with an unhandled exception dialog like the one in Figure 1-6.

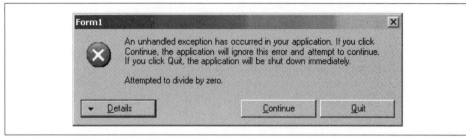

Figure 1-6. Unhandled exception dialog

There is a low-tech solution: comb through your code to make sure that you are handling all exceptions properly. But that is a lot of work, and what if you miss something? Can you protect your application from the exception that slips through? And if not, do you want the unhandled exception to jump up abruptly in your users' faces? Wouldn't you rather have it presented to them more gracefully, and maybe reported to you by logging, emailing, or some other means?

You can register a method to catch unhandled exceptions. There are two ways to achieve this. In a Windows application, you add a `ThreadExceptionEventHandler` to the `Application.ThreadException` delegate. In a console application, you add an `UnhandledExceptionEventHandler` to `AppDomain.CurrentDomain.UnhandledException`.

Examples 1-8 through Example 1-11 show a console application that uses a class in a library.

Example 1-8. Exception that goes unhandled (C# library)

✗ C# (HandleException), library code

```
//Utility.cs part of ALibrary.dll
using System;

namespace ALibrary
{
    public class Utility
    {
        public double Operate(int value1, int value2)
        {
            // Some operation
            // Of course, this is an enormous programming error
            // Never do division without making sure the denominator
            // is not zero.
            // We're just doing it here for the sake of example.
            double val = value1 / value2;
            return Math.Sqrt(val);
        }
    }
}
```

Example 1-8. Exception that goes unhandled (C# library) (continued)

}

Example 1-9. Exception that goes unhandled (C# client)

✗ C# (HandleException), client code

```
//Program.cs part of UnhandledExceptionConsoleApp.exe
using System;
using ALibrary;
using System.Threading;

namespace UnhandledExceptionConsoleApp
{
    class Program
    {
        private static void Worker()
        {
            Console.WriteLine(
                "Enter two numbers separated by a return");

            int number1 = Convert.ToInt32(Console.ReadLine());
            int number2 = Convert.ToInt32(Console.ReadLine());

            double result = new Utility().Operate(number1, number2);

            Console.WriteLine("Result is {0}", result);
        }

        [STAThread]
        static void Main(string[] args)
        {
            try
            {
                //AppDomain.CurrentDomain.UnhandledException
                //    += new UnhandledExceptionEventHandler(
                //        CurrentDomain_UnhandledException);

                new Thread(new ThreadStart(Worker)).Start();
            }
            catch(Exception ex)
            {
                Console.WriteLine("Exception: " + ex.Message);
            }
        }

        private static void CurrentDomain_UnhandledException(
            object sender, UnhandledExceptionEventArgs e)
        {
```

Example 1-9. Exception that goes unhandled (C# client) (continued)

```
            Console.WriteLine("Send the following to support");
                Console.WriteLine("Unexpected error:");
            Console.WriteLine(e.ExceptionObject);
            Console.WriteLine("Is CLR terminating: {0}",
                e.IsTerminating);
        }
    }
}
```

Example 1-10. Exception that goes unhandled (VB.NET library)

✗ VB.NET (HandleException), library code

```
'Utility.vb part of ALibrary.dll

Public Class Utility
    Public Function Operate( _
        ByVal value1 As Integer, ByVal value2 As Integer) As Double
        'Some operation
        ' Of course, this is an enormous programming error
        ' Never do division without making sure the denominator
        ' is not zero.
        ' We're just doing it here for the sake of example.
        Dim val As Double = value1 / value2

        If Double.IsInfinity(val) Then
            Throw New DivideByZeroException( _
                "Attempted to Divide by Zero")
        End If
        Return Math.Sqrt(val)
    End Function
End Class
```

Example 1-11. Exception that goes unhandled (VB.NET client)

✗ VB.NET (HandleException), client code

```
'Program.vb part of UnhandledExceptionConsoleApp.exe

Imports ALibrary
Imports System.Threading

Module Program
    Private Sub Worker( )
            Console.WriteLine( _
                "Enter two numbers separated by a return")
```

Example 1-11. Exception that goes unhandled (VB.NET client) (continued)

```
        Dim number1 As Integer = Convert.ToInt32(Console.ReadLine())
        Dim number2 As Integer = Convert.ToInt32(Console.ReadLine())

        Dim result As Double = New Utility().Operate(number1, number2)

        Console.WriteLine("Result is {0}", result)
    End Sub

    Public Sub Main()
        Try
            'AddHandler AppDomain.CurrentDomain.UnhandledException, _
            '    New UnhandledExceptionEventHandler( _
            '    AddressOf CurrentDomain_UnhandledException)

            Dim aThread As New Thread(AddressOf Worker)
            aThread.Start()
        Catch ex As Exception
            Console.WriteLine("Exception: " + ex.Message)
        End Try
    End Sub

    Private Sub CurrentDomain_UnhandledException( _
        ByVal sender As Object, ByVal e As UnhandledExceptionEventArgs)
        Console.WriteLine("Send the following to support")
        Console.WriteLine("Unexpected error:")
        Console.WriteLine(e.ExceptionObject)
        Console.WriteLine("Is CLR terminating: {0}", _
          e.IsTerminating)
    End Sub
End Module
```

In this example, you have a Utility class with an Operate() method that throws a DivisionByZeroException if its second parameter is zero. The method is invoked from a thread in Program. You don't have a try-catch block within the Worker() method to handle exceptions. When you execute the above code, the output shown in Figure 1-7 is produced.

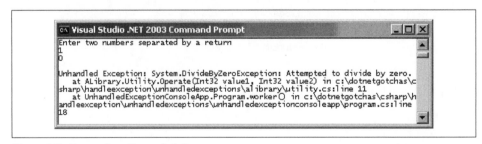

Figure 1-7. Output from Example 1-8

The exception thrown from the thread is reported as an unhandled exception. If you uncomment the first statement in Main( ), thereby registering your own handler for uncaught exceptions, you get the output shown in Figure 1-8.

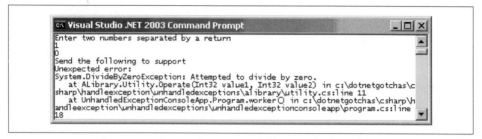

Figure 1-8. Output from Example 1-8 after registering for the UnhandledException event

By adding your handler to the AppDomain.CurrentDomain.UnhandledException event, you let the CLR know that it should send unhandled exceptions to the subscribed method.

Of course, you should not use this as a substitute for using good try-catch logic where necessary. Furthermore, your code should have finally blocks where actions have to be taken regardless of exceptions.

If your application is a Windows application, you register a handler for the Application.ThreadException event instead. Consider a simple WinForm application with one button named RunButton. The handler for that button's Click event is shown in Example 1-12, along with the Main( ) method and the exception-handler code.

Example 1-12. Taking care of unhandled exceptions in a WinForm app

✗ C# (HandleException)

```
       static void Main( )
       {
//         Application.ThreadException
//             += new ThreadExceptionEventHandler(
//                 Application_ThreadException);
           Application.Run(new Form1( ));
       }

       private void RunButton_Click(
           object sender, System.EventArgs e)
       {
           MessageBox.Show(
               new Utility( ).Operate(1, 0).ToString( ));
       }

       private static void Application_ThreadException(
```

Example 1-12. Taking care of unhandled exceptions in a WinForm app (continued)

```
        object sender,
        System.Threading.ThreadExceptionEventArgs e)
    {
        MessageBox.Show(
            "Send the following to support: " +
            e.Exception);
    }
```

✗ VB.NET (HandleException)

```
Public Shared Sub Main( )
    'AddHandler Application.ThreadException, _
    '   New ThreadExceptionEventHandler( _
    '   AddressOf Application_ThreadException)

    Application.Run(New Form1)
End Sub

Private Sub RunButton_Click( _
    ByVal sender As System.Object, _
    ByVal e As System.EventArgs) _
    Handles RunButton.Click
    MessageBox.Show(New Utility( ).Operate(1, 0).ToString( ))
End Sub

Private Shared Sub Application_ThreadException( _
ByVal sender As Object, _
ByVal e As System.Threading.ThreadExceptionEventArgs)
    MessageBox.Show( _
      "Send the following to support: " & _
      e.Exception.ToString( ))
End Sub
```

When you click the Run button, you get the output in Figure 1-6. If you uncomment the Application.ThreadException registration code in Main( ), you see something more like Figure 1-9.

From the event handler, you may take an appropriate action such as logging the exception for future diagnostics or sending the details to your support team. This can prove useful in development, testing, and even after deployment.

 Unlike this example, you shouldn't let your application keep running after an unhandled exception, because it's in an inconsistent state.

Refer to Jason Clark's article "Unexpected Errors in Managed Applications" (see the section "On the Web" in the Appendix).

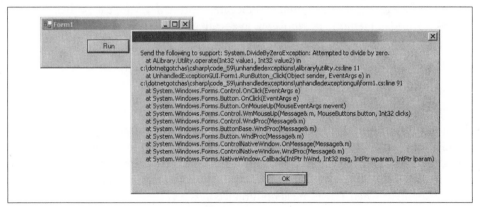

Figure 1-9. Handling the Unhandled Exception

 IN A NUTSHELL

Properly handle exceptions in your application. You can guard against unhandled exceptions by registering a handler for them. In a Windows application, you add a `ThreadExceptionEventHandler` to the `Application.ThreadException` delegate. In a console application, you add an `UnhandledExceptionEventHandler` to `AppDomain.CurrentDomain.UnhandledException`.

SEE ALSO

Gotcha #61, "Exceptions thrown from threads in the pool are lost."

GOTCHA
#7 Uninitialized event handlers aren't treated gracefully

Delegates are very effective for implementing callbacks in .NET. A delegate encapsulates a pointer to a method, and an instance of an object on which that method needs to be executed. A delegate can also encapsulate a pointer to a `static/Shared` method. The syntax provided to use a delegate is intuitive. You do not have to deal with messy pointers to functions as in C++.

Delegates are used to specify the handlers that will be called when an event occurs. If you want to register multiple methods of a class as event handlers, you can do so very easily without having to resort to something as complicated as anonymous inner classes, as you do in Java.

In order to call the handler that a delegate represents, you can either use the DynamicInvoke( ) method, or you can just call the delegate as if it were itself a method:

```
MyDelegate.DynamicInvoke(...)
```

Or:

```
MyDelegate(...)
```

Their ease of use sometimes obscures the fact that delegates are just classes, created when the compiler sees the delegate keyword. When you use a delegate, you are using an object through a special syntax. Of course, you know not to invoke methods on an object reference that you haven't initialized. However, it may not be readily apparent when a delegate is uninitialized.

When raising an event, you should consider the possibility that no handlers have been added or registered. Consider the code in Example 1-13.

Example 1-13. Accessing an uninitialized delegate

✗ C# (Delegate)

```csharp
// AComponent.cs
using System;

namespace UnInitializedDelegate
{
    public delegate void DummyDelegate();

    public class AComponent
    {
        public event DummyDelegate myEvent;

        protected virtual void OnMyEvent()
        {
            myEvent();
        }

        public void Fire()
        {
            Console.WriteLine("Raising event");
            OnMyEvent(); // Raising the event
            Console.WriteLine("Done raising event");
        }
    }
}

//Test.cs
using System;

namespace UnInitializedDelegate
```

Example 1-13. Accessing an uninitialized delegate (continued)

```
{
    public class Test
    {
        private void callback1( )
        {
            Console.WriteLine("callback1 called");
        }

        private void callback2( )
        {
            Console.WriteLine("callback2 called");
        }

        private void Work( )
        {
            AComponent obj = new AComponent( );

            Console.WriteLine("Registering 2 callbacks");
            obj.myEvent += new DummyDelegate(callback1);
            obj.myEvent += new DummyDelegate(callback2);
            obj.Fire( );

            Console.WriteLine("Removing 1 callback");
            obj.myEvent -= new DummyDelegate(callback2);
            obj.Fire( );

            Console.WriteLine("Removing the other callback");
            obj.myEvent -= new DummyDelegate(callback1);
            obj.Fire( );
        }

        [STAThread]
        static void Main(string[] args)
        {
            Test testObj = new Test( );
            testObj.Work( );
        }
    }
}
```

✗ VB.NET (Delegate)

```
'AComponent.vb
Public Delegate Sub DummyDelegate( )

Public Class AComponent
    Public Event myEvent As DummyDelegate
```

Example 1-13. Accessing an uninitialized delegate (continued)

```vb
    Protected Overridable Sub OnMyEvent( )
        RaiseEvent myEvent( )
    End Sub

    Public Sub Fire( )
        Console.WriteLine("Raising event")
        OnMyEvent( ) ' Raising the event
        Console.WriteLine("Done raising event")
    End Sub
End Class

'Test.vb
Public Class Test

    Private Sub callback1( )
        Console.WriteLine("callback1 called")
    End Sub

    Private Sub callback2( )
        Console.WriteLine("callback2 called")
    End Sub

    Private Sub Work( )
        Dim obj As New AComponent

        Console.WriteLine("Registering 2 callbacks")
        AddHandler obj.myEvent, New DummyDelegate(AddressOf callback1)
        AddHandler obj.myEvent, New DummyDelegate(AddressOf callback2)
        obj.Fire( )

        Console.WriteLine("Removing 1 callback")
        RemoveHandler obj.myEvent, New DummyDelegate(AddressOf callback2)
        obj.Fire( )

        Console.WriteLine("Removing the other callback")
        RemoveHandler obj.myEvent, New DummyDelegate(AddressOf callback1)
        obj.Fire( )
    End Sub
    Shared Sub Main(ByVal args As String( ))
        Dim testObj As New Test
        testObj.Work( )
    End Sub
End Class
```

When executed, the C# version of the program produces the result shown in Figure 1-10.

As Figure 1-10 shows, a NullReferenceException is thrown when the third call to the Fire( ) method tries to raise the event. The reason for this is that no event handler delegates are registered at that moment.

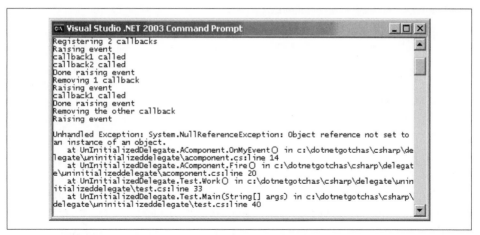

Figure 1-10. Output from the C# version of Example 1-13

The VB.NET version of the program, however, does not throw an exception. It works just fine.* Why? In the MSIL generated for RaiseEvent() (shown in Example 1-14), a check for the reference being Nothing is made.

Example 1-14. MSIL translation of a RaiseEvent() statement

```
IL_0000:  nop
IL_0001:  ldarg.0
IL_0002:  ldfld      class UnInitializedDelegate.DummyDelegate
                     UnInitializedDelegate.AComponent::myEventEvent
IL_0007:  brfalse.s  IL_0015
IL_0009:  ldarg.0
IL_000a:  ldfld      class UnInitializedDelegate.DummyDelegate
                     UnInitializedDelegate.AComponent::myEventEvent
IL_000f:  callvirt   instance void UnInitializedDelegate.DummyDelegate::Invoke()
IL_0014:  nop
IL_0015:  nop
```

 You can view the MSIL generated for your code using the tool *ildasm. exe* that comes with the .NET Framework. Simply run the tool and open the assembly you are interested in. You can view the MSIL generated for methods, properties, etc.

The correct way to implement this code in C# is to program defensively by checking for a null reference before raising the event, as shown in Example 1-15.

---

* Actually, there is a problem we are not seeing—RaiseEvent() is not thread-safe. See Gotcha #64.

Example 1-15. Checking for an uninitialized delegate

✗ C# (Delegate)

```
protected virtual void OnMyEvent()
{
    if(myEvent != null)
    {
        myEvent();
    }
}
```

Checking to see if the delegate is not `null` prevents the `NullReferenceException`. The delegate will be `null` if no one has asked to be notified when the event triggers.

Note that there is still a problem. It is possible that the last registered event handler has been removed between the line where you check if `myEvent` is `null` and the line where you raise the event, and the code may still fail. You need to consider this possibility and raise the event in a thread-safe way. See Gotcha #64, "Raising events lacks thread-safety" for details on this.

 IN A NUTSHELL

Use caution when raising an event. If no event handler has been registered, an exception is thrown in C# when you raise an event. Check to make sure that the delegate is not `null` before raising the event. In both C# and VB.NET, you need to worry about thread-safety when raising events.

SEE ALSO

Gotcha #64, "Raising events lacks thread-safety."

GOTCHA

#8 Division operation isn't consistent between types

When you divide by zero, you expect a `DivisionByZeroException` to be thrown. While this does happen for integer division, floating point division does not cause this exception. Consider Example 1-16, where I use an NUnit test to assert for division by zero.

Example 1-16. NUnit test to assert DivisionByZeroException

✔ C# (DivByZero)

```
//Calculator.cs

using System;

namespace DivisionByZeroExample
{
    public class Calculator
    {
        public int Divide(int operand1, int operand2)
        {
            return operand1 / operand2;
        }
    }
}

//Test.cs
using System;
using NUnit.Framework;

namespace DivisionByZeroExample
{
    [TestFixture]
    public class Test
    {
        private Calculator calc;

        [SetUp]
        public void Setup()
        {
            calc = new Calculator();
        }

        [Test]
        public void TestSimpleDivide()
        {
            Assert.AreEqual(2, calc.Divide(4, 2));
```

Example 1-16. NUnit test to assert DivisionByZeroException (continued)

```
        }

        [Test, ExpectedException(typeof(DivideByZeroException))]
        public void TestDivisionByZero( )
        {
            calc.Divide(4, 0);
        }
    }
}
```

✔ VB.NET (DivByZero)

```
'Calculator.vb
Public Class Calculator
    Public Function Divide(ByVal operand1 As Integer, _
        ByVal operand2 As Integer) As Integer
        Return operand1 \ operand2
    End Function
End Class

'Test.vb
Imports NUnit.Framework

<TestFixture( )> _
Public Class Test
    Private calc As Calculator

    <SetUp( )> _
    Public Sub Setup( )
        calc = New Calculator
    End Sub

    <Test( )> _
    Public Sub TestSimpleDivide( )
        Assert.AreEqual(2, calc.Divide(4, 2))
    End Sub
    <Test( ), ExpectedException(GetType(DivideByZeroException))> _
    Public Sub TestDivisionByZero( )
        calc.Divide(4, 0)
    End Sub
End Class
```

The Divide( ) method divides its first parameter by its second one. There are two test cases. The first one invokes Divide( ) with parameters 4 and 2; the second calls it with the values 4 and 0. When the code in Example 1-16 is executed in NUnit, both the test cases succeed as shown in Figure 1-11.

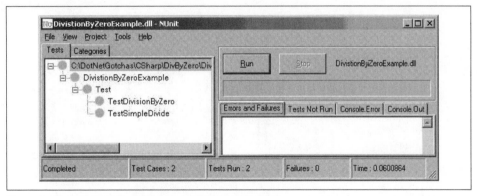

Figure 1-11. NUnit GUI output for code in Example 1-16

The TestDivisionByZero test case has declared the ExpectedException attribute, and announced that it expects a DivisionByZeroException. This test succeeds since the Divide( ) method does indeed throw a DivisionByZeroException.

Now, if the Divide( ) method performs floating-point division instead of integer division, the result will be different. Let's change the Divide( ) method of the Calculator class to use double instead of int (Integer in VB.NET), as shown in Example 1-17.

Example 1-17. Example of floating point division by zero

✗ C# (DivByZero)

```csharp
public double Divide(double operand1, double operand2)
{
    return operand1 / operand2;
}
```

✗ VB.NET (DivByZero)

```vbnet
Public Function Divide(ByVal operand1 As Double, _
    ByVal operand2 As Double) As Double
    Return operand1 / operand2
End Function
```

The effect of the code change in Example 1-17 can be seen in the NUnit GUI shown in Figure 1-12.

Note that the TestDivisionByZero test case fails because the DivisionByZeroException is not thrown. What is the result then? If either of the operands is a System.Double or System.Single, then the operation appears to succeed; no exception is thrown. But the result is an invalid number defined as either Double.PositiveInfinity or Double.NegativeInfinity, depending on the signs of the operands. However, you cannot do a simple comparison to test this; you must call Double.IsInfinity( ). Floating-point operations do not throw exceptions.

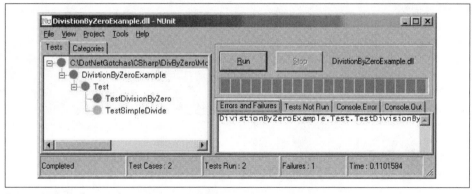

Figure 1-12. Failure to throw DivisionByZeroException

(If the operands are `Single` instead of `Double`, the appropriate values are `Single.`
`PositiveInfinity` and `Single.NegativeInfinity`. `Single` also offers the `IsInfinity( )`
method.)

 IN A NUTSHELL

If dealing with integer division, expect a `DivisionByZeroException`. Otherwise, check
the result by calling the `IsInfinity( )` method of `System.Double` or `System.Single` as
appropriate. Remember that floating-point operations don't throw exceptions. You
can avoid problems like this by checking the denominator before you perform the
operation.

SEE ALSO

Gotcha #29, "Unit testing private methods is tricky."

GOTCHA
#9 Typeless ArrayList isn't type-safe

Boxing and unboxing enable value types to be treated as objects. *Boxing* is an
implicit conversion of a value type to the `System.Object` type; i.e., an `Object` instance
is created (on the heap) and the value is copied into it. *Unboxing* is an explicit conversion from the `Object` type to a value type.

Collections (i.e., non-generic collections) treat every one of their elements as the
`Object` type. When dealing with primitive value types, adding a value to a collection
involves boxing, and accessing it from the collection involves unboxing. As a result,
you have two problems to worry about. One, the boxing and unboxing will affect
performance due to the copy overhead. Second, the value has to be unboxed to the
proper type. In this gotcha we focus mainly on the latter problem. Code like that in
Example 1-18 might compile OK but fail at run time.

Example 1-18. Behavior of ArrayList

✗ C# (ArrayList)

```csharp
using System;
using System.Collections;

namespace ArrayListClassCastException
{
    class Test
    {
        [STAThread]
        static void Main(string[] args)
        {
            ArrayList myList = new ArrayList( );

            myList.Add(3.0);
            myList.Add(3);
                // Oops. 3 is boxed in as int not double

            double total = 0;
            foreach(double val in myList) // Exception here.
            {
                total += val;
            }

            Console.WriteLine(total);
        }
    }
}
```

✗ VB.NET (ArrayList)

```vbnet
Module Test

    Sub Main( )
        Dim myList As New ArrayList

        myList.Add(3.0)
        myList.Add(3)
        ' Oops. 3 is boxed in as integer not double

        Dim total As Double = 0
        Dim val As Double
        For Each val In myList ' No Exception here.
            total += val
        Next

        Console.WriteLine(total)
    End Sub

End Module
```

The behavior of the C# code is different from the equivalent VB.NET version (even with Option Strict On).

Let's first consider the C# code. In the example, you first add 3.0 to the ArrayList myList. This gets boxed in as a double. Then you add a 3. However, this gets boxed in as an integer. When you enumerate over the items in the collection and treat them as doubles, an InvalidCastException is thrown as shown in Figure 1-13.

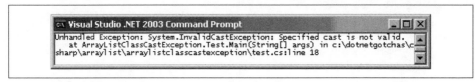

Figure 1-13. Output from the C# version of Example 1-18

What is the reason for this exception? The value 3 that was boxed as an int is unboxed as a double.

Let's now consider the VB.NET code. The VB.NET version appears to be doing the same thing as the C# version. That is, you add 3.0 to the ArrayList myList. This is boxed in as a Double. Then you add a 3. This is boxed in as an Integer. But when you enumerate the items in the collection and treat them as Double, you get the correct total, 6, as shown in Figure 1-14.

Figure 1-14. Output from the VB.NET version of Example 1-18

That is interesting! Why would C# fail, but not VB.NET? The answer is in the translation of source to MSIL. Let's take a look at the MSIL generated from C# and the MSIL generated from VB.NET.

Example 1-19 shows what MSIL command is generated from the C# code for unboxing. It is the unbox statement, which instructs the CLR to unbox the object to a System.Double.

Example 1-19. Unboxing in MSIL translated from C#

```
IL_0041:  unbox      [mscorlib]System.Double
```

Example 1-20, on the other hand, shows the MSIL that VB.NET produces. Instead of a simple unbox statement, it invokes the FromObject method on the DoubleType class in the Microsoft.VisualBasic namespace.

This method silently converts the Integer to Double, so you get the correct answer rather than an exception.

Example 1-20. Unboxing in MSIL translated from VB.NET

```
IL_0051:  call       float64 [Microsoft.VisualBasic]
   Microsoft.VisualBasic.CompilerServices.DoubleType::FromObject(
object)
```

Of course, if you modify the VB.NET code to add a Char instead of an Integer, you will get an exception. Let's take a look at this in Example 1-21.

Example 1-21. Adding a Character in the VB.NET example of ArrayList

✗ VB.NET (ArrayList)

```
Dim myList As New ArrayList

myList.Add(3.0)
myList.Add(3)
' Oops. 3 is boxed in as integer not double
myList.Add("a"c)
' Boxing "a" as Char not double

...
```

Now the VB.NET version behaves like the C# one, although the exception originates in the DoubleType class instead of the unbox command, as shown in Figure 1-15.

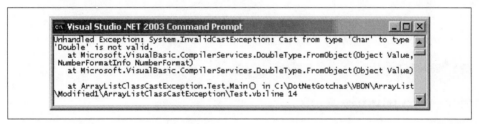

Figure 1-15. Output from Example 1-21

The problems mentioned in this gotcha are specific to non-generic collections. This will not be a problem in .NET 2.0 if you use generics. Generics provide type-safe data structures that resemble C++ templates in some ways (though they differ in their capabilities and implementation). This leads to code that's more reusable and better in performance.

The C# code that utilizes generics to perform the same function as in Example 1-18 is shown in Example 1-22. The corresponding VB.NET code is shown in Example 1-23.

Example 1-22. Generics version of the C# code from Example 1-18

✔ **C# (ArrayList)**

```
using System;
using System.Collections.Generic;

namespace ArrayListClassCastException
{
    class Test
    {
        [STAThread]
        static void Main(string[] args)
        {
            Collection<double> myList = new Collection<double>();

            myList.Add(3.0);
            myList.Add(3); // No problem. 3 is stored as 3.0.

            double total = 0;
            foreach(double val in myList)
            {
                total += val;
            }

            Console.WriteLine(total);
        }
    }
}
```

Example 1-23. Generics version of the VB.NET code from Example 1-21

✔ **VB.NET (ArrayList)**

```
Imports System.Collections.Generic

Module Test

    Sub Main()
        Dim myList As New Collection(Of Double)

        myList.Add(3.0)
        myList.Add(3) 'No problem 3 stored as 3.0

        myList.Add("a"c)
        'error BC30311: Value of type 'Char'
        'cannot be converted to 'Double'

        Dim total As Double = 0
```

```
    Dim val As Double
    For Each val In myList
        total += val
    Next

    Console.WriteLine(total)
  End Sub

End Module
```

When you use generics, there is no boxing and unboxing overhead. The value of 3 is converted to 3.0 at compile time based on the parametric type double/Double of the Collection. (You can see this by looking at the MSIL code generated.) In the case of the VB.NET code, if you pass a character to the Collection's Add( ) method, you get a compilation error since it can't be converted to double/Double.

 IN A NUTSHELL

Be careful with collections that treat elements as objects. For one thing, you may incur some boxing and unboxing overhead; for another, you may trigger an InvalidCastException. This problem goes away with Generics, so once they are available use them for type safety and performance.

SEE ALSO

Gotcha #2, "struct and class differ in behavior," Gotcha #3, "Returning value types from a method/property is risky," Gotcha #4, "You can't force calls to your value-type constructors," Gotcha #5, "String concatenation is expensive," and Gotcha #30, "Common Language Specification Compliance isn't the default."

GOTCHA

#10 Type.GetType( ) may not locate all types

The Abstract Factory pattern [Freeman04, Gamma95] is a common and useful pattern that abstracts object creation. It isolates the code that decides which type of object to create from the code that uses the objects. It is almost effortless in .NET to use Abstract Factory due to the powerful GetType( ) method of the Type class.

Suppose you need to create different kinds of objects depending on runtime conditions. Perhaps the name of the class is read from a configuration file, or provided as an input to the program. Or you may be dealing with plug-ins that are dynamically introduced when an application is launched (or even while it is running). How do you create an object when you don't know what class it belongs to until the moment you need to create it?

The `Type.GetType()` method can help you achieve this. Here's how to use it:

1. Obtain the class's type information by calling `Type.GetType()`.

2. Use the `Activator.CreateInstance()` method to create an object of that class, assuming you have a no-parameter constructor.

3. Cast the object reference (using the as operator in C# or CType function in VB.NET) to a known interface (that the class implements) and invoke the interface methods on it.

This flexibility paves the way for a lot of extensibility in applications.

The core of this facility is the `Type` class's `GetType()` method. In writing an application, if you pass the `GetType()` method the name of a class in your assembly, it will fetch the `Type` metadata for that class. However, when you ask for type information for a class or plug-in from another assembly, `GetType()` will fail.

Consider Example 1-24. It is a simple WinForm application with a button. When the button is clicked, you get the `Type` object for three types and display the information on them.

Example 1-24. Behavior of Type.GetType()

✘ C# (GetType)

```csharp
private void CallGetTypeButton_Click(object sender,
    System.EventArgs e)
{
    try
    {
        Type theType;

        theType = Type.GetType(
            "CallingGetType.Form1", true);
        MessageBox.Show("First type is "
            + theType.FullName);

        theType = Type.GetType(
            "System.Collections.Queue", true);
        MessageBox.Show("Second type is "
            + theType.FullName);

        theType = Type.GetType(
            "System.Windows.Forms.Form",
            true);
        MessageBox.Show("Third type is "
            + theType.FullName);
    }
    catch(Exception ex)
```

Example 1-24. Behavior of Type.GetType( ) (continued)

```
        {
            MessageBox.Show("Error: " + ex.Message);
        }
    }
```

✗ VB.NET (GetType)

```
Private Sub CallGetTypeButton_Click( _
    ByVal sender As System.Object, _
    ByVal e As System.EventArgs) _
    Handles CallGetTypeButton.Click
    Try
        Dim theType As Type

        theType = Type.GetType( _
         "CallingGetType.Form1", True)
        MessageBox.Show("First type is " _
         & theType.FullName)

        theType = Type.GetType( _
         "System.Collections.Queue", True)
        MessageBox.Show("Second type is " _
         & theType.FullName)

        theType = Type.GetType( _
         "System.Windows.Forms.Form", _
         True)

        MessageBox.Show("Third type is " _
         & theType.FullName)

    Catch ex As Exception

        MessageBox.Show("Error: " & ex.Message)
    End Try
End Sub
```

Figure 1-16, Figure 1-17, and Figure 1-18 show the output from the code in Example 1-24.

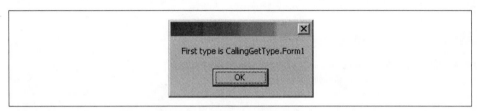

Figure 1-16. CallingGetType.Form1

Figure 1-17. System.Collections.Queue

Figure 1-18. System.Windows.Forms.Form

While there was no problem getting the Type metadata for Form1 and System. Collections.Queue, the call to GetType( ) with the class name System.Windows.Forms. Form failed. (The Form class is the base class of Form1 within which this code is executing).

In developing code that creates objects based on runtime class information, and applications that require the use of plug-ins, you may run into problems like this. If you test your application using plug-in components that are part of your own assembly, they'll probably work just fine. However, when you try to load a class from another assembly, things won't work quite so well. The reason is that GetType( ), if given a class name, only looks in the calling object's assembly and mscorlib.dll. Since Form1 belongs to the calling assembly and System.Collections.Queue belongs to mscorlib.dll, there is no problem with them.

There is a workaround that enables you to load classes from other assemblies, like System.Windows.Forms. When you tell GetType( ) which class you need, you must specify the full name of the class including the full identity of the assembly. This identity includes the name, version, culture information, and the strong name public key token.

An example of correct usage of GetType( ) for getting information on the System. Windows.Forms.Form class is shown in Example 1-25.

Example 1-25. Correct usage of GetType( )

✔ **C# (GetType)**

```
...
        theType = Type.GetType(
            "System.Windows.Forms.Form, " +
            "System.Windows.Forms, " +
```

Example 1-25. Correct usage of GetType( ) (continued)

```
                  "Version=1.0.5000.0, " +
                  "Culture=neutral, " +
                  "PublicKeyToken=b77a5c561934e089",
                  true);
```

✔ VB.NET (GetType)

```
...

        theType = Type.GetType( _
          "System.Windows.Forms.Form, " & _
            "System.Windows.Forms, " & _
            "Version=1.0.5000.0, " & _
            "Culture=neutral, " & _
            "PublicKeyToken=b77a5c561934e089", _
          True)
```

In Example 1-25, the class name System.Windows.Forms.Form is followed (comma separated) by the name of the assembly in which that class is located (System.Windows.Forms), the version number (1.0.5000.0), the culture (neutral), and the public key token of that assembly (b77a5c561934e089). The public key token for an assembly can be obtained by using the *sn* (strong name) tool. Only if you specify the fully qualified class name along with the assembly identity will you correctly retrieve the type information. As long as the application can locate the specified assembly, the type information will be loaded.

How does the application find the assembly? First the CLR looks for it in the Global Assembly Cache (GAC). Then it looks in the application base directory. If the assembly is still not found, it searches for subdirectories with the assembly name or the specific culture under the application base directory. If it still hasn't found the assembly, it continues looking for directories specified in the codebase setting in the application's configuration file. You can also explicitly load the assembly using the LoadFrom( ) method of the System.Reflection.Assembly class.

If you are using some API or library that expects you to send the name of a class, you have to follow the recommendations in this gotcha. If the class name is specified in a configuration file or is given as input for the program during runtime, you must make sure that the fully qualified name as discussed above is provided.

IN A NUTSHELL

When specifying class names in a configuration file or providing them as input for dynamically creating objects, make sure you provide the fully qualified class name, along with the full identity of the assembly.

SEE ALSO

Gotcha #11, "Public key reported by sn.exe is inconsistent" and Gotcha #14, "Type.GetType( ) might fail at run-time"

#11 Public key reported by sn.exe is inconsistent

The utility *sn.exe* creates a strong name to sign your code with a public/private key pair. When you specify the assembly identity as in Example 1-25, or when you define the binding redirect for assembly version forwarding in the configuration file, you need to specify the public key token of the assembly. If you have a strong name key (*.snk*) file for your assembly, use caution in extracting the public key token from it. The -t option of *sn.exe* gives you the public key token. However, I have seen a number of developers fall into a trap when extracting the public key token from the *.snk* file.

Let's look at an example. Suppose you use the .NET command prompt to execute *sn.exe* as shown in Example 1-26.

Example 1-26. Using the sn utility to create key and extract public key token

```
>sn  -k mykey.snk

Microsoft (R) .NET Framework Strong Name Utility
Version 1.1.4322.573
Copyright (C) Microsoft Corporation 1998-2002. All
 rights reserved.

Key pair written to mykey.snk

>sn -t mykey.snk

Microsoft (R) .NET Framework Strong Name Utility
Version 1.1.4322.573
Copyright (C) Microsoft Corporation 1998-2002. All
 rights reserved.

Public key token is 1cf34646172fcb74

>sn -p mykey.snk mykeypublic.snk

Microsoft (R) .NET Framework Strong Name Utility
Version 1.1.4322.573
Copyright (C) Microsoft Corporation 1998-2002. All
 rights reserved.

Public key written to mykeypublic.snk

>sn -t mykeypublic.snk

Microsoft (R) .NET Framework Strong Name Utility
```

Example 1-26. Using the sn utility to create key and extract public key token (continued)

```
Version 1.1.4322.573
Copyright (C) Microsoft Corporation 1998-2002. All
 rights reserved.
```

Public key token is **bab446454bf67c07**

In this example, you first run sn –k mykey.snk. This creates the strong-name file named *mykey.snk* that contains the public and private key pair. Then you run sn -t mykey.snk on the generated file. This command prints the public key token. Then you execute the command sn -p mykey.snk mykeypublic.snk to extract the public key from *mykey.snk* and save it in *mykeypublic.snk*. Finally, you run sn -t mykeypublic.snk on the public key file. Note that the tokens displayed are not the same! Which one should you use? Which one is correct?

When I ran into this problem, I scratched my head wondering why my binding redirect didn't work properly. Eventually, when I used *ildasm.exe* to view the manifest of the assembly that was linking to my assembly, I realized that the public key token was not the same as the one I had in the configuration file.

If you read through the documentation for sn -t, you'll find the statement:

> Displays the token for the public key stored in infile. The contents of infile must be previously generated using -p.

So this was the problem: the first time I ran sn -t, it extracted the public key from a file that had not been generated using sn -p. The next time I executed sn -t, it targeted *mykeypublic.snk*, which had been created using sn -p. The first sn -t was incorrect; the second was right.

It would be nice if there were an error or warning when you use -t on an input file that wasn't generated using the -p option.

How does this differ in .NET 2.0 Beta 1? This problem has been fixed in .NET 2.0 Beta 1. When you run sn -t mykey.snk, you get the following error:

```
Microsoft (R) .NET Framework Strong Name Utility  Version 2.0.40607.16
Copyright (C) Microsoft Corporation. All rights reserved.

Failed to convert key to token -- Bad Version of provider.
```

IN A NUTSHELL

Do not extract the public key token from a *.snk* file directly. Instead use the file generated from the -p option. Or better still, get it from the manifest of a binding assembly by viewing it in *ildasm.exe*.

SEE ALSO

Gotcha #10, "Type.GetType( ) may not locate all types."

CHAPTER 2

Visual Studio and Compiler Gotchas

.NET provides a very productive development environment, thanks to two main factors. One is the .NET Framework with its rich class library. The other is Visual Studio .NET, with its many wizards.

The code you write in C# or VB.NET is translated into MSIL by the C# compiler (*csc.exe*) or the VB.NET compiler (*vbc.exe*). A few idiosyncrasies of the compilers, and how Visual Studio presents them, can cause frustration in some cases and outright trouble in others. And several things get lost in the translation to MSIL. Not all source-code statements are translated quite as you might expect. This will come to light, for instance, when I discuss the odd behavior related to re-throwing an exception.

In this chapter I will focus on Visual Studio- and compiler-related gotchas.

GOTCHA
#12 Compiler warnings may not be benign

A compiler aids developers by checking for syntax consistency, and tries to eliminate (or at least reduce) the possibility of errors. However, there are certain anomalies that the compiler takes less seriously than you might want it to. Reporting them as warnings instead of errors may lead to code that compiles but does not behave the way you expect. I urge you to treat warnings as errors to make sure they don't escape your notice.

I have been preaching this since I started working with .NET. There were times when I wondered how much I should emphasize it, but I was reminded recently when a client asked me to help integrate a new product with an existing one.

I began by fetching the code from the source code control system and compiled it on my machine. Since I had not registered all the necessary components, I got errors.

When I went to resolve them, I found several warnings scattered among the errors. My first impulse was to ignore my principles and practices, fix the errors, and finish my task. (After all, I was asked to integrate, not to preach.) However, I get very nervous leaving warnings in my code. So, out of curiosity, I started browsing through the warnings. I could not believe my eyes when I saw the following "warning":

```
warning CS0665: Assignment in conditional expression is always
constant; did you mean to use == instead of = ?
```

The offending code resembled the following if-clause:

```
if (m_theTextBox.Visible = true)
```

It was scary to see this crucial mistake in production code. Somehow, it had slipped through the testing and debugging process.

Once I saw this, I looked at the other warnings with a suspicious eye. The next one I encountered said that a method was hiding a method in its base class, and suggested that I use the new keyword (shadows in VB.NET). Here's the problem: first a method is marked virtual in the base class (overridable in VB.NET); then a derived class implements a method with the same name and signature without marking it as override (overrides in VB.NET).

The result (as discussed in Gotcha #44, "Compilers are lenient toward forgotten override/overrides") is that the derived method ends up hiding or shadowing the base method instead of overriding it. This leads to behavior that is outright wrong. What is worse is that Visual Studio hides the warning under the rug, so to speak, as Example 2-1 shows.

Example 2-1. Warnings reported by Visual Studio

✗ C# (Warnings)

```
using System;

namespace TreatWarningsAsError
{
    public class Base
    {
        public virtual void foo() {}
    }

    public class Derived : Base
    {
        public void foo() {}
    }

    public class Test
    {
        [STAThread]
        static void Main(string[] args)
        {
```

Example 2-1. Warnings reported by Visual Studio (continued)

```
        int val;

        Console.WriteLine("Test");
    }
  }
}
```

✗ VB.NET (Warnings)

```
Public Class Base

    Public Overridable Sub foo( )

    End Sub
End Class

Public Class Derived
    Inherits Base
    Public Sub foo( )

    End Sub
End Class
Public Class Test
    Public Shared Sub Main(ByVal args( ) As String)
        Dim val As Integer

        Console.WriteLine("Test")
    End Sub
End Class
```

When you compile the C# code in Example 2-1, the output window displays what you see in Figure 2-1.

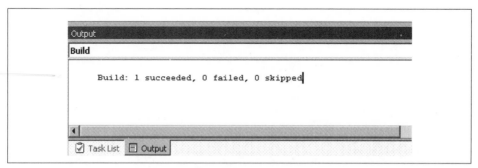

Figure 2-1. Visual Studio output window for C# code in Example 2-1

Since the build succeeded, you have no reason to look for warnings, right? Well, no, not exactly.

If you scroll up to view the compiler messages, you will find:

```
: warning CS0114: 'TreatWarningsAsError.Derived.foo()' hides
inherited member 'TreatWarningsAsError.Base.foo()'. To make the
current member override that implementation, add the override
keyword. Otherwise add the new keyword.
: warning CS0168: The variable 'val' is declared but never used
```

There are two warnings. One says that the method foo() in Derived hides the method foo() in Base. The other says that the variable val is declared but never used. While the second is benign, the first one definitely is not.

You may notice that Visual Studio points out warnings by putting a squiggly line on the offending statement. So why not just find the squiggly lines and fix the problems? Well, that might work in a small application. But in a large system, where you may have hundreds of classes, a change in one class can ripple through the entire system. You can't search every single file looking for squiggly lines.

The problem here is more fundamental: Certain cases, such as the missing override/ overrides or the use of = instead of ==, are key programming mistakes and should be treated as errors, not warnings.

I strongly recommend that you configure the compiler to treat warnings as errors. In Visual Studio, you can do this by going into your project's properties.

In a C# project, right click on the project name in the Solutions Explorer and click on Properties. In the resulting dialog, go to the Build entry under Configuration Properties. Change the value for the Treat Warnings As Errors property from False to True (you can easily do this with just a double click on the property name), as shown in Figure 2-2. (Figure 2-3 shows how to change the settings for a VB.NET project.)

After you make these changes, the incorrect override of the foo() method appears as an error. However, the benign warning of val not being used has disappeared in the C# version. In the VB.NET version, it did not appear in the first place.

Fortunately, you don't have to change these settings for every project you create. You can change them at the system level so each new project will have this setting. You do that by modifying the appropriate template.

For C#, you can find these templates in the *VC#\VC#Wizards* directory where Visual Studio .NET is installed. For instance, on my machine, it is under the *C:\ Program Files\Microsoft Visual Studio .NET 2003\VC#\VC#Wizards* directory. There are four template files: *default.csproj* (for console applications), *DefaultDll.csproj* (for DLL class library projects), *DefaultWebProject.csproj* (for ASP.NET applications), and *DefaultWinExe.csproj* (for Windows applications). Example 2-2 shows you how

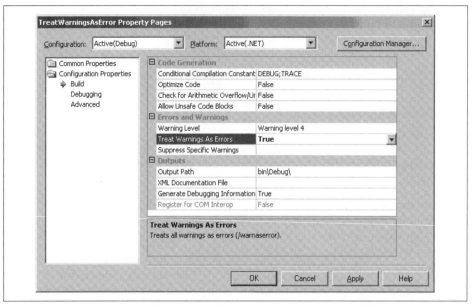

Figure 2-2. Setting Treat Warnings as Errors in a C# project

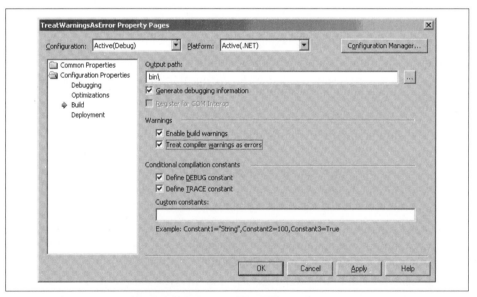

Figure 2-3. Setting Treat Warnings as Errors in a VB.NET project

to add an entry to the template file to set Treat Warnings As Errors to true for every C# console project you create.

Example 2-2. Template entry to set Treat Warnings As Errors on C# projects

```
<VisualStudioProject>
    <CSHARP>
      <Build>
          <Settings OutputType = "Exe" NoStandardLibraries = "false" >
              <Config
                  Name = "Debug"
                  DebugSymbols = "true"
                  Optimize = "false"
                  OutputPath = ".\bin\Debug"
                  EnableUnmanagedDebugging = "false"
                  DefineConstants = "DEBUG;TRACE"
                  WarningLevel = "4"
                IncrementalBuild = "false"
                TreatWarningsAsErrors = "true"
                />
                <Config
                    Name = "Release"
                    DebugSymbols = "false"
                    Optimize = "true"
                    OutputPath = ".\bin\Release"
                    EnableUnmanagedDebugging = "false"
                        DefineConstants = "TRACE"
                            WarningLevel = "4"
                IncrementalBuild = "false"
                TreatWarningsAsErrors = "true"
                />
            </Settings>
        </Build>
        <Files>
            <Include/>
            <Exclude/>
        </Files>
    </CSHARP>
</VisualStudioProject>
```

For VB.NET, the templates for different types of projects are located in different sub-directories under the *vb7\VBWizards* directory. On my system, the file *C:\Program Files\Microsoft Visual Studio .NET 2003\Vb7\VBWizards* is the Wizard directory. The template for all console applications is the file *…\Vb7\VBWizards\ConsoleApplication\Templates\1033\ConsoleApplication.vbproj*.

Example 2-3 shows how you add an entry to the template file to set Treat Warnings As Errors to true for every new VB.NET console project.

Example 2-3. Template entry to set Treat Warnings As Errors on VB.NET projects

```
<VisualStudioProject>
    <VisualBasic>
        <Build>
            <Settings OutputType = "Exe" StartupObject = "" >
```

```
            <Config
                Name = "Debug"
                DebugSymbols = "true"
                DefineDebug = "true"
                DefineTrace = "true"
                IncrementalBuild = "true"
                OutputPath = "bin"
                TreatWarningsAsErrors = "true"
            />
            <Config
                Name = "Release"
                DebugSymbols = "false"
                DefineDebug = "false"
                DefineTrace = "true"
                IncrementalBuild = "false"
                Optimize = "true"
                OutputPath = "bin"
                TreatWarningsAsErrors = "true"
            />
        </Settings>
        <References>
            <Reference Name = "System" />
            <Reference Name = "System.Data" />
            <Reference Name = "System.XML" />
        </References>
        <Imports>
            <Import Namespace = "Microsoft.VisualBasic" />
            <Import Namespace = "System" />
            <Import Namespace = "System.Collections" />
            <Import Namespace = "System.Data" />
            <Import Namespace = "System.Diagnostics" />
        </Imports>
    </Build>
    <Files>
        <Include>
        </Include>
    </Files>
  </VisualBasic>
</VisualStudioProject>
```

Treating warnings as errors has side effects, however.

The main side effect of configuring the project setting to treat warnings as errors is that benign warnings will show up as errors, thus terminating the compilation. Example 2-4 shows a simple example of a class named AService created as part of a class library.

Example 2-4. Sample code with benign warnings

```csharp
using System;

namespace TreatWarningsAsErrorSideEffect
{
    /// <summary>
    /// Summary description for Class1.
    /// </summary>
    public class AService
    {
        /// <summary>
        /// Documentation for Method1
        /// </summary>
        public void Method1( )
        {
        }

        public int Method2( )
        {
            return 0;
        }
    }
}
```

In the above example, while Method1( ) has the XML documentation tags, Method2( ) does not. This is not unusual. While you may want to document each method you write, sometimes there are methods that, for some reason, you don't want to. (A method whose sole purpose is to test some feature of your code is a good example.) When you compile the above code with Treat Warnings As Errors set to True, the warning becomes an error:

```
error CS1591: Missing XML comment for publicly visible type or member
'TreatWarningsAsErrorSideEffect.AService.Method2( )'
```

There are two solutions to this problem. One is to go ahead and write some documentation, however sketchy, for each method. Or you can suppress warnings of this kind, as shown in Figure 2-4.

But be careful about suppressing warnings. You might not really want to suppress certain warnings. Depending on the case, there may be other alternatives or workarounds.

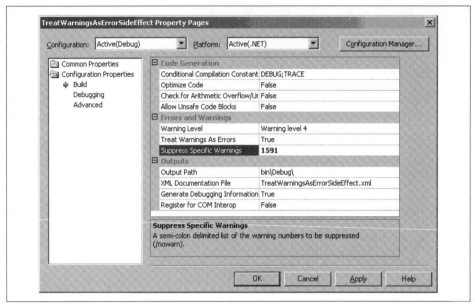

Figure 2-4. Asking certain warnings to be suppressed

 IN A NUTSHELL

Not all compiler warnings are benign. Some severe problems are reported as warnings.

Therefore, I strongly recommend that you configure the compiler to treat warnings as errors. You can do this on a per-project basis, or you can modify the Visual Studio templates to affect all future projects you create.

SEE ALSO

Gotcha #44, "Compilers are lenient toward forgotten override/overrides."

GOTCHA
#13 Ordering of catch processing isn't consist across languages

A language should avoid surprises as much as possible. Its behavior should be intuitive, consistent, and predictable. Unfortunately, both C# and VB.NET have some odd quirks. In this gotcha, I'll pick on VB.NET.

For instance, suppose you have a hierarchy of exceptions, say Exception E2 inherits from E1, which in turn inherits from System.ApplicationException. When you place catch blocks in your code, what order should you put them in? Should you write the catch for E2 before the one for E1? Or code the catch for E1 before the catch for E2?

The C# compiler tries to help by giving you a compilation error if you place them in the wrong order. However, in VB.NET, you are in for a surprise. Consider Example 2-5.

Example 2-5. Order of catch

✗ C# (CatchOrder)

```
using System;

namespace OrderOfCatch
{
    class Program
    {
        public static void AMethod()
        {
            throw new ApplicationException();
        }

        [STAThread]
        static void Main(string[] args)
        {
            try
            {
                AMethod();
            }
            catch(Exception ex)
            {
                Console.WriteLine("Caught Exception");
            }
            catch(ApplicationException ae)
                // Results in compilation error.
            {
                Console.WriteLine(
                    "Caught ApplicationException");
            }
        }
    }
}
```

✗ VB.NET (CatchOrder)

```
Module Program
    Public Sub AMethod()
        Throw New ApplicationException
    End Sub

    Sub Main(ByVal args As String())
        Try
```

Example 2-5. Order of catch (continued)

```
            AMethod( )
        Catch ex As Exception
            Console.WriteLine("Caught Exception")
        Catch ae As ApplicationException
            Console.WriteLine("Caught ApplicationException")
        End Try
    End Sub
End Module
```

C# generates the following compilation error:

```
error CS0160: A previous catch clause already catches all exceptions of this or a
super type ('System.Exception').
```

However, VB.NET does not report an error (it does not even report a warning). Executing the VB.NET version of the code produces the output in Figure 2-5.

Figure 2-5. Output from VB.NET version of Example 2-5

Instead of the catch block for System.ApplicationException being called, you end up in the catch for System.Exception.

Now let's reverse the order of the catch blocks as shown in Example 2-6.

Example 2-6. Reversing the order of catch

✔ VB.NET (CatchOrder)

```
Module Program
    Public Sub AMethod( )
        Throw New ApplicationException
    End Sub

    Sub Main(ByVal args As String( ))
        Try
            AMethod( )
        Catch ae As ApplicationException
            Console.WriteLine("Caught ApplicationException")
        Catch ex As Exception
            Console.WriteLine("Caught Exception")
        End Try
    End Sub
End Module
```

The program now produces the desired output, as shown in Figure 2-6.

Figure 2-6. Output for code in Example 2-6

When writing VB.NET code, you have to pay attention to the order of your catch blocks. The runtime is going to find the first matching type for a catch. If the base type appears before the derived type, even though a more specific type appears later in the catch sequence, the base type will handle the exception. This is why you see the difference in output between the two VB.NET code versions above.

You can use the .NET Reflector tool (see the section "On the Web" in the Appendix) to find the relationship between classes by examining the Base Types and Derived Types nodes, as shown in Figure 2-7.

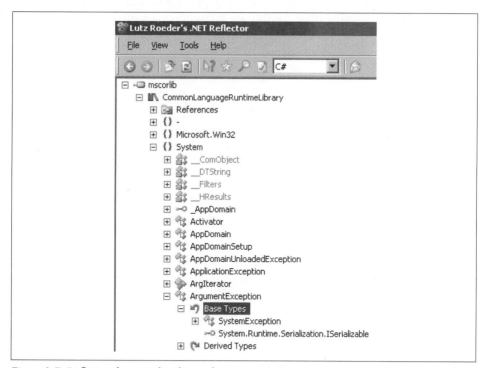

Figure 2-7. Reflector showing class hierarchy

How does this differ in .NET 2.0 Beta 1? For the VB.NET code, the compiler gives a warning (though still not an error):

```
warning BC42029: Catch block never reached, because 'System.ApplicationException'
inherits from 'System.Exception'.
```

IN A NUTSHELL

In VB.NET, if you write multiple catch statements, make sure you place them in the proper order, with catch handlers for derived exception types appearing before the catch handlers for their base types.

SEE ALSO

Gotcha #15, "rethrow isn't consistent" and Gotcha #26, "Details of exception may be hidden."

GOTCHA
#14 Type.GetType( ) might fail at run-time

Sometimes you need to retrieve the metadata (type information) from a class whose name you know at compile time. If you are going to experience an error in doing this, it is better for it to occur at compile time than at runtime. Consider Example 2-7.

Example 2-7. Failure of Type.GetType( )

✗ C# (Typeof)

```
using System;

namespace TypeOfKnownClass
{
    class Test
    {
        [STAThread]
        static void Main(string[] args)
        {
            Type theType = Type.GetType("Test");

            Console.WriteLine(theType.FullName);
        }
    }
}
```

✗ VB.NET (Typeof)

```
Module Test

    Sub Main()
        Dim theType As Type = Type.GetType("Test")
```

Example 2-7. Failure of Type.GetType( ) (continued)

```
        Console.WriteLine(theType.FullName)
    End Sub

End Module
```

While the code looks simple, executing it results in a `NullReferenceException`. The reason for the exception is that `Type.GetType( )` does not recognize the type `Test`. You must pass `Type.GetType( )` the fully qualified name of the type prefixed by its namespace. And even if you write the fully qualified name, what if you misspell the namespace? While you can easily identify and fix this in testing, you may still waste a few minutes in the process. If the type is known at compile time, it is better to get the metadata using an alternate mechanism, shown in Example 2-8.

Example 2-8. Getting the Type metadata

✔ C# (Typeof)

```
using System;

namespace TypeOfKnownClass
{
    class Test
    {
        [STAThread]
        static void Main(string[] args)
        {
            Type theType = typeof(Test);

            Console.WriteLine(theType.FullName);
        }
    }
}
```

✔ VB.NET (Typeof)

```
Module Test

    Sub Main( )
        Dim theType As Type = GetType(Test)

        Console.WriteLine(theType.FullName)
    End Sub

End Module
```

When you use typeof( ) (C#) and GetType( ) (VB.NET), the compiler automatically resolves the name Test to its fully qualified name. If there is any ambiguity, the compiler alerts you. This saves time and effort by moving the checking to compile time instead of run time.

 IN A NUTSHELL

Finding problems at compile time is better than waiting for them to surface at run time. If possible, that is, if the class name is known at compile time, use typeof/ GetType instead of the Type.GetType( ) method.

SEE ALSO

Gotcha #10, "Type.GetType( ) may not locate all types."

GOTCHA
#15 rethrow isn't consistent

In some situations, you may need to continue propagating an exception up the call stack. For instance, you may feel that you have not handled it successfully, or perhaps you just want to log the exception. In these cases, you can throw the exception again. If e is a reference to an exception object, the call that comes to mind is throw e. But what is the consequence of this statement? This is a good example of things getting lost in the translation to MSIL. Consider Example 2-9.

Example 2-9. Behavior of a throw statement

✗ C# (rethrow)

```csharp
using System;

namespace ThrowingException
{
    class Test
    {
        public static void Method1( )
        {
            throw new ApplicationException( );
        }

        public static void Method2( )
        {
            try
            {
                Method1( );
            }
            catch(Exception ex)
            {
                // Code to log may go here.
                throw ex;
```

Example 2-9. Behavior of a throw statement (continued)

```csharp
        }
    }

    public static void Method3()
    {
        try
        {
            Method1();
        }
        catch(Exception)
        {
            // Code to log may go here.
            throw;
        }
    }

    [STAThread]
    static void Main(string[] args)
    {
        try
        {
            Console.WriteLine("----- Calling Method2");
            Method2();
        }
        catch(Exception ex)
        {
            Console.WriteLine(ex);
        }

        try
        {
            Console.WriteLine("----- Calling Method3");
            Method3();
        }
        catch(Exception ex)
        {
            Console.WriteLine(ex);
        }
    }
}
}
```

✗ VB.NET (rethrow)

```vbnet
Module Test

    Public Sub Method1()
        Throw New ApplicationException
    End Sub
```

Example 2-9. Behavior of a throw statement (continued)

```vb
    Public Sub Method2()
        Try
            Method1()
        Catch ex As Exception
            'code to log may go here
            Throw ex
        End Try
    End Sub

    Public Sub Method3()
        Try
            Method1()
        Catch ex As Exception
            'code to log may go here
            Throw
        End Try
    End Sub

    Public Sub Main()
        Try
            Console.WriteLine("----- Calling Method2")

            Method2()
        Catch ex As Exception
            Console.WriteLine(ex)
        End Try

        Try
            Console.WriteLine("----- Calling Method3")

            Method3()
        Catch ex As Exception
            Console.WriteLine(ex)
        End Try
    End Sub
End Module
```

In Example 2-9, Method2() uses throw ex to propagate the exception it caught. Method3(), on the other hand, uses only throw. The output from the above program is shown in Figure 2-8.

Note that when the exception is caught in Main() from Method2() (the one that uses throw ex), the stack trace does not indicate that Method1() was the origin of the exception. However, when the exception is caught in Main() from Method3() (the one that uses throw without the ex), the stack trace points all the way to Method1(), where the exception originated.

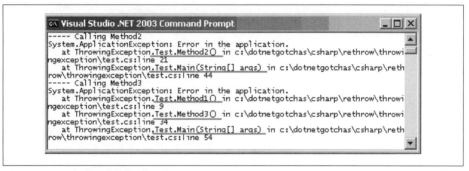

Figure 2-8. Output from Example 2-9

What is the reason for this difference? It becomes clear if you use *ildasm.exe* to examine the assembly for Method2( ) and Method3( ), shown in Example 2-10 as generated from the C# code.

Example 2-10. MSIL with difference between throw ex and throw

```
.method public hidebysig static void  Method2() cil managed
{
  // Code size       11 (0xb)
  .maxstack  1
  .locals init ([0] class [mscorlib]System.Exception ex)
  .try
  {
    IL_0000:  call       void ThrowingException.Test::Method1()
    IL_0005:  leave.s    IL_000a
  } // end .try
  catch [mscorlib]System.Exception
  {
    IL_0007:  stloc.0
    IL_0008:  ldloc.0
    IL_0009:  throw
  } // end handler
  IL_000a:  ret
} // end of method Test::Method2

.method public hidebysig static void  Method3() cil managed
{
  // Code size       11 (0xb)
  .maxstack  1
  .try
  {
    IL_0000:  call       void ThrowingException.Test::Method1()
    IL_0005:  leave.s    IL_000a
  } // end .try
  catch [mscorlib]System.Exception
  {
    IL_0007:  pop
```

```
  IL_0008:  rethrow
} // end handler
  IL_000a:  ret
} // end of method Test::Method3
```

As you can see from the MSIL, throw ex translates to a fresh throw on the call stack. However, throw by itself translates to a rethrow statement at the MSIL level. The latter results in the true rethrow of the original exception, whereas the former is treated as a new exception. So you would want to use throw instead of throw ex.

Another option is to use the InnerException property of the Exception class to propagate the exception details. In the catch block for Method2( ) you can create an exception and set the exception you caught as its constructor argument, as in the following C# code segment:

```
catch(Exception ex)
{
    // Code to log may go here.
    //throw ex;
    throw new ApplicationException(
            "Exception logged", ex);
}
```

The VB.NET version is:

```
Catch ex As Exception
    'code to log may go here
    'Throw ex
    Throw New ApplicationException("Exception logged", ex)
End Try
```

As a result of this change you will see the output shown in Figure 2-9.

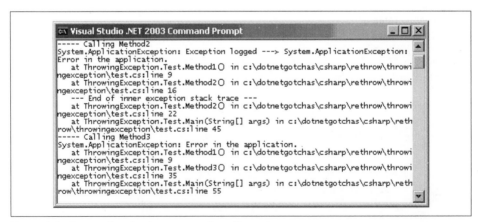

Figure 2-9. Output after the change to use InnerException

The catch blocks in Main( ) call Console.WriteLine(ex). This in turn calls the ToString( ) method on the Exception, which prints the details of that exception instance. If the Exception contains a non-null InnerException, the ToString( ) method of Exception will also print the details of the inner exception. You can see this in the output between the "--->" (in the second line from the top of Figure 2-9) and "--- End of inner exception stack trace ---."

 IN A NUTSHELL

Use throw instead of throw ex to propagate an exception. Alternately, use InnerException.

SEE ALSO

Gotcha #26, "Details of exception may be hidden."

GOTCHA
#16 Default of Option Strict (off) isn't good

C# is a strongly typed language. VB.NET, on the other hand, is not by default, unless you turn on the Option Strict option. When you create a VB.NET project in Visual Studio, Option Strict is set to Off. Should you leave it as Off? Or should you consider setting it to On? I will present arguments for both sides here. Let's start with the code in Example 2-11.

Example 2-11. Effect of Option Strict Off

✔ C# (OptionStrict)

```
This concept does not apply to C#.
```

✔ VB.NET (OptionStrict)

```
Public Class Program

    Public Sub foo( )
        Console.WriteLine("foo called")
    End Sub

    Public Shared Sub Main( )

        'Very simple case
        Dim val As Integer = 2.3
        Console.WriteLine(val)

        'This one is more killing
```

Example 2-11. Effect of Option Strict Off (continued)

```
    Dim obj As Program = New Object

    obj.foo( )

End Sub
```

```
End Class
```

In the above example Option Strict is Off (the default). The code first assigns a double value to an Integer variable. Then it goes on to assign an Object to a reference of type Program. This has disaster written all over it, and in fact the program fails at runtime. Its output is shown in Figure 2-10.

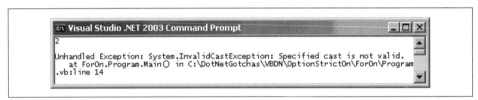

Figure 2-10. Output from Example 2-11

A compiler error would really be nice in this case. As much as possible, you want to eliminate problems at compile time, not runtime. Fortunately, the VB.NET compiler will help if you set Option Strict to On.

You can do this in the project settings, as shown in Figure 2-11.

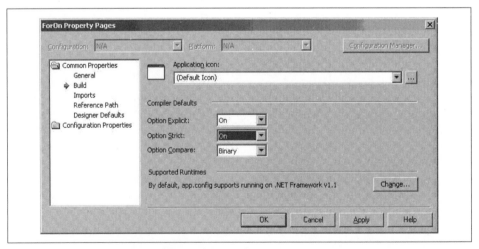

Figure 2-11. Project Setting to set Option Strict to On

Once this is set, you get the following compilation errors in the code:

- Option Strict On disallows implicit conversions from Double to Integer
- Option Strict On disallows implicit conversions from System.Object to ForOn. Program (where ForOn is the namespace for the Program class)
- So Option Strict On can help you catch errors early, at compile time rather than runtime. It should be the default on all your projects.

Are there situations where you might prefer to have Option Strict Off? Well, not many, but sometimes it comes in handy. For instance, Option Strict Off may make for simpler code by eliminating a number of CType or DirectCast statements when interoperating with some COM components. In cases where the code is easier to write with Option Strict Off, set Option Strict to Off in the source file for those classes only.

In an application that my colleagues and I developed in C#, I had to resort to writing one of the modules in VB.NET. The reason was that I had to integrate a COM component that published only the IDispatch interface. After struggling with it for hours, I could find no way to communicate with this component using C# or VB.NET with Option Strict On.

To illustrate the point, Example 2-12 shows a scripting component representing a bank account.

Example 2-12. An example scripting COM component

```
<?xml version="1.0"?>
<!-- Scripting Component eBankAccount.wsc -->
<!-- This is a strip down from a component
 that does more serious work accessing a database.
 I have cut it down to bare minimum.
-->
<component>

<?component error="true" debug="true"?>

<registration
    description="eBankAccount"
    progid="eBank.Account"
    version="1.00"
    classid="{7607496c-bfae-4200-9ffb-14c04a93d009}"
>
</registration>

<public>
    <property name="balance">
        <get/>
    </property>
    <method name="deposit">
        <PARAMETER name="purpose"/>
        <PARAMETER name="amount"/>
    </method>
```

Example 2-12. An example scripting COM component (continued)

```
    <method name="withdraw">
        <PARAMETER name="purpose"/>
        <PARAMETER name="amount"/>
    </method>
</public>

<implements type="ASP" id="ASP"/>

<script language="VBScript">
<![CDATA[
OPTION EXPLICIT

dim accountNumber
dim balance

balance = 0


function get_balance( )
    get_balance = balance
end function

function deposit(purpose, amount)
    balance = balance + amount
end function

function withdraw(purpose, amount)
    balance = balance - amount
end function

]]>
</script>

</component>
```

I wanted to access this component from within my .NET code. I tried generating a
type library from the component. However, when I used *tlbimp.exe* to import the
type library, I got this error:

```
TlbImp error: System.TypeLoadException - Error: Signature has invalid ELEMENT_TYPE_*
(element type:0x.
```

So how can you communicate with components like this? Because it only exposes the
IDispatch interface, you can only bind to it at runtime. It has no distinct signature
(methods and properties); you call all its features indirectly through the IDispatch
Invoke( ) method.

Option Strict Off and late binding through System.Object come to the rescue (see
Example 2-13).

Example 2-13. Using late binding to communicate with the component

```
Option Strict Off

Module Program

    Sub Main( )
        Dim theComType As Type = _
            Type.GetTypeFromProgID("eBank.Account")

        Dim theComponent As Object = _
            Activator.CreateInstance(theComType)

        Console.WriteLine("Balance = {0}", _
            theComponent.balance)

        Console.WriteLine("Depositing $100")
        theComponent.deposit("deposit", 100)

        Console.WriteLine("Balance = {0}", _
            theComponent.balance)

    End Sub

End Module
```

In the code in Example 2-13, even though the project level setting is Option Strict On, in this class file I have set Option Strict Off. Without this setting at the top of the file, I would have gotten compilation errors when I accessed the balance property and when I invoked the deposit( ) method.

But with Option Strict Off, I was able to dynamically create an instance of the component using the Activator.CreateInstance( ) method of the Type object obtained from the prog ID ("eBank.Account"). The above code produces the output shown in Figure 2-12.

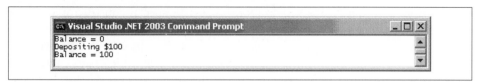

Figure 2-12. Output from Example 2-13

Set Option Strict to On to improve type checking of your VB.NET code. On rare occasions, you may find setting Option Strict Off to be of benefit, especially when you need to interoperate with late-binding COM Components exposing only the IDispatch interface. In these cases, set Option Strict Off only in those isolated files (classes) that interact with the components.

SEE ALSO

Gotcha #70, "Spattering access to COM components makes code hard to maintain."

GOTCHA
#17 Versioning may lead to Serialization headaches

Serialization is a mechanism that allows converting an object tree into a series of bytes. The most effective use of serialization is in remoting, where objects are passed by value between AppDomains or between applications. Another use of serialization is to store a snapshot of your object tree into a storage medium like a file. You can get a minimum level of support by just marking the type with a Serializable attribute. This is quite powerful, and almost effortless to implement.

If a type is flagged as Serializable, it indicates to the Serializer that an instance of the class may be serialized. If any type in the graph of the object being serialized is not Serializable, the CLR will throw a SerializationException. All fields in your type are serialized except those you mark with the NonSerialized attribute.

However, there are problems. The biggest problem with serializing to a file is versioning. If the version of a class changes after one of its objects is serialized, then the object can't be deserialized. One way to get around this limitation is to implement the ISerializable interface.

When a class implements ISerializable, the ISerializable.GetObjectData( ) method is invoked during the serialization process. A special constructor with the same signature as GetObjectData( ) is called during deserialization. Both these methods are passed a SerializationInfo object. Think of this object as a data bag or a hash table. During serialization, you can store key-value pairs into the SerializationInfo object. When you deserialize the object, you can ask for these values using their keys.

So how do you deal with versioning? If you remove a field from the class, just don't ask for its value during deserialization. But what if you add a field to the class? When you ask for that field during deserialization, an exception is thrown if the object being deserialized is from an older version. Consider Examples 2-14 and 2-15.

Example 2-14. A serialization example (C#)

```csharp
//Engine.cs
using System;

namespace Serialization
{
    [Serializable]
    public class Engine
    {
        private int power;

        public Engine(int thePower)
        {
            power = thePower;
        }

        public override string ToString()
        {
            return power.ToString();
        }

    }
}

//Car.cs
using System;
using System.Runtime.Serialization;

namespace Serialization
{
    [Serializable]
    public class Car : ISerializable
    {
        private int yearOfMake;
        private Engine theEngine;

        public Car(int year, Engine anEngine)
        {
            yearOfMake = year;
            theEngine = anEngine;
        }

        public override string ToString()
        {
            return yearOfMake + ":" + theEngine;
        }

        #region ISerializable Members
```

Example 2-14. A serialization example (C#) (continued)

```csharp
        public Car(SerializationInfo info,
            StreamingContext context)
        {
            yearOfMake = info.GetInt32("yearOfMake");
            theEngine = info.GetValue("theEngine",
                    typeof(Engine)) as Engine;
        }

        public void GetObjectData(SerializationInfo info,
            StreamingContext context)
        {
            info.AddValue("yearOfMake", yearOfMake);
            info.AddValue("theEngine", theEngine);
        }

        #endregion
    }
}

//Test.cs
using System;
using System.IO;
using System.Runtime.Serialization.Formatters.Binary;

namespace Serialization
{
    class Test
    {
        [STAThread]
        static void Main(string[] args)
        {
            Console.WriteLine(
                "Enter s to serialize, d to deserialize");
            string input = Console.ReadLine();

            if (input.ToUpper() == "S")
            {
                Car aCar = new Car(2004, new Engine(500));

                Console.WriteLine("Serializing " + aCar);

                FileStream strm = new FileStream("output.dat",
                    FileMode.Create, FileAccess.Write);
                BinaryFormatter formatter =
                    new BinaryFormatter();
                formatter.Serialize(strm, aCar);
                strm.Close();
            }
            else
            {
```

Example 2-14. A serialization example (C#) (continued)

```
            FileStream strm = new FileStream("output.dat",
                FileMode.Open, FileAccess.Read);
            BinaryFormatter formatter
                = new BinaryFormatter();
            Car aCar = formatter.Deserialize(strm) as Car;
            strm.Close();
            Console.WriteLine("DeSerialized " + aCar);
        }
    }
  }
}
```

Example 2-15. A serialization example (VB.NET)

✔ **VB.NET (ReflectionToSerialize)**

```
'Engine.vb
<Serializable()> _
Public Class Engine
    Private power As Integer

    Public Sub New(ByVal thePower As Integer)
        power = thePower
    End Sub

    Public Overrides Function ToString() As String
        Return power.ToString()
    End Function
End Class

'Car.vb
Imports System.Runtime.Serialization

<Serializable()> _
Public Class Car
    Implements ISerializable

    Private yearOfMake As Integer
    Private theEngine As Engine

    Public Sub New(ByVal year As Integer, ByVal anEngine As Engine)
        yearOfMake = year
        theEngine = anEngine
    End Sub

    Public Overrides Function ToString() As String
        Return yearOfMake & ":" & theEngine.ToString()
    End Function
```

Example 2-15. A serialization example (VB.NET) (continued)

```
    Public Sub New( _
        ByVal info As SerializationInfo, _
        ByVal context As StreamingContext)
        yearOfMake = info.GetInt32("yearOfMake")
        theEngine = CType(info.GetValue("theEngine", _
            GetType(Engine)), Engine)
    End Sub
    Public Sub GetObjectData(ByVal info As SerializationInfo, _
        ByVal context As StreamingContext) _
            Implements ISerializable.GetObjectData
        info.AddValue("yearOfMake", yearOfMake)
        info.AddValue("theEngine", theEngine)
    End Sub
End Class

'Test.vb
Imports System.IO
Imports System.Runtime.Serialization.Formatters.Binary

Module Test

    Public Sub Main( )
        Console.WriteLine( _
            "Enter s to serialize, d to deserialize")

        Dim input As String = Console.ReadLine( )

        If input.ToUpper( ) = "S" Then
            Dim aCar As Car = New Car(2004, New Engine(500))

            Console.WriteLine("Serializing " & aCar.ToString( ))

            Dim strm As FileStream = New FileStream("output.dat", _
                FileMode.Create, FileAccess.Write)

            Dim formatter As New BinaryFormatter
            formatter.Serialize(strm, aCar)
            strm.Close( )
        Else
            Dim strm As FileStream = New FileStream("output.dat", _
                FileMode.Open, FileAccess.Read)
            Dim formatter As New BinaryFormatter
            Dim aCar As Car = CType(formatter.Deserialize(strm), Car)
            strm.Close( )
            Console.WriteLine("DeSerialized " & aCar.ToString( ))
        End If
    End Sub
End Module
```

In the previous code, you either serialize or deserialize a Car object. The code is pretty straightforward so far. Now, let's run it once to serialize the Car object and then run it again to deserialize it. You get the outputs shown in Figures 2-13 and 2-14.

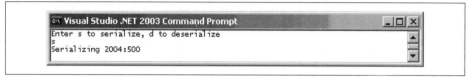

Figure 2-13. Output from Example 2-14: Serializing

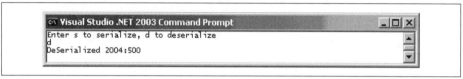

Figure 2-14. Output from Example 2-14: Deserializing

Now let's modify the Car class by adding a miles field. How can you handle this during deserialization from an older version? If you simply write the code to fetch the miles field within the special constructor you will get an exception; the deserialization will fail because the field is missing. Now, how can you process this in your code? One way is to just handle the exception and move on.

The Car class with the required code change is shown in Example 2-16.

Example 2-16. Handling an exception during deserialization

✗ C# (ReflectionToSerialize)

```
//Car.cs
using System;
using System.Runtime.Serialization;

namespace Serialization
{
    [Serializable]
    public class Car : ISerializable
    {
        private int yearOfMake;
        private Engine theEngine;
        private int miles = 0;

        public Car(int year, Engine anEngine)
        {
            yearOfMake = year;
            theEngine = anEngine;
        }
```

Example 2-16. Handling an exception during deserialization (continued)

```csharp
        public override string ToString( )
        {
            return yearOfMake + ":" + miles + ":" + theEngine;
        }

        #region ISerializable Members

        public Car(SerializationInfo info,
            StreamingContext context)
        {
            yearOfMake = info.GetInt32("yearOfMake");
            theEngine = info.GetValue("theEngine",
                typeof(Engine)) as Engine;

            try
            {
                miles = info.GetInt32("miles");
            }
            catch(Exception)
            {
                //Shhhhh, let's move on quietly.
            }
        }

        public void GetObjectData(SerializationInfo info,
            StreamingContext context)
        {
            info.AddValue("yearOfMake", yearOfMake);
            info.AddValue("theEngine", theEngine);
            info.AddValue("miles", miles);
        }

        #endregion
    }
}
```

✗ VB.NET (ReflectionToSerialize)

```vbnet
'Car.vb
Imports System.Runtime.Serialization

<Serializable( )> _
Public Class Car
    Implements ISerializable

    Private yearOfMake As Integer
    Private theEngine As Engine
    Private miles As Integer = 0
```

Example 2-16. Handling an exception during deserialization (continued)

```
    Public Sub New(ByVal year As Integer, ByVal anEngine As Engine)
        yearOfMake = year
        theEngine = anEngine
    End Sub

    Public Overrides Function ToString() As String
        Return yearOfMake & ":" & miles & ":" & theEngine.ToString()
    End Function

    Public Sub New( _
        ByVal info As SerializationInfo, _
        ByVal context As StreamingContext)
        yearOfMake = info.GetInt32("yearOfMake")
        theEngine = CType(info.GetValue("theEngine", _
            GetType(Engine)), Engine)

        Try
            miles = info.GetInt32("miles")
        Catch ex As Exception
            'Shhhhh, let's move on quietly.
        End Try
    End Sub
    Public Sub GetObjectData(ByVal info As SerializationInfo, _
        ByVal context As StreamingContext) _
            Implements ISerializable.GetObjectData
        info.AddValue("yearOfMake", yearOfMake)
        info.AddValue("theEngine", theEngine)
        info.AddValue("miles", miles)
    End Sub
End Class
```

In the special deserialization constructor, you catch the exception if the miles field is missing. While this approach works, the problem with it is twofold. First, as more fields are added and more versioning happens, you might end up with several of these try-catch blocks. The code will get cluttered and difficult to read. Second, if you look for a number of missing fields, each one triggers an exception. This will impact performance. In a sense, you are using exceptions for the wrong purpose. As you are building an application and modifying your classes, fields may very well come and go. So you should handle this situation in the normal flow of your program instead of as an exception.

It would have been nice if the SerializationInfo class had provided a way to find out if a value exists for a given key without raising an exception. Since it doesn't, you can use an enumerator to loop through the available values and populate your object. You can then use reflection to identify the target fields, and only populate the ones that actually exist in the serialization stream. The code in Examples 2-17 and 2-18 does just that.

Example 2-17. Using reflection to serialize and deserialize (C#)

✔ **C# (ReflectionToSerialize)**

```csharp
//Car.cs
using System;
using System.Runtime.Serialization;

namespace Serialization
{
    [Serializable]
    public class Car : ISerializable
    {
        private int yearOfMake;
        private Engine theEngine;
        private int miles = 0;

        public Car(int year, Engine anEngine)
        {
            yearOfMake = year;
            theEngine = anEngine;
        }

        public override string ToString()
        {
            return yearOfMake + ":" + miles + ":" + theEngine;
        }

        #region ISerializable Members

        public Car(SerializationInfo info,
            StreamingContext context)
        {
            SerializationHelper.SetData(typeof(Car), this, info);
        }

        public virtual void GetObjectData(SerializationInfo info,
            StreamingContext context)
        {
            SerializationHelper.GetData(typeof(Car), this, info);
        }

        #endregion
    }
}

//SerializationHelper.cs
using System;
using System.Runtime.Serialization;
using System.Reflection;
```

```csharp
namespace Serialization
{
    public class SerializationHelper
    {
        public static void SetData(
            Type theType, Object instance, SerializationInfo info)
        {
            SerializationInfoEnumerator enumerator =
                info.GetEnumerator( );

            while(enumerator.MoveNext( ))
            {
                string fieldName = enumerator.Current.Name;

                FieldInfo theField
                    = theType.GetField(fieldName,
                    BindingFlags.Instance |
                    BindingFlags.DeclaredOnly |
                    BindingFlags.Public |
                    BindingFlags.NonPublic);
                if (theField != null)
                {
                    theField.SetValue(instance, enumerator.Value);
                }
            }
        }

        public static void GetData(
            Type theType, Object instance, SerializationInfo info)
        {
            FieldInfo[] fields = theType.GetFields(
                BindingFlags.Instance |
                BindingFlags.DeclaredOnly |
                BindingFlags.Public |
                BindingFlags.NonPublic);

            for(int i = 0; i < fields.Length; i++)
            {
                // Do not serialize NonSerialized fields
                if(!fields[i].IsNotSerialized)
                {
                    info.AddValue(fields[i].Name,
                        fields[i].GetValue(instance));
                }
            }
        }
    }
}
```

Example 2-18. Using reflection to serialize and deserialize (VB.NET)

✔ **VB.NET (ReflectionToSerialize)**

```
'Car.vb
Imports System.Runtime.Serialization
Imports System.Reflection

<Serializable()> _
Public Class Car
    Implements ISerializable

    Private yearOfMake As Integer
    Private theEngine As Engine
    Private miles As Integer = 0

    Public Sub New(ByVal year As Integer, ByVal anEngine As Engine)
        yearOfMake = year
        theEngine = anEngine
    End Sub

    Public Overrides Function ToString() As String
        Return yearOfMake & ":" & miles & ":" & theEngine.ToString()
    End Function

    Public Sub New( _
        ByVal info As SerializationInfo, _
        ByVal context As StreamingContext)

        SerializationHelper.SetData(GetType(Car), Me, info)
    End Sub

    Public Overridable Sub GetObjectData(ByVal info As SerializationInfo, _
        ByVal context As StreamingContext) _
            Implements ISerializable.GetObjectData

        SerializationHelper.GetData(GetType(Car), Me, info)
    End Sub
End Class


'SerializationHelper.vb

Imports System.Runtime.Serialization
Imports System.Reflection

Public Class SerializationHelper
    Public Shared Sub SetData( _
    ByVal theType As Type, ByVal instance As Object, _
    ByVal info As SerializationInfo)
```

```
        Dim enumerator As SerializationInfoEnumerator = _
            info.GetEnumerator( )

        While enumerator.MoveNext( )
            Dim fieldName As String = enumerator.Current.Name
            Dim theField As FieldInfo = _
                theType.GetField(fieldName, _
                    BindingFlags.Instance Or _
                    BindingFlags.DeclaredOnly Or _
                    BindingFlags.Public Or _
                    BindingFlags.NonPublic)

            If Not theField Is Nothing Then
                theField.SetValue(instance, enumerator.Value)
            End If
        End While
    End Sub

    Public Shared Sub GetData( _
        ByVal theType As Type, _
        ByVal instance As Object, _
        ByVal info As SerializationInfo)

        Dim fields( ) As FieldInfo = theType.GetFields( _
            BindingFlags.Instance Or _
            BindingFlags.Public Or _
            BindingFlags.NonPublic)

        Dim i As Integer

        For i = 0 To fields.Length - 1
            'Do not serialize NonSerializable Fields
            If Not fields(i).IsNotSerialized Then
                info.AddValue(fields(i).Name, _
                    fields(i).GetValue(instance))
            End If
        Next
    End Sub

End Class
```

Let's first take a look at the GetObjectData( ) method that performs the serialization. It calls the SerializationHelper's GetData( ) method. This method serializes all fields that are not marked with a NonSerialized attribute.

In the special deserialization constructor, you call the SerializationHelper's SetData( ) method, which enumerates the keys in the SerializationInfo object. For each key found, the method checks if it exists in the class, and if so, sets its value.

Notice that the GetObjectData( ) method is virtual/Overridable and that it only serializes its own members, not those in its base class. Classes further derived from your class can take care of serializing their own members by overriding GetObjectData( ) and writing a special deserialization constructor, as shown in Example 2-19.

Example 2-19. Serialization and deserialization of a derived class

✔ C# (ReflectionToSerialize)

```
//DerivedCar.cs

    public DerivedCar(SerializationInfo info,
        StreamingContext context)
        : base(info, context)
    {
        SerializationHelper.SetData(
            typeof(DerivedCar), this, info);
    }

    public override void GetObjectData(SerializationInfo info,
        StreamingContext context)
    {
        base.GetObjectData(info, context);
        SerializationHelper.GetData(
            typeof(DerivedCar), this, info);
    }
```

✔ VB.NET (ReflectionToSerialize)

```
'DerivedCar.vb

  Public Sub New( _
      ByVal info As SerializationInfo, _
      ByVal context As StreamingContext)

      MyBase.New(info, context)

      SerializationHelper.SetData( _
          GetType(DerivedCar), Me, info)
  End Sub

  Public Overrides Sub GetObjectData( _
      ByVal info As SerializationInfo, _
      ByVal context As StreamingContext)

      MyBase.GetObjectData(info, context)
      SerializationHelper.GetData(GetType(DerivedCar), Me, info)
  End Sub
```

The serialization code that uses reflection will work for fields added and removed between versions. But it does not handle a field that gets removed in one version and then added back in a later one, with the same name but with a different intent, different semantics, or a different type. The difference in type can be handled by putting in a few more checks and balances, but the difference in semantics is a hard one. Further, this approach will fail if local security settings prohibit querying for private fields using reflection.

One option to get around these problems is to use a version number and to serialize or deserialize appropriate fields based on the version number. You can use this somewhat lengthy approach if the above options will not work.

 IN A NUTSHELL

Using exceptions to determine if a member should be deserialized is expensive, and is also an inappropriate use of exceptions. It is better to rely on reflection to achieve this goal, and the code is more extensible. Or handle the versioning yourself by using the version number.

SEE ALSO

Gotcha #22, "enum lacks type-safety" and Gotcha #24, "Clone( ) has limitations."

GOTCHA

#18 Creating Web apps can be painful

It is better to create a blank solution and create projects in it rather than starting out creating a project. The advantages of this are:

- You can add other projects to the solution as desired (and in a typical application you will want to).

- In a large application you can create different solutions with a subset of projects for different purposes. A project may belong to more than one solution at a time.

Say you have created a blank solution named MyApp in the *C:\projects* directory. Also assume you have created projects like a class library named MyLib from within this solution. By default, the MyLib project is placed in the *C:\projects\MyApp\MyLib* directory. Now say you want to create a Web project within the same solution, either an ASP.NET Web Application or an ASP.NET Web Service. If you specify the location of the service as http://localhost/MyWebApp, then the project for MyWebApp is unfortunately created in the *C:\inetpub\wwwroot* directory (or wherever IIS is installed). This is undesirable, as you would like to keep all files related to your solution together, or at least in your own preferred location. The problem is worse if you move an existing solution to a new machine by bringing it over from a source code control system.

In this gotcha I discuss two things:

- how to create a solution with a Web project
- how to open a solution that contains a Web project and is stored in Visual Source Safe.

Before creating a Web project, create a virtual directory. The easiest way to do that is in Windows Explorer.

In the following example, I assume that you have already created a blank solution named CreatingWebApp. In that solution you want to create an ASP.NET Web Application. If you click on Add → New Project in Solution Explorer, a project will be created under the *C:\inetpub\wwwroot* directory. However, you would like for the project to reside under the *CreatingWebApp* directory.

First you use Windows Explorer to create *MyWebApp* as a subdirectory of *CreatingWebApp*. Then you right click on it (in Windows Explorer) and select Properties. In the Properties window, you go to the Web Sharing tab as shown in Figure 2-15.

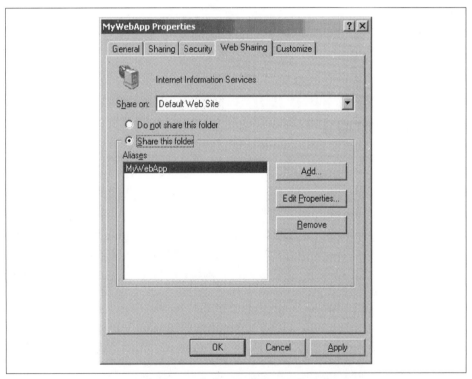

Figure 2-15. Creating a Virtual Directory before creating a Web Application

In this tab select the "Share this folder" radio button. In the dialog that pops up, accept the defaults and click OK. This process tells IIS that your new directory is the location of the virtual directory *MyWebApp*. Now in Visual Studio you can create the Web application simply by providing the location as `http://localhost/MyWebApp`, as shown in Figure 2-16.

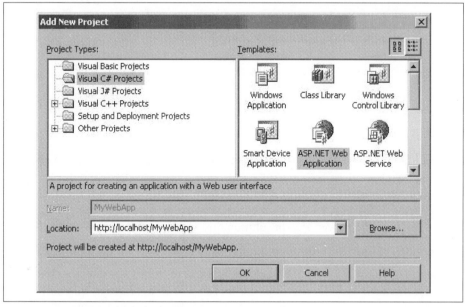

Figure 2-16. Creating a Web Application

The project-related files will now be created under the *CreatingWebApp\MyWebApp* directory.

You should take a similar approach before opening any solution containing a Web App project for the first time. First make the directory a virtual directory, then open the solution in Visual Studio.

Things get a bit more complicated when you open projects that are stored in Visual Source Safe (VSS). Suppose you have a solution in VSS containing one or more Web projects. You want to open it on a new machine belonging to a new developer on your team. I have wasted significant time on this whenever I forgot to follow the correct sequence of steps. When you open a solution in Visual Studio, if that solution is in VSS, Visual Studio tries to get the latest version. For non-Web applications, this is not much of a problem. However, if the project is a Web App, you'll be presented with the Set Project Location – CreatingWebApp dialog shown in Figure 2-17.

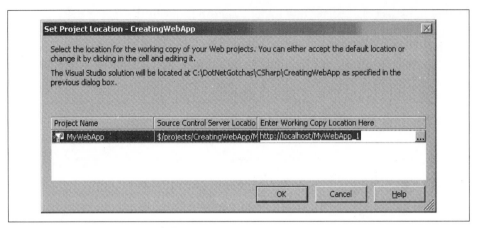

Figure 2-17. Error opening a Web App

Let's examine the problem scenario. First, you placed the solution created above in VSS. Then you removed the directory from your local hard drive and got the latest version of the solution from VSS. You made sure that *MyWebApp* is a virtual directory referring to the physical location of the *MyWebApp* directory. Then you double-clicked on the *CreatingWebApp.sln* solution file.

That is when you got the error message shown in Figure 2-17. What's the problem?

When you open the Web App, Visual Studio looks in the virtual directory and finds the project-related files. Overwriting the files in a Web application may not be the best thing to do. So, as a precaution, Visual Studio asks you to enter a different working directory. How do you avoid this problem? Here are the steps to follow:

1. Fetch the source code and related files from VSS.
2. Create the virtual directory for your Web project.
3. Leave the Web project directory in place, but remove all its contents.
4. Double-click on the *.sln* file and open the solution with Web projects in it.

This will automatically pull your Web project files from VSS.

The above steps are only needed the first time you bring the files over, or if you change the location where you keep your source code locally.

 IN A NUTSHELL

It is better to start by creating a blank solution and then creating projects in it. Also, set up a virtual directory before creating a Web App on localhost. Further, if the solution has Web Apps and you have it checked into Visual Source Safe, opening the solution the first time on a new machine requires following a specific set of steps:

1. Fetch the files.
2. Create a virtual directory.
3. Delete the contents of the virtual directory.
4. Open the solution.

SEE ALSO

Gotcha #19, "Naming XML documentation for IntelliSense support isn't intuitive."

#19 Naming XML documentation for IntelliSense support isn't intuitive

Writing XML-style documentation is supported in C# out of the box. Third-party tools can be used to generate XML documentation for VB.NET code. The next version of Visual Basic (Visual Basic 2005, which is also known as the Whidbey release) will support XML comments directly. There are two advantages to writing this documentation. One, it serves to specify what your code does, without regard to how it does it. This can be useful for users of your API—both internal users and external users. Second, it provides IntelliSense when your classes are used.

However, the XML document must have the same name as your assembly and must have the *.xml* extension. When an assembly is referenced in a project, Visual Studio brings over not only the assembly, but also the related XML documentation file. If it is named something other than the exact name of the assembly, this process does not happen and IntelliSense does not provide the details of your classes, methods, properties, etc.

As mentioned, the usefulness of the XML documentation goes beyond IntelliSense. Open source tools like NDoc (See the section "On the Web" in the Appendix) may be used to produce MSDN-like or HTML documentation. Figure 2-18 shows an example of what NDoc produces.

Figure 2-19 shows how you can configure the C# project settings to generate the XML document. Given that the XML documentation file name should be the same as the assembly name, a checkbox instead of a textbox for XML Documentation File would have been appropriate.

 IN A NUTSHELL

Name the XML documentation file the same as your assembly name to ensure that IntelliSense will work properly.

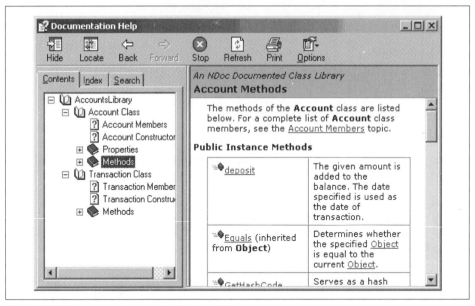

Figure 2-18. Documentation produced using NDoc

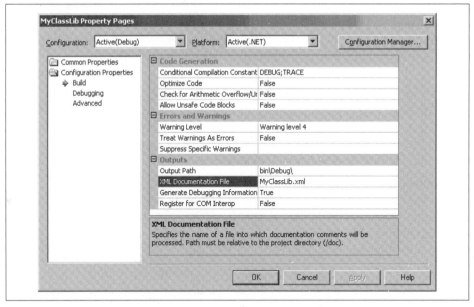

Figure 2-19. C# project settings to generate XML documentation

SEE ALSO

Gotcha #18, "Creating Web apps can be painful."

CHAPTER 3

Language and API Gotchas

Languages like C# and VB.NET allow you to develop object-oriented code without the complexity of syntax found in languages like C++. Nevertheless, there are features of the C# and VB.NET languages, and the .NET Framework types, that are likely to run counter to your intuitions. In particular, your experience with other languages may lead you to expect that certain features will behave in familiar ways in .NET and that the .NET languages will be consistent in how they handle common tasks. If so, you'll be in for some surprises. For example, .NET takes a different approach to copy constructors than C++ does. The .NET XML reader needs some help to work as quickly as you might expect. And the VB.NET and C# language compilers don't handle object initialization in the same way; nor do they spot bad enumerations at compile time, as you might expect.

In this chapter I focus on gotchas at the language and API level of the .NET platform.

GOTCHA

#20 Singleton isn't guaranteed process-wide

A static/Shared field belongs to the class and is not part of any instance. Typically, when you see a static/Shared field, you know that no matter how many instances of the class exist, there is one and only one occurrence of this field. Often a static/Shared field is used to limit the number of instances of an object—the concept of *Singleton*. (Refer to "Exploring the Singleton Design Pattern" and "Implementing the Singleton Pattern in C#" in the section "On the Web" in the Appendix for very good articles on this topic.) A singleton takes measures to make sure that no more than one instance of its type can be created in an application. One way to do this is to make the constructor of the class protected or private, and to provide a static/Shared method to fetch the object, as shown in Example 3-1.

Example 3-1. Example of a singleton

✗ C# (SingletonAppDomain)

```
using System;

namespace Singleton
{
    public class MySingleton
    {
        public readonly DateTime creationTime;

        protected MySingleton( )
        {
            creationTime = DateTime.Now;
        }

        protected static MySingleton theInstance =
            new MySingleton( );

        public static MySingleton GetInstance( )
        {
            return theInstance;
        }
    }
}
```

✗ VB.NET (SingletonAppDomain)

```
Public Class MySingleton
    Public ReadOnly creationTime As DateTime

    Protected Sub New( )
        creationTime = DateTime.Now
    End Sub

    Protected Shared theInstance As New MySingleton

    Public Shared Function GetInstance( ) As MySingleton
        Return theInstance
    End Function

End Class
```

The MySingleton class is written so that at most one instance can be created. But here's the gotcha: the unit of granularity for static/Shared fields in .NET is not the process, but the AppDomain. (Application domains provide isolation, unloading, and security boundaries for executing managed code.) And a process can contain more than one AppDomain. So the above code restricts MySingleton to one instance only within its AppDomain, but not within the entire process, as the code in Example 3-2 demonstrates.

Example 3-2. Singleton within AppDomain

✗ C# (SingletonAppDomain)

```csharp
using System;
using System.Threading;
using System.Reflection;

namespace Singleton
{
    class Test : MarshalByRefObject
    {
        public void Run( )
        {
            MySingleton object1 = MySingleton.GetInstance( );

            Console.WriteLine("Object created at {0}",
                object1.creationTime.ToLongTimeString( ));

            Thread.Sleep(1000);

            MySingleton object2 = MySingleton.GetInstance( );
            Console.WriteLine("Object created at {0}",
                object1.creationTime.ToLongTimeString( ));
        }

        [STAThread]
        static void Main(string[] args)
        {
            Test anObject = new Test( );

            anObject.Run( );
            Thread.Sleep(1000);

            AppDomain domain =
                AppDomain.CreateDomain("MyDomain");
            Test proxy =
                domain.CreateInstance(
                    Assembly.GetExecutingAssembly( ).FullName,
                    typeof(Test).FullName).Unwrap( ) as Test;
            proxy.Run( );

            Thread.Sleep(1000);
            anObject.Run( );

        }
    }
}
```

Example 3-2. Singleton within AppDomain (continued)

✗ VB.NET (SingletonAppDomain)

```
Imports System.Threading

Public Class Test
        Inherits MarshalByRefObject
    Public Sub Run( )
        Dim object1 As MySingleton = MySingleton.GetInstance( )

        Console.WriteLine("Object created at {0}", _
          object1.creationTime.ToLongTimeString( ))

        Thread.Sleep(1000)

        Dim object2 As MySingleton = MySingleton.GetInstance( )
        Console.WriteLine("Object created at {0}", _
          object1.creationTime.ToLongTimeString( ))
    End Sub

    Public Shared Sub Main( )
        Dim anObject As Test = New Test

        anObject.Run( )
        Thread.Sleep(1000)

        Dim domain As AppDomain = _
            AppDomain.CreateDomain("MyDomain")

        Dim proxy As Test = _
          CType( _
              domain.CreateInstance( _
                System.Reflection. _
                Assembly.GetExecutingAssembly( ).FullName, _
                GetType(Test).FullName).Unwrap( ), Test)

        proxy.Run( )

        Thread.Sleep(1000)
        anObject.Run( )
    End Sub
End Class
```

In the above code you call the GetInstance( ) method of MySingleton from within the Test class's Run( ) method. Then you create an object of Test within another AppDomain and call Run( ) on it. The output from the program is shown in Figure 3-1.

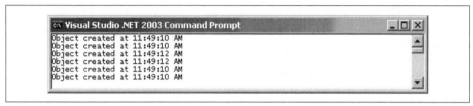

Figure 3-1. Output from Example 3-2

Notice that the four calls to GetInstance( ) made from within the default AppDomain (that is, calls to Run( ) from within the Main( ) method) fetch the same object of MySingleton (as seen in the first two and the last two statements of output). However, the calls to GetInstance( ) from the AppDomain you created produce a different instance of the MySingleton class.

In the example you create an AppDomain explicitly, so you at least know of its existence. There are times, however, when an AppDomain is created by the .NET framework (like in ASP.NET) or other APIs you may use without your being aware of it. The behavior of singleton is no different in those cases.

There is an excellent discussion of how and why .NET creates new AppDomains in [Lowy03].

 IN A NUTSHELL

A class's static/Shared fields are unique only in the AppDomain where the class is loaded. Each new AppDomain created in your application produces a new copy of them.

SEE ALSO

Gotcha #27, "Object initialization sequence isn't consistent."

GOTCHA

#21 Default performance of Data.ReadXML is poor

The System.Data.DataSet class provides great flexibility for disconnected access to data. Its capabilities to transform data into XML and to read data from XML come in very handy.

One major problem with using XML is performance. Consider the simple XML document in Example 3-3.

Example 3-3. A simple XML document

```
<root>
    <row>
      <item1>0</item1>
      <item2>0.703552246887028</item2>
      <item3>0.993569961746023</item3>
      <item4>0.147870197961046</item4>
      <item5>0.740130904009627</item5>
    </row>
    <row>
      <item1>1</item1>
      <item2>0.378916004383432</item2>
      <item3>0.143134204737439</item3>
      <item4>0.419504510434114</item4>
      <item5>0.403854837363518</item5>
  </row>
...
```

The root element contains a number of row elements. Each row contains five ele-ments named item1, item2, etc. Each item contains a value of type double.

If I have 100 rows in this document, it takes 90 milliseconds to read the XML docu-ment into the DataSet using ReadXML( ).* If I have 1,000 rows, it takes 200 millisec-onds. Not too bad. But if I have 5,000 rows, it takes 5,700 milliseconds. Finally, if I have 10,000 rows, it takes an objectionable 24,295 milliseconds (about 25 seconds).

Interestingly, if I use the System.Xml.XmlDocument parser class to parse the XML docu-ment, it doesn't take that long. So what's the problem with ReadXML( )?

It turns out that ReadXML( ) spends most of its time not in parsing the XML docu-ment, but in analyzing it to understand its format. In other words, it tries to infer a schema from the XML. So you can achieve a significant speedup by preloading the schema into the DataSet before reading the XML. You can obtain the schema in sev-eral ways. For instance, you can ask the sender of the document to provide you with the schema; you can create it manually; or you can use the *xsd.exe* tool to generate it.

Example 3-4 shows the optimization realized when reading an XML document with 10,000 rows. It alternates between reading the XML without knowing its format and loading the format from an *.xsd* (XML Schema Definition) file before reading the data.

---

* Thanks to Ruby Hjelte for bringing this to my attention during a recent project.

Example 3-4. Speedup due to preloading schema

✔ **C# (DataSetXMLSpeed)**

```
using System;
using System.Data;

namespace ReadingXML
{
    class Test
    {
        private static void timeRead(bool fetchSchema)
        {
            DataSet ds = new DataSet( );
            int startTick = Environment.TickCount;

            if (fetchSchema)
            {
                ds.ReadXmlSchema(@"..\..\data.xsd");
            }

            ds.ReadXml(@"..\..\data.xml");

            int endTick = Environment.TickCount;

            Console.WriteLine(
                "Time taken to read {0} rows is {1} ms",
                ds.Tables[0].Rows.Count,
                (endTick - startTick));
        }

        [STAThread]
        static void Main(string[] args)
        {
            Console.WriteLine("Reading XML into DataSet");
            timeRead(false);

            Console.WriteLine(
            "Reading XML into DataSet after reading Schema");
            timeRead(true);
        }
    }
}
```

✔ **VB.NET (DataSetXMLSpeed)**

```
Module Test

    Private Sub timeRead(ByVal fetchSchema As Boolean)
        Dim ds As DataSet = New DataSet
```

Example 3-4. Speedup due to preloading schema (continued)

```
        Dim startTick As Integer = Environment.TickCount

        If fetchSchema Then
            ds.ReadXmlSchema("..\data.xsd")
        End If

        ds.ReadXml("..\data.xml")

        Dim endTick As Integer = Environment.TickCount

        Console.WriteLine( _
         "Time taken to read {0} rows is {1} ms", _
         ds.Tables(0).Rows.Count.ToString( ), _
         (endTick - startTick).ToString( ))
    End Sub

    Sub Main( )
        Console.WriteLine("Reading XML into DataSet")
        timeRead(False)

        Console.WriteLine( _
            "Reading XML into DataSet after reading Schema")
        timeRead(True)
    End Sub

End Module
```

In this example you read the *data.xml* file containing 10,000 rows in the format discussed in Example 3-3. In the first run, you load the DataSet with the raw XML document. In the second run, you preload the DataSet with the *data.xsd* schema file, then ask the program to read the XML document. The *data.xsd* file was generated using the *xsd.exe* tool from the .NET command prompt as follows:

```
    xsd data.xml
```

The time taken for each of these approaches is shown in the output in Figure 3-2.

Figure 3-2. Output showing the speedup from Example 3-4

Reading the XML document cold takes about 25 seconds, while reading it after preloading the schema takes just over half a second.

How does this differ in .NET 2.0 Beta 1? The speed of execution of ReadXML( ) has significantly improved in .NET 2.0. For the case of 10,000 rows without preloading the schema, it takes only around 1,000 ms. The time taken after preloading the schema was less than 420 ms. It still helps to preload the schema.

 IN A NUTSHELL

Preload the schema into the DataSet before calling ReadXML( ). It makes a significant difference in performance as the XML file size grows. This eliminates the time taken by ReadXML( ) to infer the schema from the XML document.

SEE ALSO

Gotcha #9, "Typeless ArrayList isn't type-safe."

GOTCHA
#22 enum lacks type-safety

enum provides convenience and improved productivity. The possible values get listed in IntelliSense, so it's easy to select the one you want during programming. If your method takes an enum as a parameter, the users of your API will typically select a value from the list presented by IntelliSense. But unfortunately they don't have to, which could lead to code like that shown in Example 3-5. In this program, Method1( ) receives an enum and accesses the array resource based on that value. First, you pass three valid values of the Size enum to Method1( ). Then, you pass an invalid value of 3. The output is shown in Figure 3-3.

Example 3-5. Example to study type-safety of enum

✗ C# (EnumSafety)

```
using System;

namespace EnumTypesafety
{
    class Program
    {
        private static int[] resource = new int[] {0, 1, 2};

        public enum Size
        {
            Small,
            Medium,
            Large
        }

        public static void Method1(Size theSize)
```

Example 3-5. Example to study type-safety of enum (continued)

```
        {
            Console.WriteLine(theSize);
            Console.WriteLine("Resource: {0}",
                resource[(int)theSize]);
        }

        [STAThread]
        static void Main(string[] args)
        {
            Method1(Size.Small);
            Method1(Size.Large);
            Method1((Size) 1);
            Method1((Size) 3);
        }
    }
}
```

✗ VB.NET (EnumSafety)

```
Module Program
    Private resource( ) As Integer = New Integer( ) {0, 1, 2}

    Public Enum Size
        Small
        Medium
        Large
    End Enum

    Public Sub Method1(ByVal theSize As Size)
        Console.WriteLine(theSize)
        Console.WriteLine("Resource: {0}", _
            resource(Convert.ToInt32(theSize)))
    End Sub
    Sub Main( )
        Method1(Size.Small)
        Method1(Size.Large)
        Method1(CType(1, Size))
        Method1(CType(3, Size))
    End Sub
End Module
```

So what happens if the value sent in for the enum does not match one of the permissible values? At compile time, no error or warning is reported. Users are allowed to send Method1( ) an invalid value of 3 for the enum.

What's going on here? The answer lies in the translation to MSIL. The MSIL generated from the above code is shown in Figure 3-4.

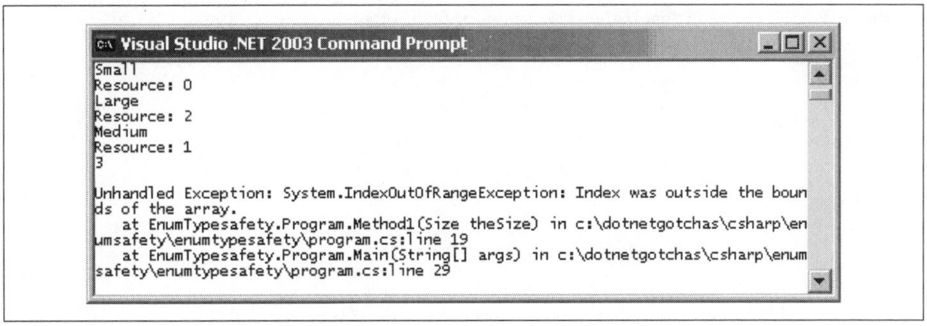

```
Visual Studio .NET 2003 Command Prompt

Small
Resource: 0
Large
Resource: 2
Medium
Resource: 1
3

Unhandled Exception: System.IndexOutOfRangeException: Index was outside the boun
ds of the array.
   at EnumTypesafety.Program.Method1(Size theSize) in c:\dotnetgotchas\csharp\en
umsafety\enumtypesafety\program.cs:line 19
   at EnumTypesafety.Program.Main(String[] args) in c:\dotnetgotchas\csharp\enum
safety\enumtypesafety\program.cs:line 29
```

Figure 3-3. Output from Example 3-5

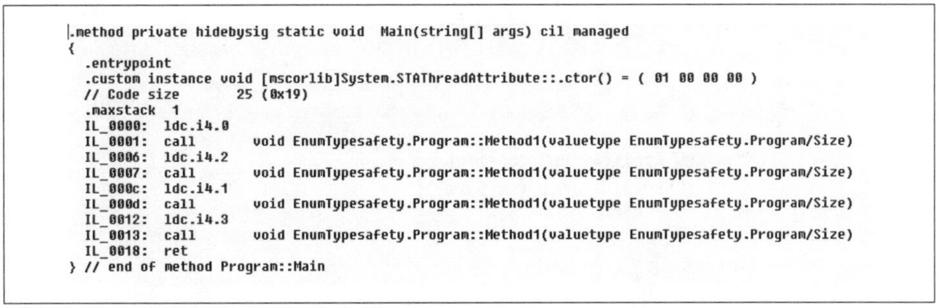

```
.method private hidebysig static void  Main(string[] args) cil managed
{
  .entrypoint
  .custom instance void [mscorlib]System.STAThreadAttribute::.ctor() = ( 01 00 00 00 )
  // Code size       25 (0x19)
  .maxstack  1
  IL_0000:  ldc.i4.0
  IL_0001:  call       void EnumTypesafety.Program::Method1(valuetype EnumTypesafety.Program/Size)
  IL_0006:  ldc.i4.2
  IL_0007:  call       void EnumTypesafety.Program::Method1(valuetype EnumTypesafety.Program/Size)
  IL_000c:  ldc.i4.1
  IL_000d:  call       void EnumTypesafety.Program::Method1(valuetype EnumTypesafety.Program/Size)
  IL_0012:  ldc.i4.3
  IL_0013:  call       void EnumTypesafety.Program::Method1(valuetype EnumTypesafety.Program/Size)
  IL_0018:  ret
} // end of method Program::Main
```

Figure 3-4. MSIL for the Main method in Example 3-5

There is no difference between passing one of the correct values and one of the incorrect ones. Under the hood, there is no type safety or range checking in place. That's why you get a runtime exception instead of a compile-time error when you access the array with the index provided. Too bad the compiler does not catch this or even give you a warning.

What can you do about this? Within methods that receive an enum, make sure the given value is valid. You have to do this before using an enum parameter to make your code robust. A modified `Method1( )` that takes care of this checking is shown in Example 3-6, along with a `Main( )` modified to catch the thrown exception. The output is shown in Figure 3-5.

Example 3-6. Example of type-safe usage of enum

✗ C# (EnumSafety)

```
using System;

namespace EnumTypesafety
{
    class Program
    {
        private static int[] resource = new int[] {0, 1, 2};
```

Example 3-6. Example of type-safe usage of enum (continued)

```
public enum Size
{
    Small,
    Medium,
    Large
}

public static void Method1(Size theSize)
{
    if(System.Enum.IsDefined(typeof(Size), theSize))
    {
        Console.WriteLine(theSize);
        Console.WriteLine("Resource: {0}",
            resource[(int)theSize]);
    }
    else
    {
        throw new ApplicationException(
                "Invalid input for Size");
    }
}

[STAThread]
static void Main(string[] args)
{
    try
    {
        Method1(Size.Small);
        Method1(Size.Large);
        Method1((Size)(1));
        Method1((Size)(3));
    }
    catch(ApplicationException ex)
    {
        Console.WriteLine(ex.Message);
        Console.WriteLine(ex.StackTrace);
    }
}
}
}
```

✗ VB.NET (EnumSafety)

```
Module Program
    Private resource() As Integer = New Integer() {0, 1, 2}

    Public Enum Size
        Small
        Medium
```

Example 3-6. Example of type-safe usage of enum (continued)

```
      Large
  End Enum

  Public Sub Method1(ByVal theSize As Size)
      If System.Enum.IsDefined(GetType(Size), theSize) Then
          Console.WriteLine(theSize)
          Console.WriteLine("Resource: {0}", _
              resource(Convert.ToInt32(theSize)))
      Else
          Throw New ApplicationException( _
              "Invalid input for Size")
      End If
  End Sub
  Sub Main( )
      Try
          Method1(Size.Small)
          Method1(Size.Large)
          Method1(CType(1, Size))
          Method1(CType(3, Size))
      Catch ex As ApplicationException
          Console.WriteLine(ex.Message)
          Console.WriteLine(ex.StackTrace)
      End Try
  End Sub
End Module
```

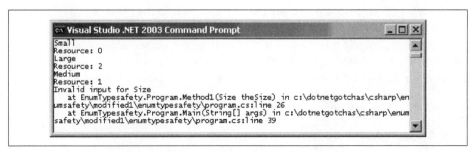

Figure 3-5. Output after the modifications in Example 3-6

This code verifies that the enum value you've been passed is valid by calling System. Enum.IsDefined( ). If it is not, it throws an exception. This prevents you from accessing the resource array with an invalid index. While using System.Enum.IsDefined( ) to verify the enum value may appear logical, there are some inherent problems in using it. First, the call to IsDefined() is expensive, as it relies heavily on reflection and metadata. Second, IsDefined() checks if the value is one of the possible values, not necessarily the ones you expect. This will be a problem if a new value is added to the enum during versioning. Refer to *http://blogs.msdn.com/brada/archive/2003/11/ 29/50903.aspx* for more details on this.

Another problem with enum types relates to serialization. The deserialization of an enum may break if you change a value in the enum after serializing an object.

 IN A NUTSHELL

Do not assume that the value of an enum received as a method parameter is within range. Check to verify it. This will make your code more robust. Program defensively.

SEE ALSO

Gotcha #15, "rethrow isn't consistent," and Gotcha #16, "Default of Option Strict (off) isn't good."

GOTCHA
#23 Copy Constructor hampers exensibility

You use classes to model concepts in an object-oriented system and create instances of your classes throughout an application. You may be interested in making a copy of an object at runtime. How do you make such a copy? In C++, you don't have to do anything special; C++ gives you a default copy constructor, a constructor that takes an instance of the class as its parameter. But this is a mixed blessing (or is it a curse?). The default C++ copy constructor makes what is called a *shallow copy*; i.e., the contents of the source object are bit-wise copied into the other object. *Deep copy* is when not only the contents of an object are copied, but also the contents of the objects that this object refers to. A deep copy does not copy just one object; it copies a tree of objects. Whether you need a shallow copy or a deep copy depends on the relationship between the object and its contents. For instance, consider Example 3-7.

Example 3-7. A class with different relationships with its contents

✔ **C# (CopyingObjects)**

```
public class Person
{
    private int age;
    private Brain theBrain;
    private City cityOfResidence;
}
```

✔ **VB.NET (CopyingObjects)**

```
Public Class Person
    Private age as Integer
    Private theBrain as Brain
    Private cityOfResidence as City
End Class
```

If you make a copy of a Person object, you most likely want the new person to have a separate Brain, but may want to refer to (share) the City of the other person. From the object modeling point of view, the person aggregates the Brain but associates with the City. Generally you want to deep-copy the aggregated object, but you may want to shallow-copy the associated object, or just set it to null/Nothing. At the code level, you use a reference to represent both aggregation and association. There is a semantic mismatch between the object model and how it is expressed in the language. There is no way for the compiler or the runtime to figure out whether an object is being associated or aggregated. You have to implement the logic to properly copy an object. Without it, any effort to do so is just a guess, and probably not correct.

This is the problem with the C++ approach. Unfortunately, C++ decided to err on the side of shallow copy. Instead of saying, "Hum, I have no idea how to make a copy so I won't even try," C++ decided, "Hum, I have no idea how to make a copy so I'll make a shallow copy."

.NET decided to err on the side of caution. It says "I can't possibly make a copy of an object without the programmer clearly specifying the intent." So .NET doesn't provide a default copy constructor.

Thus if you want to make a copy of an object, you just write your own copy constructor, right? Let's explore this further in Example 3-8.

Example 3-8. Writing a copy constructor

✗ C# (CopyingObjects)

```csharp
//Brain.cs
using System;

namespace Copy
{
    public class Brain
    {
        public Brain() {}

        public Brain(Brain another)
        {
            //Code to properly copy Brain can go here
        }

        public override string ToString()
        {
            return GetType().Name + ":" + GetHashCode();
        }

    }
```

Example 3-8. Writing a copy constructor (continued)

```csharp
}


//Person.cs

using System;

namespace Copy
{
    public class Person
    {
        private int theAge;
        private Brain theBrain;

        public Person(int age, Brain aBrain)
        {
            theAge = age;
            theBrain = aBrain;
        }

        public Person(Person another)
        {
            theAge = another.theAge;
            theBrain = new Brain(another.theBrain);
        }

        public override string ToString()
        {
            return "This is person with age " +
                        theAge + " and " +
                        theBrain;
        }

    }
}


//Test.cs
using System;

namespace Copy
{
    class Test
    {
        [STAThread]
        static void Main(string[] args)
        {
            Person sam = new Person(1, new Brain());
            Person bob = new Person(sam);
            // You rely on the copy constructor of Brain
            //to make a good deep copy
```

Example 3-8. Writing a copy constructor (continued)

```
            Console.WriteLine(sam);
            Console.WriteLine(bob);
        }
    }
}
```

```vb
'Brain.vb
Public Class Brain
    Public Sub New( )

    End Sub

    Public Sub New(ByVal another As Brain)
        ' Code to properly copy Brain can go here
    End Sub

    Public Overrides Function ToString( ) As String
        Return Me.GetType( ).Name & ":" & GetHashCode( )
    End Function

End Class


'Person.vb
Public Class Person
    Private theAge As Integer
    Private theBrain As Brain

    Public Sub New(ByVal age As Integer, ByVal aBrain As Brain)
        theAge = age
        theBrain = aBrain
    End Sub

    Public Sub New(ByVal another As Person)
        theAge = another.theAge
        theBrain = New Brain(another.theBrain)
        ' You rely on the copy constructor of Brain
        ' to make a good deep copy
    End Sub

    Public Overrides Function ToString( ) As String
        Return "This is person with age " & _
            theAge & " and " & _
            theBrain.ToString( )
    End Function
End Class
```

Example 3-8. Writing a copy constructor (continued)

```vb
'Test.vb
Module Test

    Sub Main( )
        Dim sam As New Person(1, New Brain)
        Dim bob As Person = New Person(sam)

        Console.WriteLine(sam)
        Console.WriteLine(bob)
    End Sub

End Module
```

This example has a Person class with theAge and theBrain as its members. Person has a constructor and a copy constructor. The Main( ) method in Test copies Person sam to Person bob. The output is shown in Figure 3-6.

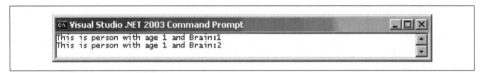

Figure 3-6. Output from Example 3-8

When it prints the first Person (sam), the age is 1 and the Brain's hash code value is 1. When it prints the second Person (bob), which was copied from the instance sam, the age is 1 but the Brain's hash code is 2.

 Generally speaking you should not use the hash code to determine identity. Even if the hash code values are the same, it does not mean the objects are identical. Here, however, since the hash code is different, you can infer that the objects are different. In reality you might use something like a GUID in each object to determine its uniqueness, or you could test the references to the Brain of the two objects to confirm that they are different. (The issues of dealing with the hash code and determining the identity of objects can get complicated. For good discussions on these topics refer to "Common Object Operations," "Equals vs. ==," and "Hashcode," in the section "On the Web" in the Appendix.)

So, in Example 3-8 we created a copy of the Person with his own Brain. Have you solved the problem of properly copying the object? Not really, because the Person's copy constructor depends on the Brain class. It specifically creates an instance of Brain. What if you have a class that derives from Brain, as shown in Example 3-9?

Example 3-9. Incorrect copying

✗ C# (CopyingObjects)

```csharp
//SmarterBrain.cs
using System;

namespace Copy
{
    public class SmarterBrain : Brain
    {
        public SmarterBrain()
        {
        }

        public SmarterBrain(SmarterBrain another) : base(another)
        {
        }
    }
}


//Test.cs
using System;

namespace Copy
{
    class Test
    {
        [STAThread]
        static void Main(string[] args)
        {
            Person sam = new Person(1, new SmarterBrain());
            Person bob = new Person(sam);

            Console.WriteLine(sam);
            Console.WriteLine(bob);
        }
    }
}
```

✗ VB.NET (CopyingObjects)

```vbnet
'SmarterBrain.vb

Public Class SmarterBrain
    Inherits Brain


    Public Sub New()
```

Example 3-9. Incorrect copying (continued)

```
    End Sub

    Public Sub New(ByVal another As SmarterBrain)
        MyBase.New(another)
    End Sub
End Class


'Test.vb
Module Test

    Sub Main()
        Dim sam As New Person(1, New SmarterBrain)
        Dim bob As Person = New Person(sam)

        Console.WriteLine(sam)
        Console.WriteLine(bob)
    End Sub

End Module
```

SmarterBrain inherits from Brain. In the Main() method of Test you create an instance of SmarterBrain and send it to the Person object. The output after this enhancement is shown in Figure 3-7.

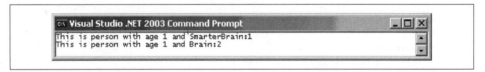

Figure 3-7. Output after change in Example 3-9

While the first Person instance (sam) has an instance of SmarterBrain, the copied instance (bob) is left with just a regular plain vanilla Brain. What went wrong? The Person's copy constructor is asking a new instance of Brain to be created regardless of the actual object referred to by theBrain. How about the fix in Example 3-10?

Example 3-10. A fix?

✗ C# (CopyingObjects)

```
    public Person(Person another)
    {
        theAge = another.theAge;

        if(another.theBrain is SmarterBrain)
        {
            theBrain = new SmarterBrain(
```

Example 3-10. A fix? (continued)

```
                (SmarterBrain) another.theBrain);
        }
        else
        {
            theBrain = new Brain(another.theBrain);
        }
    }
```

✗ VB.NET (CopyingObjects)

```
Public Sub New(ByVal another As Person)
    theAge = another.theAge

    If TypeOf another.theBrain Is SmarterBrain Then
        theBrain = New SmarterBrain( _
            CType(another.theBrain, SmarterBrain))
    Else
        theBrain = New Brain(another.theBrain)
    End If
End Sub
```

Here you have modified the copy constructor of the Person class to use Runtime Type Identification (RTTI). It seems to fix the problem.

But what do you think about this solution? Not exactly elegant, is it? Actually, it's awful. It requires Person, which aggregates Brain, to know about all the subclasses of Brain. (The upside of code like this is job security. You will be around forever fixing and tweaking it.)

As it stands, the Person class is not extensible for the addition of new types of Brains. It fails the Open-Closed Principle (OCP). Refer to [Martin03] for details on this and other object-oriented design principles.

The Open-Closed Principle (OCP)

The Open-Closed Principle (OCP), proposed by Bertrand Myers, states that a software module must be open for extension but closed for modification or change. In other words, you should not have to modify the code to make it extensible.

How can you fix the code so it makes a proper copy of the object? The correct option is the prototype pattern, which is based on abstraction and polymorphism [Freeman04, Gamma95]. You depend on a prototypical instance to create a copy. This is discussed in the next gotcha, "Clone() has limitations"

 *IN A NUTSHELL*

Writing a public copy constructor leads to extensibility problems. You should not use a public copy constructor in C++, Java, and the .NET languages.

SEE ALSO

Gotcha #20, "Singleton isn't guaranteed process-wide," Gotcha #24, "Clone() has limitations," Gotcha #27, "Object initialization sequence isn't consistent," and Gotcha #28, "Polymorphism kicks in prematurely."

GOTCHA
#24 Clone( ) has limitations

You saw the extensibility problems posed by the use of a public copy constructor in Gotcha #23, "Copy Constructor hampers exensibility." How do you make a good copy of an object?

If all you need is a shallow copy, do you have to write all the code yourself? No, . NET provides a MemberwiseClone() method that performs a shallow copy. However, to make sure this is not inadvertently used like the default copy constructor in C++, it is protected, not public. If you need to do a simple shallow copy, you provide a method that you implement using MemberwiseClone(). However, there are a couple of problems with this:

- You can't invoke MemberwiseClone() from within a copy constructor. This is because MemberwiseClone() creates and returns an object, and there is no way to return this from a copy constructor.

- MemberwiseClone() does not use a constructor to create an object and can't deal with objects that have readonly fields, as discussed later in this gotcha.

It is better to rely on polymorphism to create an object of the appropriate class. This is the intent of the System.ICloneable interface. You can implement ICloneable on the Brain class and call its Clone() method to copy the object, as shown in Example 3-11.

Example 3-11. Using ICloneable

✗ C# (CopyingObjects)

```
//Brain.cs
using System;

namespace Copy
{
    public class Brain : ICloneable
```

Example 3-11. Using ICloneable (continued)

```
    {
        //...
        #region ICloneable Members

        public object Clone()
        {
            return MemberwiseClone();
        }

        #endregion
    }
}


//Person.cs
//...

    public class Person
    {
        //...
        public Person(Person another)
        {
            theAge = another.theAge;

            theBrain = another.theBrain.Clone() as Brain;
        }
    }
```

✗ VB.NET (CopyingObjects)

```
'Brain.vb
Public Class Brain
    Implements ICloneable


    '...
    Public Function Clone() As Object _
        Implements System.ICloneable.Clone
        Return MemberwiseClone()
    End Function
End Class


'Person.vb
Public Class Person

    '...
    Public Sub New(ByVal another As Person)
        theAge = another.theAge
```

Example 3-11. Using ICloneable (continued)

```
        theBrain = CType(another.theBrain.Clone( ), Brain)
    End Sub

End Class
```

In this version, you implement ICloneable on the Brain class, and in its Clone( ) method do a shallow copy using MemberwiseClone( ). For now, a shallow copy is good enough. The output of the program is shown in Figure 3-8.

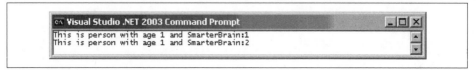

Figure 3-8. Output from Example 3-11

The Clone( ) method copies the object correctly. The Person class is extensible to adding new types of Brain classes as well. Looks good. Are you done?

Well, unfortunately, not yet! Let's think about this some more. Say the Brain has an identifier. (Brains don't usually, but just for the sake of this example, assume that the idea makes sense.) So, here is the Brain class with its identifier in Example 3-12.

Example 3-12. A class with an identifier

✗ C# (CopyingObjects)

```
//Brain.cs
using System;

namespace Copy
{
    public class Brain : ICloneable
    {
        private int id;
        private static int idCount;

        public Brain( )
        {
            id =
            System.Threading.Interlocked.Increment(ref idCount);
        }

        public Brain(Brain another)
        {
            //Code to properly copy Brain can go here
        }
```

Example 3-12. A class with an identifier (continued)

```csharp
public override string ToString( )
{
    return GetType( ).Name + ":" + id;
}

#region ICloneable Members

public object Clone( )
{
    return MemberwiseClone( );
}

#endregion
    }
}
```

✗ VB.NET (CopyingObjects)

```vb
'Brain.vb
Public Class Brain
    Implements ICloneable

    Private id As Integer
    Private Shared idCount As Integer

    Public Sub New( )
        id = System.Threading.Interlocked.Increment(idCount)
    End Sub

    Public Sub New(ByVal another As Brain)
        ' Code to properly copy Brain can go here
    End Sub

    Public Overrides Function ToString( ) As String
        Return Me.GetType( ).Name & ":" & id
    End Function

    Public Function Clone( ) As Object _
        Implements System.ICloneable.Clone
        Return MemberwiseClone( )
    End Function
End Class
```

The Brain class has an id and a static/Shared field idCount. Within the constructor you increment (in a thread-safe manner) the idCount and store the value in the id field. You use this id instead of the hash code in the ToString( ) method. When you execute the code you get the output as in Figure 3-9.

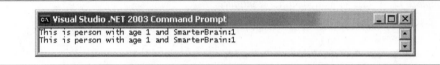

Figure 3-9. Output from Example 3-12

Both the objects of SmarterBrain end up with the same id. Why's that? It's because the MemberwiseClone( ) method does not call any constructor. It just creates a new object by making a copy of the original object's memory. If you want to make id unique among the instances of Brain, you need to do it yourself. Let's fix the Clone( ) method, as shown in Example 3-13, by creating a clone using the MemberwiseClone( ) method, then modifying its id before returning the clone. The output after this change is shown in Figure 3-10.

Example 3-13. Fixing the Clone() to maintain unique id

✗ C# (CopyingObjects)

```csharp
public object Clone( )
{
    Brain theClone = MemberwiseClone( ) as Brain;
    theClone.id =
        System.Threading.Interlocked.Increment(ref idCount);

    return theClone;
}
```

✗ VB.NET (CopyingObjects)

```vbnet
Public Function Clone( ) As Object _
    Implements System.ICloneable.Clone
    Dim theClone As Brain = CType(MemberwiseClone( ), Brain)
    theClone.id = _
        System.Threading.Interlocked.Increment(idCount)
    Return theClone
End Function
```

Figure 3-10. Output from Example 3-13

That looks better. But let's go just a bit further with this. If id is a unique identifier for the Brain object, shouldn't you make sure it doesn't change? So how about making it readonly? Let's do just that in Example 3-14.

Example 3-14. Problem with readonly and Clone( )

✗ C# (CopyingObjects)

```
//Brain.cs
// ...
    public class Brain : ICloneable
    {
        private readonly int id;
        private static int idCount;

        // ...
```

✗ VB.NET (CopyingObjects)

```
'Brain.vb
Public Class Brain
    Implements ICloneable

    Private ReadOnly id As Integer
    Private Shared idCount As Integer

    '...
```

As a result of this change, the C# compiler gives the error:

```
A readonly field cannot be assigned to (except in a constructor or a variable
initializer).
```

In VB.NET, the error is:

```
'ReadOnly' variable cannot be the target of an assignment.
```

A readonly field can be assigned a value at the point of declaration or within any of the constructors, but not in any other method. But isn't the Clone( ) method a special method? Yes, but not special enough. So if you have a readonly field that needs to have unique values, the Clone( ) operation will not work.

Joshua Bloch discusses cloning very clearly in his book *Effective Java* [Bloch01]. He states, "... you are probably better off providing some alternative means of object copying or simply not providing the capability." He goes on to say, "[a] fine approach to object copying is to provide a copy constructor."

Unfortunately, as you saw in Gotcha #23, "Copy Constructor hampers exensibility," the use of a copy constructor leads to extensibility issues. Here's the dilemma: I say copy constructors are a problem and Bloch says you can't use Clone( ). So what's the answer?

Providing a copy constructor is indeed a fine approach, as Bloch states—as long as it's with a slight twist. The copy constructor has to be protected and not public, and it should be invoked within Brain.Clone( ) instead of within the copy constructor of Person. The modified code is shown in Example 3-15.

Example 3-15. A copy that finally works

✔ **C# (CopyingObjects)**

```
//Brain.cs
using System;

namespace Copy
{
    public class Brain : ICloneable
    {
        private readonly int id;
        private static int idCount;

        public Brain( )
        {
            id =
            System.Threading.Interlocked.Increment(ref idCount);
        }

        protected Brain(Brain another)
        {
            id = System.Threading.Interlocked.Increment(ref idCount);
        }

        public override string ToString( )
        {
            return GetType( ).Name + ":" + id;
        }

        #region ICloneable Members

        public virtual object Clone( )
        {
            return new Brain(this);
        }

        #endregion
    }
}


//SmarterBrain.cs
using System;

namespace Copy
{
    public class SmarterBrain : Brain
    {
        public SmarterBrain( )
```

Example 3-15. A copy that finally works (continued)

```
        {
        }

        protected SmarterBrain(SmarterBrain another)
            : base(another)
        {
        }

        public override object Clone()
        {
            return new SmarterBrain(this);
        }

    }
}
```

✔ VB.NET (CopyingObjects)

```
'Brain.vb
Public Class Brain
    Implements ICloneable

    Private ReadOnly id As Integer
    Private Shared idCount As Integer

    Public Sub New()
        id = System.Threading.Interlocked.Increment(idCount)
    End Sub

    Protected Sub New(ByVal another As Brain)
        id = System.Threading.Interlocked.Increment(idCount)
    End Sub

    Public Overrides Function ToString() As String
        Return Me.GetType().Name & ":" & id
    End Function

    Public Overridable Function Clone() As Object _
        Implements System.ICloneable.Clone
        Return New Brain(Me)
    End Function
End Class


'SmarterBrain.vb

Public Class SmarterBrain
    Inherits Brain
```

Example 3-15. A copy that finally works (continued)

```
    Public Sub New( )

    End Sub

    Protected Sub New(ByVal another As SmarterBrain)
        MyBase.New(another)
    End Sub


    Public Overrides Function Clone( ) As Object
        Return New SmarterBrain(Me)
    End Function
End Class
```

Now you have made the copy constructors of Brain and SmarterBrain protected. Also, you have made the Brain.Clone( ) method virtual/overridable. In it, you return a copy of the Brain created using the copy constructor. In the overridden Clone( ) method of SmarterBrain, you use the copy constructor of SmarterBrain to create a copy. When the Person class invokes theBrain.Clone( ), polymorphism assures that the appropriate Clone( ) method in Brain or SmarterBrain is called, based on the real type of the object at runtime. This makes the Person class extensible as well. The output after the above modifications is shown in Figure 3-11.

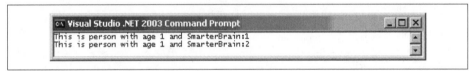

Figure 3-11. Output from Example 3-15

A similar change to the Person class results in the code shown in Example 3-16.

Example 3-16. Proper copying of Person class

✔ **C# (CopyingObjects)**

```
//Person.cs

using System;

namespace Copy
{
    public class Person : ICloneable
    {
        private int theAge;
        private Brain theBrain;

        public Person(int age, Brain aBrain)
```

Example 3-16. Proper copying of Person class (continued)

```
        {
            theAge = age;
            theBrain = aBrain;
        }

        protected Person(Person another)
        {
            theAge = another.theAge;

            theBrain = another.theBrain.Clone() as Brain;
        }

        public override string ToString()
        {
            return "This is person with age " +
                    theAge + " and " +
                    theBrain;
        }

        #region ICloneable Members

        public virtual object Clone()
        {
            return new Person(this);
        }

        #endregion
    }
}


//Test.cs
using System;

namespace Copy
{
    class Test
    {
        [STAThread]
        static void Main(string[] args)
        {
            Person sam = new Person(1, new SmarterBrain());
            //Person bob = new Person(sam);
            Person bob = sam.Clone() as Person;

            Console.WriteLine(sam);
            Console.WriteLine(bob);
        }
    }
}
```

Example 3-16. Proper copying of Person class (continued)

✔ **VB.NET (CopyingObjects)**

```
'Person.vb
Public Class Person
    Implements ICloneable

    Private theAge As Integer
    Private theBrain As Brain

    Public Sub New(ByVal age As Integer, ByVal aBrain As Brain)
        theAge = age
        theBrain = aBrain
    End Sub

    Protected Sub New(ByVal another As Person)
        theAge = another.theAge

        theBrain = CType(another.theBrain.Clone( ), Brain)
    End Sub

    Public Overrides Function ToString( ) As String
        Return "This is person with age " & _
            theAge & " and " & _
            theBrain.ToString( )
    End Function

    Public Overridable Function Clone( ) As Object _
        Implements System.ICloneable.Clone
        Return New Person(Me)
    End Function
End Class



'Test.vb
Module Test

    Sub Main( )
        Dim sam As New Person(1, New SmarterBrain)
        'Dim bob As Person = New Person(sam)
        Dim bob As Person = CType(sam.Clone( ), Person)

        Console.WriteLine(sam)
        Console.WriteLine(bob)
    End Sub

End Module
```

IN A NUTSHELL

Avoid public copy constructors and do not rely on MemberwiseClone( ). Invoke your protected copy constructor from within your Clone( ) method. Public copy constructors lead to extensibility problems. Using MemberwiseClone( ) can also cause problems if you have readonly fields in your class. A better approach is to write a Clone( ) method and have it call your class's protected copy constructor.

SEE ALSO

Gotcha #20, "Singleton isn't guaranteed process-wide," Gotcha #23, "Copy Constructor hampers exensibility," Gotcha #27, "Object initialization sequence isn't consistent," and Gotcha #28, "Polymorphism kicks in prematurely."

GOTCHA

#25 Access to static/Shared members isn't enforced consistently

A static/Shared method belongs to a class and not to any specific instance. Furthermore, it is never polymorphic. C# has taken the high road of disallowing the call to static members using an object reference. Unfortunately, VB.NET does not impose the same restriction. The downside to calling Shared members on a reference is that it may lead to confusion at times. Consider Example 3-17.

Example 3-17. Invoking Shared member using a reference

✔ **C# (Shared)**

C# does not allow the call to static members using an object reference. So this is not an issue for C# programmers. It only concerns VB.NET, C++, and Java programmers.

✔ **C# (VB.NET (Shared))**

```vb
'Base.vb
Public Class Base
 Public Overridable Sub Method1()
Console.WriteLine("Base.Method1")
 End Sub

 Public Shared Sub Method2()
 Console.WriteLine("Base Method2")
 End Sub
End Class

'Derived.vb
```

Example 3-17. Invoking Shared member using a reference (continued)

```
Public Class Derived
 Inherits Base
 Public Overrides Sub Method1( )
 Console.WriteLine("Derived.Method1")
 End Sub

 Public Shared Sub Method2( )
"Derived Method2")
 End Sub
End Class

'Test.vb
Public Class Test
 Public Shared Sub Run(ByVal b As Base)
 b.Method1( )
 b.Method2( )
 End Sub
 Public Shared Sub Main( )
 Dim object1 As New Derived

 Console.WriteLine("--------- Using object of Derived")
 object1.Method1( )
 object1.Method2( )
 Run(object1)
 End Sub
End Class
```

In the VB.NET version of Example 3-17, there is a class named Base and a class named Derived that inherits from Base. Base has an overridable method named Method1( ) and a Shared method named Method2( ). The Derived class overrides Method1( ) and also provides a Shared method named Method2( ).

In the Test code, you create a Derived object, then call Method1( ) and Method2( ) on it using the object reference object1. Next you pass the reference object1 to a method Run( ), which treats it as a Base type. Within the Run( ) method you are still dealing with an object of Derived. When the Run( ) method invokes the two methods using the Base type reference, the method invoked for the call to Method1( ) is on Derived due to polymorphism. However, the method invoked for the call to Method2( ) is on Base, not on Derived, even though the object being pointed to by the reference is of type Derived. When the program executes, you get the output shown in Figure 3-12.

Figure 3-12. Output from Example 3-17

Note that when the code is compiled a warning is generated for Method2() of Derived. It recommends that you mark Method2() with the Shadows keyword. Marking it Shadows will not change the output of the program, however. The call to Method1() using the Base reference is polymorphic and goes to the Derived class's Method2(). However, the call to Method2() is not polymorphic. Within the Run() method, it is statically bound to the method of Base at compile time. As a result, Method2() of Base is invoked rather than Method2() of Derived. In fact, when a Shared method is accessed using an object reference, the compiler replaces the object reference with the class name at the time of compilation. In this example, b.Method2() is replaced by Base.Method2(). While the call b.Method1() results in a polymorphic callvirt instruction in MSIL, the call to b.Method2() simply becomes a static call. Figure 3-13 shows the MSIL generated from the above code.

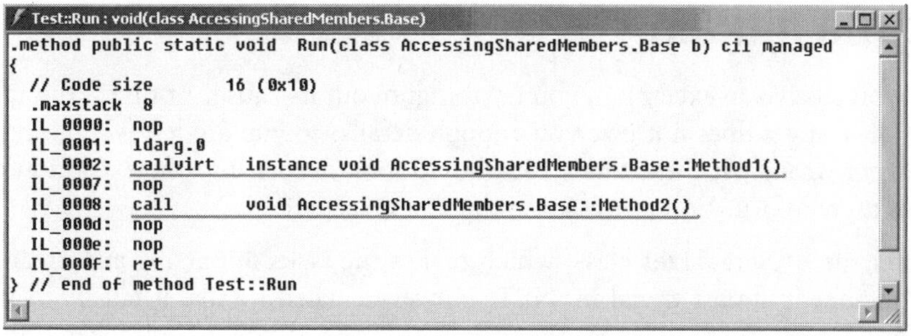

```
Test::Run : void(class AccessingSharedMembers.Base)                    _|□|x|
.method public static void  Run(class AccessingSharedMembers.Base b) cil managed
{
  // Code size        16 (0x10)
  .maxstack  8
  IL_0000:  nop
  IL_0001:  ldarg.0
  IL_0002:  callvirt    instance void AccessingSharedMembers.Base::Method1()
  IL_0007:  nop
  IL_0008:  call        void AccessingSharedMembers.Base::Method2()
  IL_000d:  nop
  IL_000e:  nop
  IL_000f:  ret
} // end of method Test::Run
```

Figure 3-13. MSIL for Run() method in Example 3-17

Given that static/shared methods are not polymorphic, it is easy to get confused if they are invoked using an object reference, especially if the static/Shared methods are part of the derived class as well. As a good coding practice, you should refrain from calling Shared members using an object reference in VB.NET (and C++ and Java as well). Instead, use the class to access them. Instead of calling b.Method2(), write Base.Method2().

How does this differ in .NET 2.0 Beta 1? The VB.NET compiler issues a warning (not an error) if you access a Shared member using an object reference. The warning generated is:

```
warning BC42025: Access of shared member through an instance; qualifying expression
will not be evaluated.
```

If you configure Visual Studio to treat warnings as errors (see Gotcha #12, "Compiler warnings may not be benign"), you will avoid this gotcha.

 **IN A NUTSHELL**

Refrain from accessing Shared members of a class through an object reference. Use the class to access them.

SEE ALSO

Gotcha #12, "Compiler warnings may not be benign, Gotcha #27, "Object initialization sequence isn't consistent," and Gotcha #28, "Polymorphism kicks in prematurely."

GOTCHA

#26 Details of exception may be hidden

When you receive an exception, you try to figure out its cause. At times, though, the exception you get does not give you enough details, so you are left wondering what really went wrong. At these times you should look deeper into the exception object to see if more information is present in the InnerException.

Consider the XMLSerializer class, which makes the tasks of parsing and creating an XML document almost trivial in .NET. However, when it fails, it fails with style. I have found it painful to diagnose the problems. Then somehow I discovered that the actual error message is hidden in the InnerException property. Look at the example in Example 3-18.

Example 3-18. Failure of XMLSerializer

> ✗ **C# (XMLSerializer)**

```
//SomeType.cs
using System;

namespace XmlSerializerException
{
    public class SomeType
    {
        private int val;

        public int TheValue
        {
            get { return val; }
            set { val = value; }
        }
    }
}
```

Example 3-18. Failure of XMLSerializer (continued)

```
//Program.cs
using System;
using System.Collections;
using System.Xml.Serialization;
using System.IO;

namespace XmlSerializerException
{
    class Program
    {
        [STAThread]
        static void Main(string[] args)
        {
            ArrayList myList = new ArrayList( );
            myList.Add(new SomeType( ));

            try
            {
                using(FileStream fileStrm
                        = new FileStream("output.xml",
                        FileMode.Create))
                {
                    XmlSerializer theSerializer
                        = new XmlSerializer(
                            typeof(ArrayList));
                    theSerializer.Serialize(fileStrm, myList);
                }
            }
            catch(InvalidOperationException ex)
            {
                Console.WriteLine(
                    "OOps: The Problem is \"{0}\"",
                    ex.Message);
            }
            catch(Exception catchAllEx)
            {
                Console.WriteLine(
                    "OOps: The Problem is \"{0}\"",
                    catchAllEx.Message);
                throw;
            }
        }
    }
}
```

Example 3-18. Failure of XMLSerializer (continued)

✗ VB.NET (XMLSerializer)

```
'SomeType.vb

Public Class SomeType
    Private val As Integer

    Public Property TheValue() As Integer
        Get
            Return val
        End Get
        Set(ByVal Value As Integer)
            val = Value
        End Set
    End Property
End Class

'Program.vb
Imports System.IO
Imports System.Xml.Serialization

Module Program

    Sub Main()
        Dim myList As New ArrayList
        myList.Add(New SomeType)

        Try
            Dim fileStrm As New FileStream("output.xml", _
                FileMode.Create)

            Dim theSerializer As New XmlSerializer(GetType(ArrayList))

            theSerializer.Serialize(fileStrm, myList)
        Catch ex As InvalidOperationException
            Console.WriteLine( _
             "OOps: The Problem is ""{0}""", _
             ex.Message)
        Catch catchAllEx As Exception
            Console.WriteLine( _
             "OOps: The Problem is ""{0}""", _
             catchAllEx.Message)
            Throw
        End Try
    End Sub

End Module
```

In this example you create an ArrayList and populate it with one SomeType Object. Then you create an XMLSerializer and ask it to serialize the ArrayList to the file output.xml. This looks pretty straightforward. But when you execute the code, you get the exception shown in Figure 3-14.

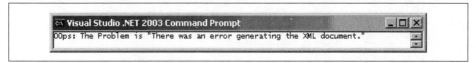

Figure 3-14. Exception from Example 3-18

Not a very helpful message, is it? You could sit there scratching your head until all your hair falls out. If the code is a bit more complicated, it can be even more frustrating to find the real problem. But if you modify the catch statement to print the details from the InnerException property, you get more meaningful information. The modified catch block is shown in Example 3-19.

Example 3-19. Looking for InnerException

✔ **C# (XMLSerializer)**

```csharp
catch(InvalidOperationException ex)
{
    Console.WriteLine(
        "OOps: The Problem is \"{0}\"",
        ex.Message);
    if (ex.InnerException != null)
    {
        Console.WriteLine(
            "The real problem is {0}",
            ex.InnerException);
    }
}
```

✔ **VB.NET (XMLSerializer)**

```vbnet
Catch ex As InvalidOperationException
    Console.WriteLine( _
     "OOps: The Problem is ""{0}""", _
    ex.Message)

    If Not ex.InnerException Is Nothing Then
        Console.WriteLine( _
            "The real problem is {0}", ex.InnerException)
    End If
```

In addition to displaying the information from the exception, it also displays details of its InnerException. The output after the code change appears in Figure 3-15.

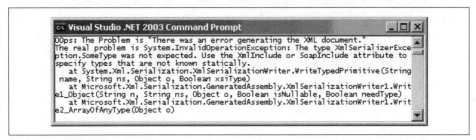

Figure 3-15. Detailed error reported from change in Example 3-19

The inner exception clearly tells you what the problem is, and now it seems obvious: the XmlSerializer has no idea what types of objects will be held in the ArrayList. Now this is disappointing—if you specify all the types that may be in the ArrayList then the code is non-extensible; it will violate the Open-Closed Principle (See the sidebar "The Open-Closed Principle (OCP)" in Gotcha #23, "Copy Constructor hampers exensibility," for more details on this principle.) In this case, you have to use the XmlInclude attribute to indicate what types the ArrayList can hold. (You will have to change the attribute declaration if you decide to add an object of a new type to it. But that is another problem.) The point here is that you can get the information about what went wrong by examining the InnerException of the received exception.

An easy way to examine the InnerException of an exception is to use the Exception. ToString( ) method to display its information, instead of using its Message property. (See Gotcha #15, "rethrow isn't consistent.")

IN A NUTSHELL

Look at the InnerException for a fuller understanding of the problem when you receive an exception. In general, examine the InnerException if there is one. If you will be logging an exception, remember to log not only the exception details, but the InnerException information as well. And remember that the InnerException is itself an Exception; it might contain its own InnerException.

SEE ALSO

Gotcha #15, "rethrow isn't consistent" and Gotcha #23, "Copy Constructor hampers exensibility."

#27 Object initialization sequence isn't consistent

When you create an object, the memory for the instance is allocated, each of its fields is initialized with the default value defined by the CTS, and then the constructor is invoked. If you create an object of a derived class, then all fields of the base are initialized and the constructor of the base is invoked before any field of the derived class is initialized. This is conventional wisdom derived from languages such as C++ and Java. But it is *not* the sequence that is followed in C#. In fact, *the sequence of initialization is not the same between C# and VB.NET*. Take a look at Example 3-20.

 The object initialization sequence in C# is well-documented in section 10.10.3 of the C# Language Specification (see "On the Web" in the Appendix"). My worry is not the fact that the object initialization sequence differs in C#, as compared to C++ or Java. It is that the sequence is not consistent between .NET languages—for instance, between C# and VB.NET.

Example 3-20. Object initialization sequence

> ✔ **C# (Initialization)**

```
//SomeClass1.cs
using System;

namespace ObjectInitSequence
{
    public class SomeClass1
    {
        public SomeClass1( )
        {
            Console.WriteLine("Constructor of SomeClass1 called");
        }
    }
}

// SomeClass2.cs
using System;

namespace ObjectInitSequence
{
    public class SomeClass2
    {
        public SomeClass2( )
        {
            Console.WriteLine("Constructor of SomeClass2 called");
```

Example 3-20. Object initialization sequence (continued)

```
        }
    }
}

//Base.cs
using System;

namespace ObjectInitSequence
{
    public class Base
    {
        private SomeClass1 obj1 = new SomeClass1( );

        public Base( )
        {
            Console.WriteLine("Constructor of Base called");
        }
    }
}

//Derived.cs
using System;

namespace ObjectInitSequence
{
    public class Derived : Base
    {
        private SomeClass2 obj2 = new SomeClass2( );

        public Derived( )
        {
            Console.WriteLine("Constructor of Derived called");
        }
    }
}

//Test.cs
using System;

namespace ObjectInitSequence
{
    class Test
    {
        [STAThread]
        static void Main(string[] args)
        {
            Derived obj = new Derived( );
        }
    }
}
```

Example 3-20. Object initialization sequence (continued)

```
'SomeClass1
Public Class SomeClass1
    Public Sub New( )
        Console.WriteLine("Constructor of SomeClass1 called")
    End Sub
End Class

'SomeClass2.vb
Public Class SomeClass2
    Public Sub New( )
        Console.WriteLine("Constructor of SomeClass2 called")
    End Sub
End Class

'Base.vb
Public Class Base
    Private obj1 As SomeClass1 = New SomeClass1

    Public Sub New( )
        Console.WriteLine("Constructor of Base called")
    End Sub
End Class

'Derived.vb
Public Class Derived
    Inherits Base
    Private obj2 As SomeClass2 = New SomeClass2

    Public Sub New( )
        Console.WriteLine("Constructor of Derived called")
    End Sub
End Class

'Test.vb
Module Test
    Sub Main( )
        Dim obj As Derived = New Derived
    End Sub

End Module
```

In the above code, the class Base has a field of type SomeClass1. The class Derived, which inherits from Base, has a field of type SomeClass2. Each of these classes has a constructor that prints a message announcing itself. What is the sequence of field initialization and constructor calls when an object of Derived is created? Before you answer, you may want to ask, which language?! The C# code given above produces the output shown in Figure 3-16.

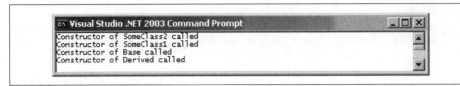

Figure 3-16. Output from C# version of Example 3-20

However, the VB.NET version of the code produces different results, shown in Figure 3-17.

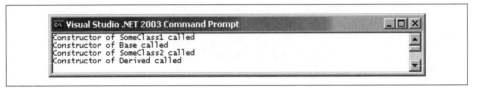

Figure 3-17. Output from VB.NET version of Example 3-20

While the two programs are identical except for the language used to write them, the behavior is different. In C#, the Derived class's fields are initialized, then those of the Base class. Next, the constructors are called top-down, the Base constructor first and then the Derived constructor. In the case of the VB.NET program, however, the sequence is different (and conformant with the sequence in C++ and Java). The initialization of fields in Base and the invocation of the Base class constructor complete before any field of the Derived class is initialized.

While you are wondering about this, let me throw you some even more interesting things. What is the sequence if I derive a C# class from a VB.NET class? What happens if I derive a VB.NET class from a C# class which in turn is derived from another VB.NET class? If I derive a C# class from a VB.NET class, then the derived members will be initialized before the base members. However, if I derive a VB.NET class from a C# class, then the base members will be initialized before any derived members. In case you have more than two levels of inheritance and you mix languages between levels, the sequence depends on the language of the derived class at each level (good luck).

 IN A NUTSHELL

Clearly understand the sequence in which objects are initialized in C# versus VB.NET. Understanding the sequence will help avoid surprises from this rather odd inconsistency.

SEE ALSO

Gotcha #23, "Copy Constructor hampers exensibility," Gotcha #24, "Clone() has limitations," and Gotcha #28, "Polymorphism kicks in prematurely."

#28 Polymorphism kicks in prematurely

Polymorphism is the most cherished feature in object-oriented programming. An important tenet in object modeling is that objects be kept in a valid state at all times. Ideally, you should never be able to invoke methods on an object until it has been fully initialized. Unfortunately in .NET, it isn't difficult to violate this with the use of polymorphism. Unlike C++, in .NET polymorphism kicks in even before the execution of the constructor has completed. This behavior is similar to Java.

Let's review polymorphism for a moment. It assures that the virtual/overridable method that is called is based on the real type of the object, and not just the type of the reference used to invoke it. For instance, say foo( ) is a virtual/overridable method on a base class, and a class that derives from the base overrides that method. Assume also that you have two references baseReference and derivedReference of the base type and derived type. Let both of these references actually refer to the same instance of the derived class. Now, regardless of how the method is called, either as baseReference.foo( ) or derivedReference.foo( ), the same method foo( ) in the derived class is invoked. This is due to the effect of polymorphism or dynamic binding.

While this sounds great, the problem is that polymorphism enters into the picture before the derived class's constructor is even called. Consider Example 3-21.

Example 3-21. Polymorphism during construction

✗ C# (PolymorphismTooSoon)

```
//Room.cs
using System;

namespace ProblemPolymorphismConstruction
{
    public class Room
    {
        public void OpenWindow( )
        {
            Console.WriteLine("Room window open");
        }
        public void CloseWindow( )
        {
            Console.WriteLine("Room window closed");
        }
    }
}
```

Example 3-21. Polymorphism during construction (continued)

```
//ExecutiveRoom.cs.
using System;

namespace ProblemPolymorphismConstruction
{
    public class ExecutiveRoom : Room
    {
    }
}

//Employee.cs
using System;

namespace ProblemPolymorphismConstruction
{
    public class Employee
    {
        public Employee()
        {
            Console.WriteLine("Employee's constructor called");

            Work();
        }

        public virtual void Work()
        {
            Console.WriteLine("Employee is working");
        }
    }
}

//Manager.cs
using System;

namespace ProblemPolymorphismConstruction
{
    public class Manager : Employee
    {
        private Room theRoom = null;
        private int managementLevel = 0;

        public Manager(int level)
        {
            Console.WriteLine("Manager's constructor called");

            managementLevel = level;

            if (level < 2)
                theRoom = new Room();
            else
```

Example 3-21. Polymorphism during construction (continued)

```
                theRoom = new ExecutiveRoom( );
        }

        public override void Work( )
        {
            Console.WriteLine("Manager's work called");

            theRoom.OpenWindow( );
            base.Work( );
        }
    }
}

//User.cs
using System;

namespace ProblemPolymorphismConstruction
{
    class User
    {
        static void Main(string[] args)
        {
            Console.WriteLine("Creating Manager");
            Manager mgr = new Manager(1);

            Console.WriteLine("Done");
        }
    }
}
```

✗ VB.NET (PolymorphismTooSoon)

```
'Room.vb

Public Class Room
    Public Sub OpenWindow( )
        Console.WriteLine("Room window open")
    End Sub

    Public Sub CloseWindow( )
        Console.WriteLine("Room window closed")
    End Sub
End Class


'ExecutiveRoom.vb
Public Class ExecutiveRoom
    Inherits Room
End Class
```

Example 3-21. Polymorphism during construction (continued)

```vb
'Employee.vb

Public Class Employee
    Public Sub New( )
        Console.WriteLine("Employee's constructor called")

        Work( )
    End Sub

    Public Overridable Sub Work( )
        Console.WriteLine("Employee is working")
    End Sub
End Class

'Manager.vb
Public Class Manager
    Inherits Employee
    Private theRoom As Room = Nothing
    Private managementLevel As Integer = 0

    Public Sub New(ByVal level As Integer)
        Console.WriteLine("Manager's constructor called")

        managementLevel = level

        If level < 2 Then
            theRoom = New Room
        Else
            theRoom = New ExecutiveRoom
        End If
    End Sub
    Public Overrides Sub Work( )
        Console.WriteLine("Manager's work called")

        theRoom.OpenWindow( )
        MyBase.Work( )
    End Sub
End Class

'User.vb
Module User

    Sub Main( )
        Console.WriteLine("Creating Manager")
        Dim mgr As New Manager(1)

        Console.WriteLine("Done")
    End Sub
End Module
```

In the example given above, you have a Room class with OpenWindow( ) and CloseWindow( ) methods. The ExecutiveRoom derives from Room, but does not have any additional functionality as yet. The Employee has a constructor that invokes its Work( ) method. The Work( ) method, however, is declared virtual/overridable in the Employee class.

In the Manager class, which inherits from Employee, you have a reference of type Room. Depending on the Manager's level, in the constructor of the Manager, you assign the theRoom reference to either an instance of Room or an instance of ExecutiveRoom. In the overridden Work( ) method in the Manager class, you invoke the method on theRoom to open the window and then invoke the base class's Work( ) method. Looks reasonable so far, doesn't it? But when you execute this program you get a NullReferenceException as shown in Figure 3-18.

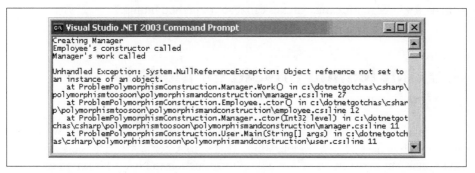

Figure 3-18. Exception from Example 3-21

Notice that in the creation of the Manager object, the Employee's constructor is called first. From the Employee's constructor, the call to Work( ) polymorphically calls Manager.Work( ).

Why? In the Employee constructor, even though the self reference this/Me is of type Employee, the real instance is of type Manager. But at this point, the constructor of Manager has not been invoked. As a result, the reference theRoom is still null/Nothing. The Work( ) method, however, assumes that the object has been constructed and tries to access theRoom. Hence the NullReferenceException.

Ideally, no method should ever be called on an object until its constructor has completed. However, the above example shows that there are situations where this can happen.

As a side note, if you initialize theRoom at the point of declaration to a Room instance, you half-fix the problem. The C# code will run fine, but the VB.NET code will still throw the exception. The reason for this? The difference in the sequence of initialization between the two languages, as discussed in Gotcha #27, "Object initialization sequence isn't consistent."

Understand the consequence of calling virtual/overridable methods from within a constructor. If you need to further initialize your object, provide an Init( ) method that users of your object can call after the constructor completes. This even has a name: two-phase construction.

SEE ALSO

Gotcha #23, "Copy Constructor hampers exensibility," Gotcha #24, "Clone() has limitations," Gotcha #27, "Object initialization sequence isn't consistent," Gotcha #43, "Using new/shadows causes "hideous hiding"," Gotcha #44, "Compilers are lenient toward forgotten override/overrides," Gotcha #45, "Compilers lean toward hiding virtual methods," and Gotcha #47, "Signature mismatches can lead to method hiding."

GOTCHA
#29 Unit testing private methods is tricky

NUnit is an excellent tool that allows you to write unit-testing code, thereby improving the robustness of your application. (Refer to Gotcha #8, "Division operation isn't consistent between types" for a brief introduction to NUnit.) It serves as a critical aid in refactoring—helping you identify the code changes you need to make as your design evolves. Developers who have started using the tool find it hard to imagine writing any code and refactoring it without the test harness and the support provided by NUnit.

Where should your test cases go? The pundits recommend that you place the test classes (called the "test fixture") in the same assembly as the code you're testing. This allows you to test not only the public members of a class, but the internal members as well. While this sounds great, there is one problem. Doing so might force you to make some of the class's methods internal instead of private in order to test them. Also, just to make your class testable, sometimes you might find yourself writing methods that aren't otherwise needed. I've even heard the suggestion to use compiler flags to make a method internal for testing and private for release. Such options make the code less readable and result in some very unpleasant code-maintenance nightmares. Relaxing the access control for the sake of testing is also not desirable, especially when there is an alternative. Consider Example 3-22 to test a simple User class.

Example 3-22. NUnit test for a simple User

✗ C# (TestPrivate)

```
//Test.cs
using System;
using NUnit.Framework;
using System.Security.Cryptography;

namespace UnitTest
{
    [TestFixture]
    public class Test
    {
        private User theUser;

        [SetUp]
        public void CreateUser()
        {
            theUser = new User();
        }

        [Test]
        public void TestSetPassword()
        {
            string PASSWORD = "Cod!ng";

            theUser.ChangePassword(null, PASSWORD);
            // How do you assert that the password has been set?
            // You can rely on calling the GetPassword method to do this.
            // However, do you really want to provide a
            // method to get the password?

            // OK, let's write one for now.

            byte[] hashCode = new SHA256Managed().ComputeHash(
                System.Text.Encoding.ASCII.GetBytes(PASSWORD));

            string hashCodeString = BitConverter.ToString(hashCode);

            Assert.AreEqual(hashCodeString, theUser.GetPassword());
        }
    }
}

//User.cs
using System;
using System.Security.Cryptography;

namespace UnitTest
{
```

Example 3-22. NUnit test for a simple User (continued)

```csharp
public class User
{
    private string password;

    public void ChangePassword(
            string oldPassword, string thePassword)
    {
        // Make sure that the caller is either creating
        // a new password, or knows the old password

        if ((password == null && oldPassword == null)
            || CreateHash(oldPassword) == password)
        {
            password = CreateHash(thePassword);
        }
        else
        {
            throw new ApplicationException("Invalid password");
        }
    }

    internal string GetPassword( )
    {
        return password;
    }

    private string CreateHash(string input)
    {
        byte[] hashCode = new SHA256Managed( ).ComputeHash(
            System.Text.Encoding.ASCII.GetBytes(input));

        return BitConverter.ToString(hashCode);
    }
}
}
```

✗ VB.NET (TestPrivate)

```vbnet
'Test.vb
Imports NUnit.Framework
Imports System.Security.Cryptography

<TestFixture( )> _
Public Class Test

    Private theUser As User

    <SetUp( )> _
    Public Sub CreateCalculator( )
```

Example 3-22. NUnit test for a simple User (continued)

```vbnet
        theUser = New User
    End Sub

    <Test()> _
  Public Sub TestSetPassword()
        Dim PASSWORD As String = "Cod!ng"

        theUser.ChangePassword(Nothing, PASSWORD)
        'How do you assert that the password has been set?
        'You can rely on calling the GetPassword method to do this.
        'However, do you really want to provide a
        'method to get the password?

        'OK, let's write one for now.

        Dim hashCode() As Byte = New SHA256Managed().ComputeHash( _
                    System.Text.Encoding.ASCII.GetBytes(PASSWORD))

        Dim hashCodeString As String = BitConverter.ToString(hashCode)

        Assert.AreEqual(hashCodeString, theUser.GetPassword())
    End Sub
End Class


'User.vb
Imports System
Imports System.Security.Cryptography

Public Class User
    Private password As String

    Public Sub ChangePassword(ByVal oldPassword As String, _
          ByVal thePassword As String)
        'Make sure that the caller is either creating a new password,
        'or knows the old password
        If (password Is Nothing And oldPassword Is Nothing) OrElse _
              CreateHash(oldPassword) = password Then
            password = CreateHash(thePassword)
        Else
            Throw New ApplicationException("Invalid password")
        End If
    End Sub

    Friend Function GetPassword() As String
        Return password
    End Function
```

Example 3-22. NUnit test for a simple User (continued)

```
    Private Function CreateHash(ByVal input As String) As String
        Dim hashCode( ) As Byte = New SHA256Managed( ).ComputeHash( _
                    System.Text.Encoding.ASCII.GetBytes(input))

        Return BitConverter.ToString(hashCode)

    End Function
End Class
```

In this example, you have a User class that needs to be tested. You are writing a test case for the SetPassword( ) method. After the call to SetPassword( ), you want to check if the password has been set correctly. How do you do that? From within the Test class, you can access the public members and internal/friend members of the User class (since Test is in the same assembly as User). The only option I can think of here is to write an internal/friend method named GetPassword( ) in the User class to make SetPassword( ) testable. This might not be desirable. You might not want to expose the password. Furthermore, you might not need GetPassword( ) in the application, since you are writing it just to test SetPassword( ).

Why not make the test case a nested class of the User class? (Of course, I am not suggesting that you make all test fixtures nested classes. But if you need your test case to access the private inner workings of a class, writing it as a nested class accomplishes this.) The modified code with Test as a nested class is shown in Example 3-23.

Example 3-23. Test as nested class

✔ **C# (TestPrivate)**

```
using System;
using System.Security.Cryptography;
using NUnit.Framework;

namespace UnitTest
{
    public class User
    {
        private string password;

        public void ChangePassword(
            string oldPassword, string thePassword)
        {
            if ((password == null && oldPassword == null)
                || CreateHash(oldPassword) == password)
            {
                password = CreateHash(thePassword);
            }
            else
            {
```

Example 3-23. Test as nested class (continued)

```
                    throw new ApplicationException("Invalid password");
            }
        }

        private string CreateHash(string input)
        {
            byte[] hashCode = new SHA256Managed( ).ComputeHash(
                System.Text.Encoding.ASCII.GetBytes(input));

            return BitConverter.ToString(hashCode);
        }

        // In .NET 2.0, with Partial Classes, this can be
        // in a separate file
        [TestFixture]
        public class Test
        {
            private User theUser;

            [SetUp]
            public void CreateUser( )
            {
                theUser = new User( );
            }

            [Test]
            public void TestSetPassword( )
            {
                string PASSWORD = "Cod!ng";

                theUser.ChangePassword(null, PASSWORD);

                Assert.AreEqual(theUser.password,
                    theUser.CreateHash(PASSWORD));
            }
        }
    }
}
```

✔ **VB.NET (TestPrivate)**

```
'User.vb
Imports System
Imports System.Security.Cryptography
Imports NUnit.Framework

Public Class User
    Private password As String
```

Example 3-23. Test as nested class (continued)

```
    Public Sub ChangePassword(ByVal oldPassword As String, _
            ByVal thePassword As String)
        If (password Is Nothing And oldPassword Is Nothing) OrElse _
                CreateHash(oldPassword) = password Then
            password = CreateHash(thePassword)
        Else
            Throw New ApplicationException("Invalid password")
        End If
    End Sub

    Private Function CreateHash(ByVal input As String) As String
        Dim hashCode() As Byte = New SHA256Managed().ComputeHash( _
                    System.Text.Encoding.ASCII.GetBytes(input))

        Return BitConverter.ToString(hashCode)

    End Function

    'In .NET 2.0, with Partial Classes, this can be in a separate file
    <TestFixture()> _
    Public Class Test

        Private theUser As User

        <SetUp()> _
        Public Sub CreateCalculator()
            theUser = New User
        End Sub

        <Test()> _
      Public Sub TestSetPassword()
            Dim PASSWORD As String = "Cod!ng"

            theUser.ChangePassword(Nothing, PASSWORD)

            Assert.AreEqual(theUser.password, _
                theUser.CreateHash(PASSWORD))
        End Sub
    End Class

End Class
```

In this code, the Test class is a nested class of the User class. Nested classes have full access to private members of the nesting class. This allows a more convenient way to test the class implementation without compromising the encapsulation or access control. The test case being executed under NUnit is shown in Figure 3-19.

One disadvantage of this approach is that the class file *User.cs* (or *User.vb*) now becomes larger. Furthermore, you may not want to release your test cases with your

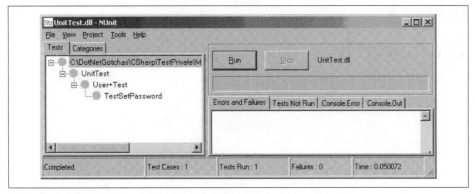

Figure 3-19. NUnit test executing a nested test fixture

assembly. This will not be an issue in the next release of .NET, where partial classes are allowed. Then you'll be able to write the User class in one or more files and keep the test cases in different files. That will also make it easier to remove test cases from the build in production.

 IN A NUTSHELL

If you find yourself changing the accessibility of fields and methods just so you can test them, or you start introducing methods only for the sake of testing other methods (e.g., GetPassword( ) in Example 3-22), consider writing those tests as nested classes. The tests that depend only on non-private members of a class should still be written as higher-level classes in the same project.

SEE ALSO

Gotcha #8, "Division operation isn't consistent between types."

CHAPTER 4

Language Interoperability Gotchas

The .NET Common Language Runtime (CLR) executes the Microsoft Intermediate Language (MSIL). Code written in one of .NET's various supported languages is translated into MSIL and metadata. Your compiled classes are referenced through metadata and used in this MSIL. This makes it possible to use code written in different languages. You can aggregate or associate an object of a class written in C#, for instance, within a VB.NET program. You can even inherit from a class written in a different language.

The exciting implication of this is that .NET does not restrict you to any language. If you are a C++ or Java programmer, you can use C# (or managed C++). If you are a VB programmer, you can use VB.NET. Or you can use one of the other 25+ languages supported in .NET. (Refer to "Languages available in .NET" in the section "On the Web" in Appendix)

However, there are a few glitches to keep in mind. Not all the languages support every MSIL feature. Furthermore, each language has its own set of keywords; although there are some commonalities in keywords between languages, there are many differences to watch out for. What kind of mess can you get into with these differences? What are the things you need to remember to make your code interoperable between languages? These issues are the focus of this chapter.

GOTCHA

#30 Common Language Specification Compliance isn't the default

When I first started learning C#, I heard that it has some C++ features that are not in Java. My first thought was templates. I was quite disappointed to find instead that one of the supported features is operator overloading. It's quite complicated in C++ [Stroustrup00, Cline99]; it gives you many ways to shoot yourself in the foot. Having offered courses on C++ for over 12 years, I know the pain people go through just learning operator overloading. Getting it right is another story [Meyers96, Meyers98]. Overloading is supposed to make your code intuitive and easier to understand, but it often has the opposite effect.

Unfortunately, in my opinion, C# took what was complicated in C++ and made it worse. For instance, you can overload the true operator. This requires that you overload the false operator as well. Arbitrarily overloading operators increases the complexity of your code and reduces its readability; its worth is questionable.

Furthermore, not all .NET languages support operator overloading. If you write a C# class with overloaded operators, those operators are not accessible from VB.NET. If you have merely overloaded the operators and have not provided equivalent regular methods, your code is not considered to be Common Language Specification (CLS) compliant. CLS compliance requires you to provide a regular method for each overloaded operator.

CLS Compliance

Proper implementation of overloaded operators (and their equivalent methods) is only one aspect of CLS compliance. If your type is to be fully usable in any .NET language, it must expose only features that are common to all languages. The basic language features needed for applications have been defined in a set of conventions called the Common Language Specification (CLS).

The Common Type System (CTS) supports a rich set of types found in many programming languages. However, not all types supported in the .NET CTS are interoperable or CLS-compliant. In this regard, the CLS rules define a subset of the CTS. By claiming CLS compliance you are indicating that your code follows the CLS rules and restrictions. This affects how you expose all the public and protected members of your public types. However, code that is private, not exposed, or local to your implementation can use any language-specific features. Furthermore, only assemblies marked with the CLSCompliant attribute are considered CLS-compliant.

The Common Language Infrastructure (CLI) is an ECMA-335 standard that defines a runtime environment for applications written in multiple high-level languages to run. For a thorough discussion of these concepts, refer to "ECMA-CLI" in the section "On the Web" in the Appendix. Also refer to [Box03].

To make sure your code is CLS-compliant, add [Assembly: System. CLSCompliant(true)] to the *AssemblyInfo.cs* file of a C# project, or add <Assembly: CLSCompliant(True)> to *AssemblyInfo.vb* for VB.NET. Then run the assembly through the FxCop tool. (See "FxCop" in the section "On the Web" in the Appendix for details about this tool.)

Consider the example of delegates in .NET. Typically a C# programmer would use the += operator to add or register a delegate. In VB.NET, you can realize the same goal using either the Combine( ) method or the special AddHandler statement. Similarly, the Remove( ) method is equivalent to the C# -= operator on delegates. Providing regular methods for each overloaded operator allows users of your class to take advantage of the operators in languages that support overloading, while making it fully usable in languages that don't.

If you want your code to be CLS-compliant, then for each operator you must provide a regular method as well. Operator overloading does not reduce the code size. In fact, you will end up writing more methods to accommodate languages that don't support it.

 IN A NUTSHELL

Always provide a regular method for each overloaded operator. Mark your assembly with the CLSCompliant attribute if you intend to provide language interoperability. Then use the FxCop tool to confirm that you are CLS-compliant.

SEE ALSO

Gotcha #31, "Optional parameters break interoperability."

GOTCHA
#31 Optional parameters break interoperability

An optional parameter in VB.NET is a parameter that is given a value at the point of declaration. When you call a method that has optional parameters, you can choose not to provide a value for them. The compiler will substitute the default values. However, not all .NET languages support optional parameters. VB.NET allows you to declare trailing arguments as optional. C# does not. What happens to interoperability if you use optional parameters in VB.NET? Consider Example 4-1.

Example 4-1. Using optional parameters

✔ **C# and VB.NET (Optional)**

```
'SomeClass1.vb part of AVBDNLibrary.dll
Public Class SomeClass1
    Public Overridable Sub SomeMethod(ByVal val1 As Integer, _
        Optional ByVal val2 As Double = 0.0)

    End Sub
End Class
```

Example 4-1. Using optional parameters (continued)

```
//Test.cs part of CSUser.exe
using System;

namespace CSUser
{
    class Test
    {
        [STAThread]
        static void Main(string[] args)
        {
            AVBDNLibrary.SomeClass1 obj
                = new AVBDNLibrary.SomeClass1();
            obj.SomeMethod(1, 2);
        }
    }
}
```

The VB.NET class SomeClass1 has a method SomeMethod( ) with two parameters, the second one marked Optional. You also have a C# class Test that, in its Main( ) method, creates an instance of the VB.NET class SomeClass1 and then calls its SomeMethod( ). If you look at this example, there seems to be no problem in calling the method SomeMethod( ) of SomeClass1. In fact, IntelliSense displays the method signature in C# without showing any indication of default or optional arguments, as seen in Figure 4-1.

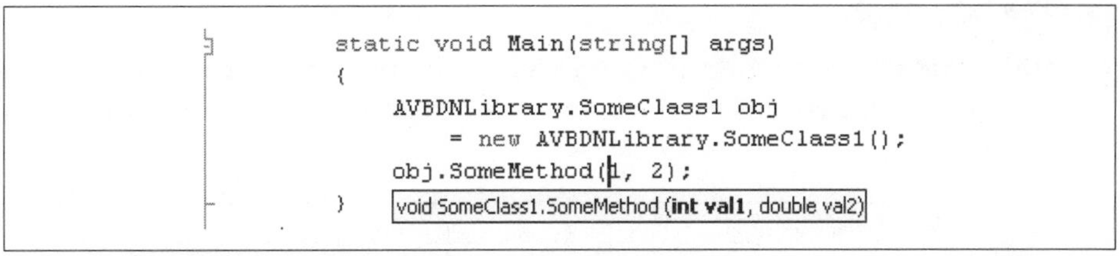

Figure 4-1. C# IntelliSense for a method with optional parameter

Well, there is no problem if this is the level of interoperability you are looking for. However, things get tricky if you go further. To illustrate what can happen, let's derive a C# class from SomeClass1. This is shown in Example 4-2.

Example 4-2. Deriving a C# class from the VB.NET class in Example 4-1

> ✔ **C# and VB.NET (Optional)**

```
//SomeClass2.cs part of CSLib.dll
using System;

namespace CSLib
{
    public class SomeClass2 : AVBDNLibrary.SomeClass1
    {
```

Example 4-2. Deriving a C# class from the VB.NET class in Example 4-1 (continued)

```
        public override void SomeMethod(int val1, double val2)
        {
            base.SomeMethod (val1, val2);
        }
    }
}
```

Note that the overridden method SomeMethod( ) takes two parameters, int val1 and double val2. Since C# does not support optional parameters, both the parameters are specified.

So far so good, right? Now say you create a VB.NET class that derives from SomeClass2, as in Example 4-3.

Example 4-3. Deriving a VB.NET class from the C# class in Example 4-2

✗ C# and VB.NET (Optional)

```
'SomeClass3.vb part of AVBDNLibrary2.dll
Public Class SomeClass3
    Inherits CSLib.SomeClass2
    Public Overrides Sub SomeMethod(ByVal val1 As Integer, _
        ByVal val2 As Double)

    End Sub
End Class
```

Now that SomeClass3 inherits from SomeClass2, the overridden method does not have any optional parameters. When you compile this code, you get the error shown in Figure 4-2.

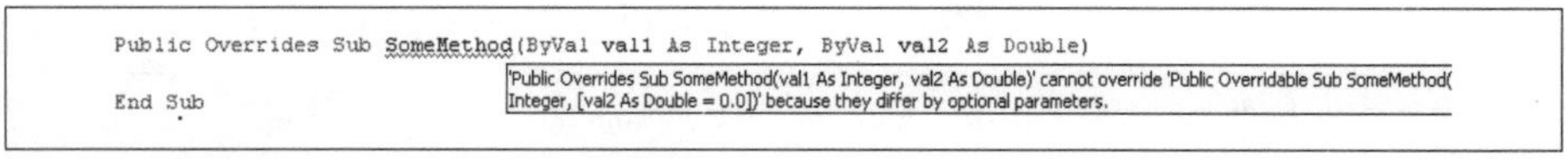

```
    Public Overrides Sub SomeMethod(ByVal val1 As Integer, ByVal val2 As Double)

    End Sub
```
'Public Overrides Sub SomeMethod(val1 As Integer, val2 As Double)' cannot override 'Public Overridable Sub SomeMethod(Integer, [val2 As Double = 0.0])' because they differ by optional parameters.

Figure 4-2. Error compiling code in Example 4-3

The error message tells you that SomeClass3 cannot override SomeMethod( ) because the base version and the overridden version differ by the optional parameter. What if you try to fix this error by placing the Optional keyword in SomeClass3.SomeMethod( ), as in Example 4-4?

Example 4-4. Placing the Optional keyword in the overriding method

✗ C# and VB.NET (Optional)

```
'SomeClass3.vb part of AVBDNLibrary2.dll
Public Class SomeClass3
    Inherits CSLib.SomeClass2
```

Example 4-4. Placing the Optional keyword in the overriding method (continued)

```
    Public Overrides Sub SomeMethod(ByVal val1 As Integer, _
        Optional ByVal val2 As Double = 0.0)

    End Sub
End Class
```

No go. You get the same error (see Figure 4-3).

```
    Public Overrides Sub SomeMethod(ByVal val1 As Integer, Optional ByVal val2 As Double = 0.0)
                         ┌─────────────────────────────────────────────────────────────────────────
    End Sub              │'Public Overrides Sub SomeMethod(val1 As Integer, [val2 As Double = 0.0])' cannot override 'Public Overrides Sub SomeMethod(va
                         │Integer, val2 As Double)' because they differ by optional parameters.
```

Figure 4-3. Error compiling code in Example 4-4

The compiler is still not happy. Why? It's because there's a conflict here. The first-level base-class method says it needs an optional parameter. The second-level immediate base class, however, says it does not have any optional parameters (being a C# class). If you look at the MSIL generated for each of these classes using *ildasm.exe*, you will notice that SomeClass1.SomeMethod( ) in the VB.NET base class has [opt] specified. However, the method in the C# class does not.

IN A NUTSHELL

Not all .NET languages support optional parameters. This may lead to interoperability problems. Consider using method overloading instead of optional parameters.

SEE ALSO

Gotcha #16, "Default of Option Strict (off) isn't good," Gotcha #30, "Common Language Specification Compliance isn't the default," Gotcha #32, "Mixing case between class members breaks interoperability," Gotcha #33, "Name collision with keywords breaks interoperability," and Gotcha #34, "Defining an array isn't consistent."

GOTCHA

#32 Mixing case between class members breaks interoperability

Do not create properties or methods that differ only by case. C# (like C++ and Java) is case-sensitive. VB.NET (like VB6) is not. So how would VB.NET handle a C# class that has two different properties with the same name (i.e., their spelling differed only by case)? This is illustrated in Example 4-5.

Example 4-5. Mixing the case

✗ C# and VB.NET (DifferInCase)

```
//SomeClass.cs part of CSLib.dll
using System;

namespace CSLib
{
    public class SomeClass
    {
        public int Value1
        {
            get { return 1; }
        }

        public int value1
        {
            get { return 2; }
        }
    }
}
```

Here you have a C# class SomeClass with two properties, Value1 and value1. The C# compiler has no objection to this. Now let's write a VB.NET class that uses the above class, as in Example 4-6.

Example 4-6. Using C# class with mixed-case members

✗ C# and VB.NET (DifferInCase)

```
'TestModule.vb part of VBUser.exe

Module TestModule

    Sub Main( )
        Dim obj As New CSLib.SomeClass

        Dim val As Integer

        val = obj.Value1
    End Sub

End Module
```

When you compile, you get the error shown in Figure 4-4.

 In .NET Version 1.0, this compilation error did not appear. Instead the first property with that name was used. In this case, Value1 would have been used instead of value1.

```
            val = obj.Value1
    -    End Sub                    Overload resolution failed because no accessible 'Value1' is most specific for these arguments:
                                    'Public ReadOnly Property value1() As Integer': Not most specific.
    - End Module                    'Public ReadOnly Property Value1() As Integer': Not most specific.
```

Figure 4-4. Error compiling code in Example 4-6

How does this differ in .NET 2.0 Beta 1? There is no compilation error; the behavior is the same as in .NET version 1.0.

These two properties can be accessed in C# without any problem. The C# compiler resolves the names properly. The VB.NET compiler, however, gets confused about this "overloading." Incidentally, you can use reflection in VB.NET to access these two properties, because the CLR uses case-sensitive matching to determine the members.

 IN A NUTSHELL

Do not write properties, methods, or fields whose names differ only by case. This breaks interoperability.

SEE ALSO

Gotcha #31, "Optional parameters break interoperability," Gotcha #33, "Name collision with keywords breaks interoperability," and Gotcha #34, "Defining an array isn't consistent."

GOTCHA
#33 Name collision with keywords breaks interoperability

When choosing names for methods or properties, avoid names that are keywords in other .NET languages. Most of the time this won't be an issue, for you would be unlikely to choose a name like new, structure, or class. However, I've been surprised at times by the names I chose. Consider Example 4-7.

Example 4-7. Method name conflict

✗ C# and VB.NET (WhatsInAName)

```
//StopWatch.cs part of CSLib.dll
using System;

namespace CSLib
{
    public class StopWatch
    {
```

Example 4-7. Method name conflict (continued)

```
    public virtual void Start() {}

    public virtual void Stop() {}

    public virtual void Reset()
    {
    }

    public int ElapasedTime
    {
        get { return 0; }
    }
  }
}
```

A C# class named StopWatch models a stopwatch that will allow you to measure the time spent in certain activities or events. It has a method named Start() that gets the stopwatch going. The Stop() method halts it. Reset() is used to simply clear the stopwatch. The ElapsedTime property gives you the time that has elapsed. Let's just leave the methods and property with a dummy implementation for this example. The code compiles without any error. So, what's the problem?

Let's create a VB.NET class that derives from this, as in Example 4-8.

Example 4-8. A VB.NET class derived from the class in Example 4-7

> ✔ **C# and VB.NET (WhatsInAName)**

```
'SpecialStopWatch.vb part of VBLib.dll

Public Class SpecialStopWatch
    Inherits CSLib.StopWatch

    Public Overrides Sub Reset()

    End Sub

    Public Overrides Sub Start()

    End Sub

    Public Overrides Sub Stop()

    End Sub
End Class
```

When you compile the code you get an error, as in Figure 4-5.

```
        Public Overrides Sub Stop()
                                    Keyword is not valid as an identifier.
        End Sub
```

Figure 4-5. Error compiling the class in Example 4-8

The problem here is that Stop is a keyword in VB.NET. A Stop statement suspends execution of the code. Yes, you do want to suspend the execution of the StopWatch, but not the execution of the program. But there is a workaround in this case. You can write the method as shown in Figure 4-6.

```
        Public Overrides Sub [Stop]()

        End Sub
```

Figure 4-6. Workaround to override Stop() method

This allows the code to compile. When invoking the method on an object of SpecialStopWatch, you simply call the Stop( ) method like you call any other method: *obj*.Stop( ), where *obj* stands for the name of the method.

While VB.NET escapes the conflicting methods by placing the name within [ ], C# uses an @ prefix. For instance, say you have a method named override( ) in a VB.NET class. If you derive from that class in C# and override the method named override( ), you have to write it as shown in Figure 4-7.

```
        public override void @override()
        {
            base.@override ();
        }
```

Figure 4-7. Keyword prefix in C#

When calling this method, you write *obj.@override( )*. This works, but it's ugly.

IN A NUTSHELL

When choosing names (for methods, properties, etc), use caution not to use names that are keywords in other languages. The other languages may have to use escape characters to access these conflicting names. Of course, as more languages become available in the .NET environment, you can't possibly know all their keywords. But if you know this is an issue, at least it won't surprise you if you bump into it.

SEE ALSO

Gotcha #31, "Optional parameters break interoperability," Gotcha #32, "Mixing case between class members breaks interoperability," and Gotcha #34, "Defining an array isn't consistent."

#34 Defining an array isn't consistent

Most of the application code I write is in C#. However, I have been involved in a few projects where I had to mix languages and write some VB.NET code. The fact that the .NET Framework class library (FCL) is the same for C# and VB.NET gives me the confidence that I can switch between the languages with maximum ease. But my confidence has been shaken when I have come across code that looks correct but doesn't work the way I expect it to.

When dealing with arrays, quite a bit of confusion is inherited from the earlier languages. While C-derived languages have zero-based indexes, VB6 used one-based indexes. However, in VB.NET, the index is zero-based. Well, can you say that all .NET languages are consistent now?

Suppose you are a C# developer and you write the code in Example 4-9.

Example 4-9. Array allocation

> ✔ **C# and VB.NET (Array)**

```
//Test.cs part of C# project Iterateover.exe
using System;

namespace IterateOver
{
    class Test
    {
        [STAThread]
        static void Main(string[] args)
        {
            object[] objects = new object[3];

            for(int i = 0; i < 3; i++)
            {
                objects[i] = new object();
            }

            foreach(Object anObj in objects)
            {
                Console.WriteLine(anObj.GetHashCode());
            }
        }
    }
}
```

You create an array of objects and set each element to an object instance. Then you use foreach to traverse the array and print the hash code of each object. The output is shown in Figure 4-8.

Figure 4-8. Output from Example 4-9

Now suppose you are asked to convert this code to VB.NET. That shouldn't be too difficult, right? So, here you go, your VB.NET version of the above code is shown in Example 4-10.

Example 4-10. VB.NET version of Example 4-9

✗ C# and VB.NET (Array)

```
'Test.vb - VB.NET Port of Test.cs

Module Test

    Sub Main( )
        Dim objects( ) As Object = New Object(3) {}

        For i As Integer = 0 To 2
            objects(i) = New Object
        Next

        For Each anObj As Object In objects
            Console.WriteLine(anObj.GetHashCode( ))
        Next
    End Sub

End Module
```

That's a straightforward port. You changed the syntax from C# to the appropriate syntax in VB.NET. But when you execute the VB.NET code, you get the output shown in Figure 4-9.

What went wrong? It first printed the hash code for the three objects as you would expect, and then it threw a NullReferenceException. The reason for this problem is that, in VB.NET, when you declared new Object(3) {}, you actually created an array of size 4 instead of size 3. Consider the code in Example 4-11.

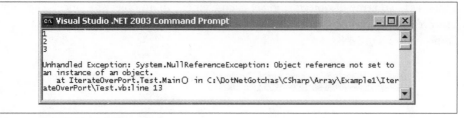

Figure 4-9. Output from Example 4-10

Example 4-11. Array size differences

✔ **C# and VB.NET (Array)**

```csharp
//MyCollection.cs part of CSLib.dll
using System;

namespace CSLib
{
    public class MyCollection
    {
        public int[] Values
        {
            get { return new int[10]; }
        }
    }
}
```

```vbnet
'MyCollection.vb part of VBLib.dll
Public Class MyCollection

    Public ReadOnly Property Values()
        Get
            Return New Integer(10) {}
        End Get
    End Property

End Class
```

```vbnet
'TestModule.vb in VBUser.exe
Module TestModule

    Sub Main()
        Dim obj1 As New CSLib.MyCollection
        Dim obj2 As New VBLib.MyCollection

        Console.WriteLine("Size of arrays")
        Console.WriteLine("C# created: {0}", obj1.Values.Length)
        Console.WriteLine("VB.NET created: {0}", obj2.Values.Length)
```

Example 4-11. Array size differences (continued)

```
    End Sub

End Module
```

In C# you create an array using the syntax `new int[10]`, while in VB.NET you use `new int(10) {}`. It looks like you're doing the same thing in both, but when you run the program you get the output shown in Figure 4-10.

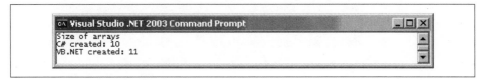

Figure 4-10. Output from Example 4-11

Here's the crux of the problem: when you create an array in VB.NET, you specify the maximum index value. In C#, you specify the maximum size (one more than the maximum index value).

 IN A NUTSHELL

Use caution creating arrays, and know the difference in how C# and VB.NET declare them. In C#, you specify the maximum size of the array. In VB.NET, you specify the maximum allowed index value.

SEE ALSO

Gotcha #31, "Optional parameters break interoperability" and Gotcha #33, "Name collision with keywords breaks interoperability."

CHAPTER 5

Garbage Collection Gotchas

Garbage collection, in general, is the process of cleaning up the memory and resources used by an object when it is no longer needed. For instance, in C++, you write a destructor to take care of this. There are two tasks that the destructor typically performs:

- deletes other objects to which the object holds pointers
- closes handles to resources

.NET, on the contrary, provides automatic garbage collection. It largely removes the burden of memory management from the programmer. But what does automatic garbage collection really do? It just reclaims the memory used by objects. What about the cleanup of resources?

When I say *resources* here, I mean unmanaged resources: those that .NET will not be able to release automatically. For example, resources created while interacting with a COM component or while using PInvoke to access some Win32 API. You, the programmer, have to write code to properly dispose of these resources.

The Finalize( ) method is provided for this purpose. When an object is garbage-collected, the CLR takes care of memory-related cleanup and calls the object's Finalize( ) method, giving it an opportunity to release any unmanaged resources.

In VB.NET, you have to actually write the Finalize( ) method. In C#, you don't. Instead, you write a specialized pseudo-destructor with the *~NameOfYourClass*( ) syntax, as in C++. But don't confuse the C# pseudo-destructor with the C++ destructor. The generated MSIL does not contain any destructor. The C# compiler creates the Finalize( ) method using the code you write in the specialized pseudo-destructor.

 Throughout the rest of this chapter, whenever I refer to the "Finalize( ) method," I am referring to the Finalize( ) method in VB.NET and the pseudo-destructor in C#.

The CLR is responsible for reclaiming memory; your object's Finalize( ) method releases unmanaged resources. This appears reasonable and straightforward, but a number of practical issues surface during development. This chapter focuses on concerns related to garbage collection, and how to write code that handles it effectively.

GOTCHA

#35 Writing Finalize() is rarely a good idea

An object is said to be accessible if traversing from a reference on the stack will lead you to it, directly or indirectly. When an object becomes inaccessible, it is ready for garbage collection, since no part of your code needs to access its content. When it is actually removed is up to the garbage collector. If this object implements a Finalize( ) method, it is executed at the time of its cleanup by the CLR.

The state change an object undergoes during the cleanup phase is shown in Figure 5-1. It first goes from accessible (A) to inaccessible (I). While in this "zombie" state, it occupies memory, but you cannot execute any of its methods or access any of its fields or properties. (But sometimes it may look like you can. See Gotcha #36, "Releasing managed resources in Finalize() can wreak havoc." The object may remain in this inaccessible state anywhere from fractions of seconds to hours (or longer), depending on the garbage collector and the memory usage of the application. When the garbage collector eventually decides to clean the object up, it inspects it to see if the Finalize( ) method needs to be executed. If so, the object is brought to the resurrected state (R) and becomes accessible once again. Once the Finalize( ) method has run, the object goes to the Inaccessible-no-need-to-finalize state (IF). Then the memory occupied by the object is reclaimed and the object becomes non-existent (N).

Jeffrey Richter explains the CLR garbage-collection mechanism in great detail. Refer to "Garbage Collection" in the section "On the Web" in the Appendix.

If the object does not have a Finalize( ) method, the cleanup will be faster. It can go from the inaccessible state (I) to the non-existent state (N) directly, as shown in Figure 5-1 by the dashed line labeled with a question mark.

Should you implement the Finalize( ) method? Consider Example 5-1.

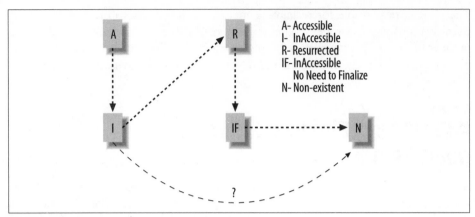

Figure 5-1. States of an object during its cleanup phase

Example 5-1. Code with Finalize()

✗ C# (Finalize)

```csharp
using System;

namespace WhyNoFinalize
{
    public class SomeClass
    {
        private SomeOtherClass ref1;

        public SomeClass(SomeOtherClass givenObject)
        {
            ref1 = givenObject;
        }

        ~SomeClass()
        {
            ref1 = null;
        }
    }
}
```

✗ VB.NET (Finalize)

```vbnet
Public Class SomeClass
    Private ref1 As SomeOtherClass

    Public Sub New(ByVal givenObject As SomeOtherClass)
        ref1 = givenObject
    End Sub
    Protected Overrides Sub Finalize()
```

Example 5-1. Code with Finalize() (continued)

```
        ref1 = Nothing
        MyBase.Finalize()
    End Sub
End Class
```

In this example, `SomeClass` holds a reference to an instance of `SomeOtherClass`. The `Finalize()` method of `SomeClass` sets the reference `ref1` to null/Nothing. Is this necessary?

No, it isn't. Whenever an instance becomes inaccessible, so do all of the other objects that are accessible only through that instance. So, when an object of `SomeClass` becomes unreachable, the object of `SomeOtherClass` that `ref1` refers to does also. Once a group of objects becomes inaccessible, all of them might be collected during the next garbage-collection sweep. There is no guarantee in which order their `Finalize()` methods will be called. So the object of `SomeOtherClass` that `ref1` refers to may have already been removed by the time `SomeClass.Finalize()` is called! Setting `ref1` to null/Nothing is redundant. But writing the `Finalize()` method provides code for the garbage collector to execute, and obliges it to resurrect the object, thus unnecessarily slowing it down. Even worse, the memory is not reclaimed until the next garbage-collection sweep, further delaying the cleanup.

 IN A NUTSHELL

Do not write the `Finalize()` method unless you have a good reason. It makes more work for the garbage collector. The main reason for implementing `Finalize()` is to make sure you free unmanaged resources, as you'll see in Gotcha #36, "Releasing managed resources in Finalize() can wreak havoc." Only write it in the context of the Dispose design pattern (see Gotcha #40, "Implementing IDisposable isn't enough").

SEE ALSO

Gotcha #36, "Releasing managed resources in Finalize() can wreak havoc," Gotcha #37, "Rules to invoke base.Finalize() are not consistent," Gotcha #38, "Depending on Finalize() can tie up critical resources," Gotcha #39, "Using Finalize() on disposed objects is costly," Gotcha #40, "Implementing IDisposable isn't enough," and Gotcha #41, "Using the Dispose Design Pattern doesn't guarantee cleanup."

#36 Releasing managed resources in Finalize() can wreak havoc

Do not access managed resources within the Finalize( ) method. Typically objects may have dependencies on other objects. In a language like C++, it is not unusual within a destructor to communicate with associated objects. However, when working with .NET, you should not carry those practices over to the Finalize( ) method.

You may ask, "So what if I access other objects within Finalize( )?" The reason you shouldn't is that the result cannot be predicted. You have no idea of the order in which the garbage collector will call the Finalize( ) method of your objects. You may write code that accesses other objects within Finalize( ), run your program, and say, "See, it works!" The phrase "it works" is a very unpleasant one in programming. It's like saying, "See, I drove the wrong direction on a one-way street and nothing went wrong." In such cases, it is not a question of *if* things will go wrong, but *when*. This is illustrated in Example 5-2.

Example 5-2. Accessing managed resources

✗ C# (NotToFinalize)

```
//SomeOtherClass.cs
using System;

namespace FinalizeAndManagedResources
{
    public class SomeOtherClass
    {
        private int[] values = new int[1000000];

        public void Notify( )
        {
            Console.WriteLine("Notify called on SomeOtherClass");
        }

        ~SomeOtherClass( )
        {
            Console.WriteLine("*** SomeOtherClass Finalized");
        }
    }
}

//SomeClass.cs
using System;

namespace FinalizeAndManagedResources
```

Example 5-2. Accessing managed resources (continued)

```csharp
{
    public class SomeClass
    {
        private SomeOtherClass other;

        public void Setother(SomeOtherClass otherObject)
        {
            other = otherObject;
        }

        ~SomeClass()
        {
            Console.WriteLine("Finalize called on SomeClass");
            if(other != null)
            {
                other.Notify();
            }
        }
    }
}

//Test.cs
using System;

namespace FinalizeAndManagedResources
{
    class Test
    {
        [STAThread]
        static void Main(string[] args)
        {
            SomeClass object1 = new SomeClass();
            SomeOtherClass object2 = new SomeOtherClass();
            object1.Setother(object2);
        }
    }
}
```

✘ VB.NET (NotToFinalize)

```vbnet
'SomeOtherClass.vb
Public Class SomeOtherClass
    Private values() As Integer = New Integer(1000000 - 1) {}

    Public Sub Notify()
        Console.WriteLine("Notify called on SomeOtherClass")
    End Sub
```

Example 5-2. Accessing managed resources (continued)

```vb
    Protected Overrides Sub Finalize()
        MyBase.Finalize()
        Console.WriteLine("*** SomeOtherClass Finalized")
    End Sub
End Class


'SomeClass.vb
Public Class SomeClass
    Private other As SomeOtherClass

    Public Sub Setother(ByVal otherObject As SomeOtherClass)
        other = otherObject
    End Sub
    Protected Overrides Sub Finalize()
        MyBase.Finalize()
        Console.WriteLine("Finalize called on SomeClass")
        If Not other Is Nothing Then
            other.Notify()
        End If
    End Sub
End Class


'Test.vb
Module Test

    Sub Main()
        Dim object1 As SomeClass = New SomeClass
        Dim object2 As SomeOtherClass = New SomeOtherClass
        object1.Setother(object2)
    End Sub

End Module
```

In this example, an instance of SomeClass has a reference to an instance of SomeOtherClass. When the object of SomeClass is finalized, it calls the Notify() method on the SomeOtherClass object. In the Main() method of the Test module, you create instances of the two classes and relate them using the SetOther() method of SomeClass. When the program completes execution, both the objects are garbage collected. The question is, in which order?

Figure 5-2 shows one possible scenario. (One of my reviewers asked how many times I had to run the program to get this output. It took only one run!)

The Notify() method is called on the object after its Finalize() method has already executed. This is strange behavior and may lead to unpredictable results. Had it thrown an exception or crashed, it would be easy to realize the problem and fix it. Because it looks like it works, the problem remains obscured and unfixed.

Figure 5-2. Output from Example 5-2

Here's another issue to consider. Suppose the method called during finalization is trying to be a good thread-safe citizen. Take a look at Example 5-3. Though this example is somewhat contrived, it starkly illustrates the risks of accessing managed resources in Finalize( ).

Example 5-3. Inadvertently locking from within Finalize()

✗ C# (NotToFinalize)

```
//SomeOtherClass.cs
using System;

namespace FinalizeAndManagedResources
{
    public class SomeOtherClass
    {
        private int[] values = new int[1000000];

        public void Notify()
        {
            Console.WriteLine("Entering Notify");
            lock(this)
            {
                Console.WriteLine("Notify called on SomeOtherClass");
            }
        }

        ~SomeOtherClass()
        {
            Console.WriteLine("*** SomeOtherClass Finalized");
        }
    }
}


//SomeClass.cs
using System;

namespace FinalizeAndManagedResources
{
    public class SomeClass
    {
```

Example 5-3. Inadvertently locking from within Finalize() (continued)

```csharp
        private SomeOtherClass other;

        public void Setother(SomeOtherClass otherObject)
        {
            other = otherObject;
        }

        ~SomeClass( )
        {
            Console.WriteLine("Finalize called on SomeClass");
            if(other != null)
            {
                other.Notify( );
            }
        }
    }
}


//Test.cs
using System;

namespace FinalizeAndManagedResources
{
    class Test
    {
        private static void ohoh(SomeOtherClass obj)
        {
            SomeClass object1 = new SomeClass( );
            object1.Setother(obj);
        }

        [STAThread]
        static void Main(string[] args)
        {
            SomeOtherClass object2 = new SomeOtherClass( );

            lock(object2)
            {
                ohoh(object2);
                GC.Collect( );
                //GC.WaitForPendingFinalizers( );
                Console.WriteLine("OK let's release lock in Main");
            }

            Console.WriteLine("Are we here");
        }
    }
}
```

Example 5-3. Inadvertently locking from within Finalize() (continued)

✗ VB.NET (NotToFinalize)

```vb
'SomeOtherClass.vb
Public Class SomeOtherClass
    Private values() As Integer = New Integer(1000000 - 1) {}

    Public Sub Notify()
        Console.WriteLine("Entering Notify")
        SyncLock Me
            Console.WriteLine("Notify called on SomeOtherClass")
        End SyncLock
    End Sub


    Protected Overrides Sub Finalize()
        MyBase.Finalize()
        Console.WriteLine("*** SomeOtherClass Finalized")
    End Sub
End Class



'SomeClass.vb
Public Class SomeClass
    Private other As SomeOtherClass

    Public Sub Setother(ByVal otherObject As SomeOtherClass)
        other = otherObject
    End Sub
    Protected Overrides Sub Finalize()
        MyBase.Finalize()
        Console.WriteLine("Finalize called on SomeClass")
        If Not other Is Nothing Then
            other.Notify()
        End If
    End Sub
End Class



'Test.vb
Module Test
    Sub ohoh(ByVal obj As SomeOtherClass)
        Dim object1 As New SomeClass
        object1.Setother(obj)
    End Sub

    Sub Main()
        Dim object2 As New SomeOtherClass
```

Example 5-3. Inadvertently locking from within Finalize( ) (continued)

```
        SyncLock object2
            ohoh(object2)
            GC.Collect()
            'GC.WaitForPendingFinalizers()
            Console.WriteLine("OK let's release lock in Main")
        End SyncLock
        Console.WriteLine("Are we here")
    End Sub

End Module
```

Within the Main( ) method you get a lock on an object of SomeOtherClass. Then you create an instance of SomeClass and the instance of SomeOtherClass is associated with it. When GC.Collect( ) is invoked, since the instance of SomeClass is no longer accessible, its Finalize( ) is called. Within this Finalize( ) method, you invoke Notify( ) on the instance of SomeOtherClass. In Notify( ), you lock the object. However, the main thread within the Main( ) method already owns a lock on the object. This blocks the garbage collector thread—it cannot continue until the Main( ) method completes. (Main( ) is able to run to completion because the call to GC.Collect( ) does not block, even though the CLR's finalization thread does.) You can see this in the output from the program, shown in Figure 5-3.

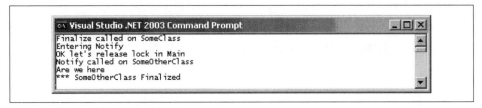

Figure 5-3. Output from Example 5-3

Let's take this a bit further. The GC class's WaitForPendingFinalizers( ) method suspends the calling thread until the finalization thread has run the Finalize( ) method on all eligible objects in its queue. Now what happens if you uncomment the GC. WaitForPendingFinalizers( ) in the Main( ) method in Example 5-3? The output is shown in Figure 5-4.

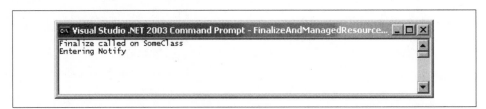

Figure 5-4. Deadlock after GC.WaitForPendingFinalizers() was uncommented in Example 5-3

The program is deadlocked. You may say, well, don't call GC.WaitForPendingFinalizers( ), or GC.Collect( ) for that matter. But what if you had called some other method on the object from another thread, and that thread holds a lock on the object while it waits for something else? There is a high probability of deadlock occurring if you access managed resources within the Finalize( ) method.

 IN A NUTSHELL

Do not touch any managed objects within the Finalize( ) method. Do not call any methods on other objects, or even set their references to null/Nothing. This could lead to unpredictable results, including the possibility of crash or deadlock. Only release unmanaged resources within Finalize( ).

SEE ALSO

Gotcha #35, "Writing Finalize() is rarely a good idea," Gotcha #37, "Rules to invoke base.Finalize() are not consistent," Gotcha #38, "Depending on Finalize() can tie up critical resources," Gotcha #39, "Using Finalize() on disposed objects is costly," Gotcha #40, "Implementing IDisposable isn't enough," and Gotcha #41, "Using the Dispose Design Pattern doesn't guarantee cleanup."

GOTCHA
#37 Rules to invoke base.Finalize() aren't consistent

Object.Finalize( ) is an odd method. It is defined as protected overridable. As mentioned in the introduction to this chapter, in C# you implement your class's Finalize( ) method with the special syntax ~NameOfClass, where NameOfClass is the actual name of your class. This pseudo-destructor is compiled into the Finalize( ) method during the MSIL translation.

Furthermore, within the C# destructor, you should not attempt to call Finalize( ) on the base class. The compiler-generated Finalize( ) takes care of calling the base class's Finalize( ), even if an exception is raised, because the call is safe inside a finally block.

For example, look at this pseudo-destructor:

```
~MyClass( )
{
    // Whatever cleanup code you write
}
```

The C# compiler will translate this into the Finalize( ) method in your assembly. A look at the generated MSIL using *ildasm.exe* will clarify this for you (see Figure 5-5).

```
MyClass::Finalize : void()                                          _|□|×|
.method family hidebysig virtual instance void
        Finalize() cil managed
{
  // Code size        10 (0xa)
  .maxstack  1
  .try
  {
    IL_0000:  leave.s     IL_0009
  } // end .try
  finally
  {
    IL_0002:  ldarg.0
    IL_0003:  call        instance void [mscorlib]System.Object::Finalize()
    IL_0008:  endfinally
  } // end handler
  IL_0009:  ret
} // end of method MyClass::Finalize
```

Figure 5-5. MSIL translation of a C# pseudo-destructor

If a C# programmer ever has to work with VB.NET code, he should remember that the rules are different. In VB.NET, you write Finalize( ) as a Protected Overrides method, and you *must* call MyBase.Finalize( ), as shown in Example 5-4.

Example 5-4. Writing Finalize() in VB.NET

```
Protected Overrides Sub Finalize( )
    Try
        'Whatever cleanup code you write
    Finally
        MyBase.Finalize( )
    End Try
End Sub
```

However, if you use the Dispose design pattern (refer to Gotcha #40, "Implementing IDisposable isn't enough"), then you most likely will not implement the Finalize( ) method in your derived classes.

IN A NUTSHELL

In C#, *do not* invoke the base class's Finalize( ) method from within the destructor. In VB.NET, *do* invoke the base class's Finalize( ) method from within the Finalize( ) method.

SEE ALSO

Gotcha #35, "Writing Finalize() is rarely a good idea," Gotcha #36, "Releasing managed resources in Finalize() can wreak havoc," Gotcha #38, "Depending on Finalize() can tie up critical resources," Gotcha #39, "Using Finalize() on disposed objects is costly," Gotcha #40, "Implementing IDisposable isn't enough," and Gotcha #41, "Using the Dispose Design Pattern doesn't guarantee cleanup."

#38 Depending on Finalize( ) can tie up critical resources

When an object becomes inaccessible it may remain in that state for an unpredictable amount of time. The garbage collector decides when the memory needs to be reclaimed based on its own heuristics, which include factors such as the amount of memory being used. The problem is that the time between when you have quit using the object and when Finalize( ) is called on it might be very long. If your object is using some critical unmanaged resources, you will be holding onto them in the meantime. This may lead to resource contention that is not detected or handled well within your .NET program.

Consider the case where a .NET object communicates with a COM component running in a different process. The .NET object is very small (say only a few bytes in size). The COM object it communicates with, however, is large. Now, say you have a loop where you create one .NET object per iteration, using it and letting go of the reference. When will the unmanaged resource be released?

The answer, based on what you've read so far in this chapter, is *eventually*—but who knows exactly when?

Fortunately, .NET provides a mechanism to support synchronous cleanup of resources used by objects. If an object implements the IDisposable interface, it lets its users know that it offers a Dispose( ) method they can call to release the object. (Dispose( ) is the only method defined by IDisposable.) Because the users call Dispose( ) while the object is still accessible, it can free both managed and unmanaged resources.

An illustration of this is shown in Example 5-5. The code defines the Wrapper class, and states that it implements IDisposable. The Dispose( ) method cleans up the COM object by calling the ReleaseComObject( ) method of the System.Runtime. InteropServices.Marshal class. As a fail-safe mechanism to make sure the COM object gets released, the Finalize( ) method does the same thing. (ReleaseComObject( ) is discussed in Gotcha #65, "Release of COM object is confusing.")

Example 5-5. Using unmanaged resources from .NET

✗ C# (ResourceHold)

```
//Wrapper.cs
using System;
using ACOMCompLib;

namespace FinalizePeril
{
```

Example 5-5. Using unmanaged resources from .NET (continued)

```
public class Wrapper : IDisposable
{
    IMyComp comp = new MyCompClass();

    public int doSomething()
    {
        int result;
        comp.doSomething(out result);
        return result;
    }

    ~Wrapper()
    {
        System.Runtime.InteropServices.Marshal.ReleaseComObject(comp);
    }

    #region IDisposable Members

    public void Dispose()
    {
        System.Runtime.InteropServices.Marshal.ReleaseComObject(comp);
    }

    #endregion
}
}

//Test.cs
using System;
using ACOMCompLib;

namespace FinalizePeril
{
    class Test
    {
        [STAThread]
        static void Main(string[] args)
        {
            int iterations = Convert.ToInt32(args[0]);
            int result = 0;
            for(int i = 0; i < iterations; i++)
            {
                Wrapper theWrapper = null;
                try
                {
                    theWrapper = new Wrapper();
                    result = theWrapper.doSomething();
                }
                finally
                {
```

Example 5-5. Using unmanaged resources from .NET (continued)

```
                theWrapper.Dispose();
            }
        }

        Console.WriteLine(result);
        Console.WriteLine("End of Main");
    }
}
}
```

✗ VB.NET (ResourceHold)

```
'Wrapper.vb

Imports ACOMCompLib

Public Class Wrapper
    Implements IDisposable
    Dim comp As IMyComp = New MyCompClass

    Public Function doSomething() As Integer
        Dim result As Integer
        comp.doSomething(result)
        Return result
    End Function

    Public Sub Dispose() Implements System.IDisposable.Dispose
        System.Runtime.InteropServices.Marshal.ReleaseComObject(comp)
    End Sub

    Protected Overrides Sub Finalize()
        MyBase.Finalize()
        System.Runtime.InteropServices.Marshal.ReleaseComObject(comp)
    End Sub

End Class

'Test.vb
Module Test

    Sub Main(ByVal args() As String)
        Dim iterations As Integer = Convert.ToInt32(args(0))
        Dim result As Integer = 0

        For i As Integer = 0 To iterations - 1
            Dim theWrapper As Wrapper

            Try
                theWrapper = New Wrapper
```

Example 5-5. Using unmanaged resources from .NET (continued)

```
            result = theWrapper.doSomething( )
        Finally
            theWrapper.Dispose( )
        End Try

        Console.WriteLine(result)
        Console.WriteLine("End of Main")
    Next
End Sub

End Module
```

In the example, one instance of `Wrapper` is created for each pass through the loop. Each object of `Wrapper` has a reference to a COM component. What would happen if you didn't call `theWrapper.Dispose( )`? Well, if the COM component is in-process, you don't have much to worry about. As the memory usage increases, the garbage collector will kick in and `Finalize( )` the inaccessible objects. However, if the COM component is out-of-process, then you are simply out of luck, especially if the COM components are large. As far as the CLR is concerned it will have no reason to garbage-collect because the memory utilization on its side is pretty low. As a result, it will not call `Finalize( )`.

A good analogy is to consider having two small tables of the same size. On one table you place very small objects, say peanuts. For each peanut you place on the first table, you place a larger object on the second table, say a watermelon. The second table will fill up pretty quickly, while the first table has a lot of free space. This is exactly what happens in the example above if you neglect to call `theWrapper.Dispose( )`. The Wrapper and the Runtime Callable Wrapper (RCW) that it uses are very small objects and thousands of these can be held in memory. However, if the related COM objects are watermelon-sized, you get into memory contention on the COM component server side. By calling `theWrapper.Dispose( )`, you make sure the COM objects get released each time through the loop.

You can't predict exactly when `Finalize( )` will be called on an object; thus, any resource not released by the programmer will be held until that happens. This could cause some undesirable side effects. By implementing the `IDisposable` interface and its `Dispose( )` method, you give users of your object a way to clean it up synchronously.

As I pointed out earlier, the `Finalize( )` and `Dispose( )` methods of the `Wrapper` class both call `ReleaseComObject( )`. Of course, you don't want to repeat the code in both. (Refer to the Don't Repeat Yourself (DRY) principle in [Hunt00].) You'll see how to refactor these in Gotcha #40, "Implementing IDisposable isn't enough."

 *IN A NUTSHELL*

Do not rely on the CLR to call the `Finalize()` method. Allow users of your object to properly clean up by implementing the `System.IDisposable` interface. This way, they can call the `Dispose()` method on the object when they are done using it.

SEE ALSO

Gotcha #35, "Writing Finalize() is rarely a good idea," Gotcha #36, "Releasing managed resources in Finalize() can wreak havoc," Gotcha #39, "Using Finalize() on disposed objects is costly," Gotcha #40, "Implementing IDisposable isn't enough," Gotcha #41, "Using the Dispose Design Pattern doesn't guarantee cleanup," and Gotcha #65, "Release of COM object is confusing."

GOTCHA
#39 Using Finalize( ) on disposed objects is costly

It is better to `Dispose()` an object than to depend on its `Finalize()` being called, because `Dispose()` lets you control the cleanup of an object (see Gotcha #38, "Depending on Finalize() can tie up critical resources"). Also, there is overhead if the garbage collector needs to call `Finalize()` (see Gotcha #39, "Using Finalize() on disposed objects is costly"). If an object has been properly disposed of (by the call to `Dispose()`), there is no need for its `Finalize()` to be called. After all, `Dispose()` should have already taken care of its resources, both managed and unmanaged. What would `Finalize()` need to do in this case?

.NET provides a mechanism (`GC.SuppressFinalize()`), which tells the CLR not to invoke `Finalize()` on an object. Calling this method eliminates the overhead of the `Finalize()` call and the accompanying delay in reclaiming memory.

Let's explore the usage of `GC.SuppressFinalize()` by studying Example 5-6.

Example 5-6. Suppressing the Finalize() call

✘ C# (SuppressingFinalize)

```
using System;

namespace SuppressFinalize
{
    public class Test : IDisposable
    {
        private readonly int id;

        public Test(int theID)
```

Example 5-6. Suppressing the Finalize() call (continued)

```csharp
    {
        id = theID;
    }

    ~Test()
    {
        Console.WriteLine("Finalize called on {0}", id);
    }

    #region IDisposable Members

    public void Dispose()
    {
        Console.WriteLine("Dispose called on {0}", id);
        GC.SuppressFinalize(this);
    }

    #endregion

    [STAThread]
    static void Main(string[] args)
    {
        int count = 1;
        Test object1 = new Test(count++);
        Test object2 = new Test(count++);

        object1.Dispose();

        Console.WriteLine("Main done");
    }
  }
}
```

✗ VB.NET (SuppressingFinalize)

```vbnet
Public Class Test
    Implements IDisposable

    Private ReadOnly id As Integer

    Public Sub New(ByVal theID As Integer)
        id = theID
    End Sub


    Protected Overrides Sub Finalize()
        MyBase.Finalize()
        Console.WriteLine("Finalize called on {0}", id)
    End Sub
```

Example 5-6. Suppressing the Finalize( ) call (continued)

```
    Public Sub Dispose( ) Implements System.IDisposable.Dispose
        Console.WriteLine("Dispose called on {0}", id)
        GC.SuppressFinalize(Me)
    End Sub

    Public Shared Sub Main( )
        Dim count As Integer = 1
        Dim object1 As New Test(count)
        count += 1
        Dim object2 As New Test(count)
        object1.Dispose( )

        Console.WriteLine("Main done")
    End Sub
End Class
```

In this example, the class Test implements the IDisposable interface. Its Dispose( ) method invokes GC.SuppressFinalize( ). In Main( ), you create two objects of Test and dispose of only one of them. When you execute the code, you get the output shown in Figure 5-6.

Figure 5-6. Output from Example 5-6

Note that Finalize( ) gets called on the second object, but not on the first. When you invoke Dispose( ) on the first object, you indicate to the CLR that it should not bother invoking Finalize( ) on this object. As a result, the memory used by the object gets released without the added delay involved with Finalize( ).

IN A NUTSHELL

Calling Finalize( ) on an object involves overhead. This should be avoided as much as possible. From within your Dispose( ) method, call GC.SuppressFinalize( ).

SEE ALSO

Gotcha #35, "Writing Finalize() is rarely a good idea," Gotcha #36, "Releasing managed resources in Finalize() can wreak havoc," Gotcha #38, "Depending on Finalize() can tie up critical resources," Gotcha #40, "Implementing IDisposable isn't enough," and Gotcha #41, "Using the Dispose Design Pattern doesn't guarantee cleanup."

#40 Implementing IDisposable isn't enough

Let's review key points from Gotcha #35, Gotcha #38, and Gotcha #39:

- The call to Finalize( ) involves overhead, which you can avoid by calling GC.SuppressFinalize( ) in Dispose( ).
- There is no guarantee when the Finalize( ) method will be called, so you may hold resources much longer than you intend.

For these reasons, it is better to use Dispose( ) instead of relying on Finalize( ).

That sounds good, except for one problem. Unfortunately, the author of a class has no way to force the user of an object to invoke the Dispose( ) method. It requires discipline on the part of the programmer to call Dispose( ) at the appropriate location in the code. What if he forgets to? You want the resources to be cleaned up anyway; doing it in Finalize( ) is better than not doing it at all. You know that Finalize( ) *will* be called eventually, you just don't know *when*.

So what code should you put in Finalize( )? Remember that you should not touch any managed resources (Gotcha #36, "Releasing managed resources in Finalize() can wreak havoc"). But you do need to clean up unmanaged resources.

What code do you write in Dispose( )? If you call GC.SuppressFinalize( ) in Dispose( ) (as you should), you won't be able to rely on Finalize( ) to clean up unmanaged resources; Dispose( ) will have to take care of them.

In addition, since Dispose( ) (unlike Finalize( )) is not executed in the middle of a garbage-collection sweep, it can safely release other managed objects. So within Dispose( ) you take care of cleaning up both managed and unmanaged resources.

How do you free unmanaged resources in Dispose( ) and Finalize( ) without duplicating code? In Gotcha #38, "Depending on Finalize() can tie up critical resources," these two methods made identical calls to ReleaseComObject( ) (see Example 5-5).

The Dispose design pattern will help properly refactor Dispose( ) and Finalize( ). (Refer to "Dispose Design Pattern" in the section "On the Web" in the Appendix.)

This pattern stipulates that both Finalize( ) and IDisposable.Dispose( ) delegate to a third protected virtual/Overridable method. According to Microsoft's specification, this method should be called Dispose( ) as well, and should take one bool/ Boolean parameter, which Microsoft calls disposing. This indicates whether the method has been called by IDisposable.Dispose( ) (true) or Finalize( ) (false). This protected Dispose( ) method does all resource cleanup. Whether the disposing argument is true or false, it cleans up unmanaged resources. But only if this argument is true, indicating that the object is still accessible, does it attend to managed resources.

The Dispose(bool disposing) method is protected because you don't want users of your class to call it directly, and you need to override it in any derived classes.

> A better name could have been chosen for the Dispose(bool) method in the Dispose Design Pattern. It is less confusing if you can clearly see the difference between the methods named Dispose. Unfortunately, a number of classes in the .NET class library (e.g., System.EnterpriseServices.ServicedComponent), expect you to use the Dispose(bool) method. I'm sticking with the method names in the pattern to be consistent.

With this pattern, only classes at the top of your class hierarchies need to implement Finalize( ) and IDisposable.Dispose( ). Those two methods call Dispose(false) and Dispose(true), respectively. Derived classes just implement the protected version of Dispose( ). Because this method is defined as virtual/Overridable in the base class, and override/Overrides in all derived classes, the correct derived implementation will execute.

> The full VB.NET prototype also includes the Overloads keyword, as follows:
>
>   Protected **Overloads** Overrides Sub Dispose(_
>   ByVal disposing As Boolean)

To complete the pattern, the derived class's Dispose( ) must invoke its base class's Dispose( ); i.e., the protected version with the disposing parameter.

Example 5-7 and Example 5-8 illustrate the Dispose Design Pattern.

Example 5-7. Dispose design pattern (C#)

✔ **C# (DisposeFinalize)**

```
//Base.cs
using System;

public class Base : IDisposable
{
    private bool disposed = false;
    private readonly int id;

    public Base(int theID)
    {
        id = theID;
    }
```

Example 5-7. Dispose design pattern (C#) (continued)

```csharp
    protected virtual void Dispose(bool disposing)
    {
        if (!disposed)
        {
            if (disposing)
            {
                Console.WriteLine(
                    "Base Cleaning up managed resources on {0}",
                    id);

                // Code to clean up managed resources
            }

            Console.WriteLine(
                "Base Cleaning up unmanaged resources on {0}", id);

            // Code to clean up unmanaged resources
        }

        disposed = true;
    }

    public void Dispose()
    {
        Dispose(true);
        GC.SuppressFinalize(this);
    }

    ~Base()
    {
        Console.WriteLine("*** Finalize called on Base {0}", id);
        Dispose(false);
    }
}

//Derived.cs
using System;

namespace DisposePattern
{
    public class Derived : Base
    {
        private bool disposed = false;

        public Derived(int theID) : base(theID) {}

        protected override void Dispose(bool disposing)
        {
            if (!disposed)
```

Example 5-7. Dispose design pattern (C#) (continued)

```csharp
        {
            try
            {
                if (disposing)
                {
                    Console.WriteLine(
                        "Derived Cleaning up managed resources");
                    // Code to clean up managed resources
                }

                Console.WriteLine(
                    "Derived Cleaning up unmanaged resources");
                // Code to clean up unmanaged resources
            }
            finally
            {
                base.Dispose(disposing);
            }
        }

        disposed = true;
    }
  }
}

//Test.cs
using System;

namespace DisposePattern
{
    class Test
    {
        [STAThread]
        static void Main(string[] args)
        {
            Derived object1 = new Derived(1);
            Derived object2 = new Derived(2);

            object1.Dispose();
        }
    }
}
```

Example 5-8. Dispose design pattern (VB.NET)

```vb
'Base.vb

Public Class Base
    Implements IDisposable
    Private disposed As Boolean = False
    Private ReadOnly id As Integer

    Public Sub New(ByVal theID As Integer)
        id = theID
    End Sub

    Protected Overridable Sub Dispose(ByVal disposing As Boolean)
        If Not disposed Then
            If disposing Then
                Console.WriteLine( _
                    "Base Cleaning up managed resources on {0}", _
                    id)

                ' Code to cleanup managed resources
            End If
            Console.WriteLine( _
             "Base Cleaning up unmanaged resources on {0}", id)

            ' Code to cleanup unmanaged resources

        End If

        disposed = True
    End Sub

    Public Sub Dispose() Implements System.IDisposable.Dispose
        Dispose(True)
        GC.SuppressFinalize(Me)
    End Sub

    Protected Overrides Sub Finalize()
        MyBase.Finalize()
        Console.WriteLine("*** Finalize called on Base {0}", id)
        Dispose(False)
    End Sub
End Class

'Derived.vb
Public Class Derived
    Inherits Base
```

Example 5-8. Dispose design pattern (VB.NET) (continued)

```
    Private disposed As Boolean = False

    Public Sub New(ByVal theID As Integer)
        MyBase.New(theID)
    End Sub


    Protected Overloads Overrides Sub Dispose(ByVal disposing As Boolean)
        Try
            If Not disposed Then

                If disposing Then
                    Console.WriteLine( _
                        "Derived Cleaning up managed resources")
                    ' Code to cleanup managed resources
                End If

                Console.WriteLine( _
                    "Derived Cleaning up unmanaged resources")
                ' Code to cleanup unmanaged resources
            End If

            disposed = True
        Finally
            MyBase.Dispose(disposing)
        End Try
    End Sub
End Class

'Test.vb
Module Module1

    Sub Main( )
        Dim object1 As New Derived(1)
        Dim object2 As New Derived(2)

        object1.Dispose( )
    End Sub

End Module
```

Take a look at the Base class. It implements IDisposable, so it must provide a Dispose( ) method with no parameter. This method invokes the Dispose(bool disposing) method with true as its argument. The Finalize( ) method invokes Dispose(bool disposing) as well, but passes false instead of true. The Dispose(bool disposing) method cleans up unmanaged resources regardless of the parameter's value. It only cleans up managed resources if disposing is true, that is, only if it's been called by the no-parameter Dispose( ) method. If invoked by the Finalize( )

method, it does not touch any managed resources. See Gotcha #36, "Releasing managed resources in Finalize() can wreak havoc."

In the Derived class, you do not have to implement the Finalize( ) method or the no-parameter Dispose( ). Instead, you simply override the Dispose( ) method that takes the bool/Boolean parameter. First you clean up managed resources, but only if the disposing parameter is true. Next, you take care of unmanaged resources. Finally, you call the corresponding Dispose( ) method of the Base class. The output from the above program is shown in Figure 5-7.

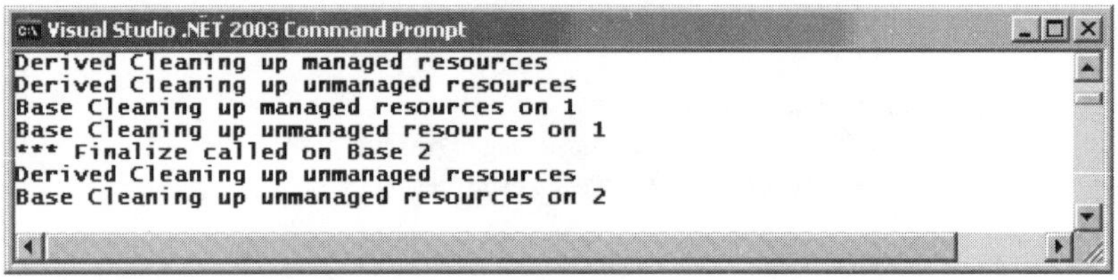

```
Visual Studio .NET 2003 Command Prompt
Derived Cleaning up managed resources
Derived Cleaning up unmanaged resources
Base Cleaning up managed resources on 1
Base Cleaning up unmanaged resources on 1
*** Finalize called on Base 2
Derived Cleaning up unmanaged resources
Base Cleaning up unmanaged resources on 2
```

Figure 5-7. Output from Example 5-7

From the output, you can see that object1 is cleaned up using the Dispose( ) method and that its Finalize( ) is not called. Both managed and unmanaged resources are cleaned up properly here. On the other hand, object2 is cleaned up in the Finalize( ) method. Only the unmanaged resources are deleted in this case, as expected.

With this code, you still need to be concerned about a couple of problems. First, you may have to make some adjustments to the Dispose(bool) method for thread-safety in a multithreaded application. Second, it is possible for a user to call the Dispose( ) method on an object more than once, and to call other methods on an object after the call to Dispose( ). In your methods, you need to check if the object has been disposed. If it has, you should raise an ObjectDisposedException.

As a final illustration of the Dispose Design Pattern, let's revisit the Wrapper class from Gotcha #38, "Depending on Finalize() can tie up critical resources" (see Example 5-5). In the previous version, both Finalize( ) and Dispose( ) call ReleaseComObject( ). By moving this call to Dispose(bool disposing), you remove the duplication. The Wrapper class in this example has no managed resources and no base class below System.Object. Therefore, it does not call base.Dispose( ).

Example 5-9 shows the refactored implementation.

Example 5-9. Refactored Wrapper Class

> ✔ **C# (RefactoredWrapper)**

```
//Wrapper.cs
using System;
using ACOMCompLib;
```

Example 5-9. Refactored Wrapper Class (continued)

```
namespace FinalizePeril
{
    public class Wrapper : IDisposable
    {
        IMyComp comp = new MyCompClass( );
        bool disposed = false;

        public int doSomething( )
        {
            if (disposed)
            {
                throw new ObjectDisposedException(null);
            }
            int result;
            comp.doSomething(out result);
            return result;
        }

        protected virtual void Dispose(bool disposing)
        {
            if (!disposed)
            {
                // No managed resources to clean up
                // Clean up unmanaged resources regardless of who called us
                System.Runtime.InteropServices.Marshal.ReleaseComObject(comp);
                GC.SuppressFinalize(this);
                disposed = true;
            }
        }

        ~Wrapper( )
        {
            Dispose(false);
        }

        #region IDisposable Members

        public void Dispose( )
        {
            Dispose(true);
        }

        #endregion
    }
}
```

Example 5-9. Refactored Wrapper Class (continued)

```vb.net
'Wrapper.vb

Imports ACOMCompLib

Public Class Wrapper
    Implements IDisposable
    Dim comp As IMyComp = New MyCompClass
    Private disposed As Boolean = False

    Public Function doSomething() As Integer
        If disposed = True Then
            Throw New ObjectDisposedException(Nothing)
        End If
        Dim result As Integer
        comp.doSomething(result)
        Return result
    End Function

    Protected Overridable Sub Dispose(ByVal disposing As Boolean)
        If Not disposed Then
            ' No managed resources to clean up
            ' Clean up unmanaged resources regardless of who called us
            System.Runtime.InteropServices.Marshal.ReleaseComObject(comp)
            GC.SuppressFinalize(Me)
            disposed = True
        End If
    End Sub

    Public Sub Dispose() Implements System.IDisposable.Dispose
        Dispose(True)
    End Sub

    Protected Overrides Sub Finalize()
        Try
            Dispose(False)
        Finally
            MyBase.Finalize()
        End Try
    End Sub

End Class
```

 IN A NUTSHELL

Follow the Dispose design pattern (with adjustments for thread-safety if needed), because it provides an effective way to clean up both managed and unmanaged resources.

Gotcha #35, "Writing Finalize() is rarely a good idea," Gotcha #36, "Releasing managed resources in Finalize() can wreak havoc," Gotcha #37, "Rules to invoke base.Finalize() are not consistent," Gotcha #38, "Depending on Finalize() can tie up critical resources," Gotcha #39, "Using Finalize() on disposed objects is costly," and Gotcha #41, "Using the Dispose Design Pattern doesn't guarantee cleanup."

GOTCHA
#41 Using the Dispose Design Pattern doesn't guarantee cleanup

While the IDisposable interface and the Dispose Design Pattern are very important to follow, these are recommendations on how you write a class, not how you use an instance of the class. If you create an object, the CLR may *eventually* call its Finalize(). On the other hand, Dispose() is never called automatically. Users of your object have the responsibility of calling it. What if they forget to?

The problem does not end there. Even if you have a call to Dispose(), what if an exception is thrown before the program reaches that statement? What can you do to ensure that Dispose() is called and thereby increase the probability of proper cleanup?

To deal with these issues, C# offers the using keyword (though there is no way to force the user to use it). Consider Example 5-10.

Example 5-10. Code that utilizes the using keyword

✔ **C# (Using)**

```
//Test.cs
using System;

namespace DisposePattern
{
    class Test
    {
        [STAThread]
        static void Main(string[] args)
        {
            using(Derived object1 = new Derived(1))
            {
                Derived object2 = new Derived(2);
            }
        }
    }
}
```

In this example, you use the using keyword when creating object1 of the Derived class. You do not call its Dispose( ) method. (The class Derived is the same as the one used in Example 5-7.) The using keyword provides a significant benefit. It not only makes the call to Dispose( ), it does so in a finally block, as the generated MSIL in Figure 5-8 shows. This ensures that the object is disposed of properly even when an exception is thrown.

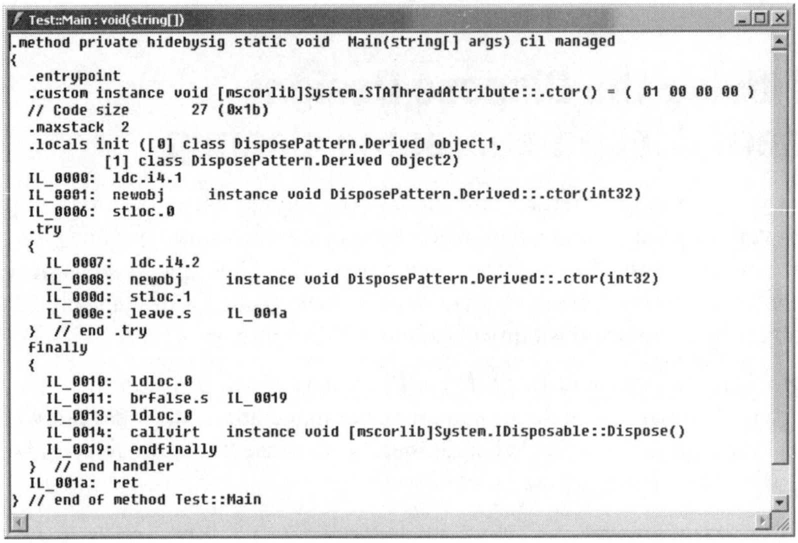

```
Test::Main : void(string[])                                                   _ □ ×
.method private hidebysig static void  Main(string[] args) cil managed
{
  .entrypoint
  .custom instance void [mscorlib]System.STAThreadAttribute::.ctor() = ( 01 00 00 00 )
  // Code size       27 (0x1b)
  .maxstack  2
  .locals init ([0] class DisposePattern.Derived object1,
           [1] class DisposePattern.Derived object2)
  IL_0000:  ldc.i4.1
  IL_0001:  newobj     instance void DisposePattern.Derived::.ctor(int32)
  IL_0006:  stloc.0
  .try
  {
    IL_0007:  ldc.i4.2
    IL_0008:  newobj     instance void DisposePattern.Derived::.ctor(int32)
    IL_000d:  stloc.1
    IL_000e:  leave.s    IL_001a
  } // end .try
  finally
  {
    IL_0010:  ldloc.0
    IL_0011:  brfalse.s  IL_0019
    IL_0013:  ldloc.0
    IL_0014:  callvirt   instance void [mscorlib]System.IDisposable::Dispose()
    IL_0019:  endfinally
  } // end handler
  IL_001a:  ret
} // end of method Test::Main
```

Figure 5-8. MSIL generated for Main() in Example 5-10

You can declare more than one reference in the using declaration:

```
using(Derived obj1 = new Derived(1), obj2 = new Derived(2))
```

The Dispose( ) method, in this case, will be called on each referenced object at the appropriate time.

Unfortunately, using is only available in C#. In VB.NET, to make sure Dispose( ) is invoked, call it in a Finally block. A VB.NET example of calling Dispose( ) in the Finally block is shown below:

```
Try
    theWrapper = New Wrapper
    result = theWrapper.doSomething( )
Finally
    theWrapper.Dispose( )
End Try
```

How does this differ in .NET 2.0 Beta 1? A Using...End Using block is being introduced in the next version of VB.NET.

 **IN A NUTSHELL**

The using keyword in C# improves your chances of cleaning up your resources properly. In VB.NET, you have to take responsibility for invoking Dispose() by calling it within a Finally block. Take advantage of the Using...End Using block when you move to .NET 2.0.

SEE ALSO

Gotcha #35, "Writing Finalize() is rarely a good idea," Gotcha #36, "Releasing managed resources in Finalize() can wreak havoc," Gotcha #37, "Rules to invoke base.Finalize() are not consistent," Gotcha #38, "Depending on Finalize() can tie up critical resources," Gotcha #39, "Using Finalize() on disposed objects is costly," and Gotcha #40, "Implementing IDisposable isn't enough."

CHAPTER 6

Inheritance and Polymorphism Gotchas

Though you can gain a superficial knowledge of C++ in a couple of weeks, and become adept at it in a few years, an experienced C++ programmer would probably never claim to be a master of the language. Its complexities are mind-boggling. (I know people who have made career changes because of it.) More recent languages have eliminated a number of its tricky features and made it much easier to write good code. However, they have their own set of challenges. While they have taken a few steps forward on a number of issues, they have gone a few steps backward on some others. This can impact the extensibility of your code, break polymorphism, and make it harder for you to derive from your classes. Learning what these challenges are, and avoiding them or handling them judiciously, is imperative to effective development. In this chapter I will discuss the things you need to be aware of in the areas of inheritance and polymorphism so you can make best use of these important concepts.

#42 Runtime Type Identification can hurt extensibility

In working with an inheritance hierarchy, how do you know which type an instance belongs to? Given a reference, you can use casting to convert it to the type you desire. However, the problem with casting is that if the conversion is not valid, it results in a runtime InvalidCastException. This is ugly and you must avoid it at all costs. What alternatives do you have?

.NET languages allow you to determine the type of an object at runtime. This feature is called *Runtime Type Identification* (RTTI). In C# you use the keyword is; in VB.NET you use TypeOf...Is. I will refer to these as RTTI operators.

What are the consequences of using RTTI operators extensively or arbitrarily? I will discuss the dark side of RTTI in a very simple example, shown in Example 6-1.

Example 6-1. Working with object hierarchy

✗ C# (RTTI)

```csharp
//Animal.cs
public class Animal
{
    public void Eat() { Console.WriteLine("Animal eating"); }
}

//Dog.cs
public class Dog : Animal
{
    public void Bark() { Console.WriteLine("Dog barking"); }
}

//Cat.cs
public class Cat : Animal
{
    public void Meow() { Console.WriteLine("Cat Meowing"); }
}

//Trainer.cs
public class Trainer
{
    public void Train(Animal anAnimal)
    {
        anAnimal.Eat();
        //Using casting

        Dog doggie = (Dog) anAnimal;
        doggie.Bark();

        Cat aCat = (Cat) anAnimal;
        aCat.Meow();
    }
}

//Test.cs
class Test
{
    [STAThread]
    static void Main(string[] args)
    {
        Dog spencer = new Dog();
        Cat snow = new Cat();
        Trainer jimmy = new Trainer();

        jimmy.Train(spencer);
        jimmy.Train(snow);
    }
}
```

Example 6-1. Working with object hierarchy (continued)

✗ VB.NET (RTTI)

```
'Animal.vb
Public Class Animal
    Public Sub Eat()
        Console.WriteLine("Animal eating")
    End Sub
End Class

'Dog.vb
Public Class Dog
    Inherits Animal

    Public Sub Bark()
        Console.WriteLine("Dog barking")
    End Sub
End Class


'Cat.vb
Public Class Cat
    Inherits Animal

    Public Sub Meow()
        Console.WriteLine("Cat Meowing")
    End Sub
End Class


'Trainer.vb
Public Class Trainer
    Public Sub Train(ByVal anAnimal As Animal)
        anAnimal.Eat()

        'Using Casting

        Dim doggie As Dog = CType(anAnimal, Dog)
        doggie.Bark()

        Dim aCat As Cat = CType(anAnimal, Cat)
        aCat.Meow()
    End Sub
End Class


'Test.vb
Module Module1
```

Example 6-1. Working with object hierarchy (continued)

```
Sub Main( )
    Dim spencer As New Dog
    Dim snow As New Cat
    Dim jimmy As New Trainer

    jimmy.Train(spencer)
    jimmy.Train(snow)
End Sub

End Module
```

In this example, the Trainer wants to train an Animal. In the process of training, she first feeds the animal by calling the Eat( ) method. In the next activity, she wants the animal to express itself. In this example, the animal may be either a Dog or a Cat, so you cast it to these types and call the Bark( ) and the Meow( ) methods. But this code, while flawless in compilation, throws an InvalidCastException at runtime, as shown in Figure 6-1.

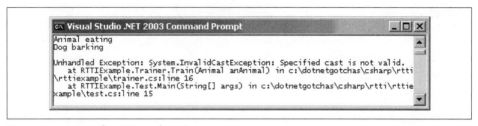

Figure 6-1. Output from Example 6-1

The CLR does not like your casting a Dog object to a Cat. (It is only natural that dogs do not like to be treated as cats—do not try that at home.) The worst you can do at this point is to surround the casting code with try/catch statements, suppress the exception in the catch and claim that you have taken care of the situation. This is undesirable for a couple of reasons. For one thing, using exceptions in situations like this is expensive. For another, you have not properly handled the condition where the given Animal is not a type you expect. *Casting is ugly.*

Let's consider the use of RTTI. In the code in Example 6-2, I show only the changes to the Trainer class (the only class I have changed).

Example 6-2. Using RTTI

✗ C# (RTTI)

```
//Trainer.cs
public class Trainer
{
    public void Train(Animal anAnimal)
```

Example 6-2. Using RTTI (continued)

```
    {
        anAnimal.Eat( );

        //Using RTTI

        if (anAnimal is Dog)
        {
            Dog doggie = (Dog) anAnimal;
            doggie.Bark( );
        }
        else if (anAnimal is Cat)
        {
            Cat aCat = (Cat) anAnimal;
            aCat.Meow( );
        }
    }
}
```

✗ VB.NET (RTTI)

```
'Trainer.vb
Public Class Trainer
    Public Sub Train(ByVal anAnimal As Animal)
        anAnimal.Eat( )

        'Using RTTI

        If TypeOf anAnimal Is Dog Then
            Dim doggie As Dog = CType(anAnimal, Dog)
            doggie.Bark( )
        ElseIf TypeOf anAnimal Is Cat Then
            Dim aCat As Cat = CType(anAnimal, Cat)
            aCat.Meow( )
        End If
    End Sub
End Class
```

In the Train( ) method you check to see if, at run time, the given reference points to an instance of Dog. If so, then you perform the cast. Similarly, you check to see if the reference points to an object of Cat and make the cast only if it is. You will not trigger an exception in this case. Figure 6-2 shows the output from the modified program.

Figure 6-2. Output after the code change in Example 6-2

In C#,

```
        Dog doggie = anAnimal as Dog;
        if (doggie != null)
        {
            doggie.Bark( );
        }
```

is equivalent to

```
        if (anAnimal is Dog)
        {
            Dog doggie = (Dog) anAnimal;
            doggie.Bark( );
        }
```

Both the as and is operators represent the use of RTTI. However, the as operator can only be used with reference types.

Is this better than using casting? Well, at least the exceptions go away. But what happens if you add another type of Animal to your system in the future, say a Horse? When an instance of Horse is sent to the Train( ) method, it invokes the Eat( ) method, but not any of the other methods on Horse, for example Neighs( ). If you ask the horse if it had a good time at the trainer, it will probably say, "The trainer fed me, then he asked if I was a dog and I said no. He then asked if I was a cat and I said no. Then he just walked away. He is not an equal opportunity trainer."

The code that uses RTTI in this manner is not extensible. It fails the Open-Closed Principle (OCP), which states that a software module must be open for extension but closed for modification. That is, you should be able to accommodate changes in the requirements by adding small new modules of code, not by changing existing code (see Gotcha #23, "Copy Constructor hampers exensibility").

While RTTI is better than casting, it is still bad. It is better to rely on polymorphism. You should abstract the methods of the derived class into the base class. In this example, the Bark( ) of Dog and the Meow( ) of Cat can be abstracted as, say, MakeNoise( ) in Animal. However, Animal doesn't know how to implement that method, so it's marked as abstract/MustOverride. This alerts derived classes that they are responsible for implementing it. The code in Example 6-3 shows these changes.

Example 6-3. Relying on abstraction and polymorphism

✔ C# (RTTI)

```
//Animal.cs
public abstract class Animal
{
    public void Eat( )
```

Example 6-3. Relying on abstraction and polymorphism (continued)

```
    {
        Console.WriteLine("Animal eating");
    }

    public abstract void MakeNoise();
}

//Dog.cs
public class Dog : Animal
{
    public void Bark( )
    {
        Console.WriteLine("Dog barking");
    }

    public override void MakeNoise( )
    {
        Bark( );
    }

}

//Cat.cs
public class Cat : Animal
{
    public void Meow( )
    {
        Console.WriteLine("Cat Meowing");
    }

    public override void MakeNoise( )
    {
        Meow( );
    }

}

//Trainer.cs
public class Trainer
{
    public void Train(Animal anAnimal)
    {
        anAnimal.Eat( );

        //Using Abstraction and Polymorphism

        anAnimal.MakeNoise( );
    }
}
```

Example 6-3. Relying on abstraction and polymorphism (continued)

✔ **VB.NET (RTTI)**

```vb
'Animal.vb
Public MustInherit Class Animal
    Public Sub Eat( )
        Console.WriteLine("Animal eating")
    End Sub

    Public MustOverride Sub MakeNoise( )
End Class


'Dog.vb

Public Class Dog
    Inherits Animal

    Public Sub Bark( )
        Console.WriteLine("Dog barking")
    End Sub

    Public Overrides Sub MakeNoise( )
        Bark( )
    End Sub
End Class


'Cat.vb
Public Class Cat
    Inherits Animal

    Public Sub Meow( )
        Console.WriteLine("Cat Meowing")
    End Sub

    Public Overrides Sub MakeNoise( )
        Meow( )
    End Sub
End Class


'Trainer.vb
Public Class Trainer
    Public Sub Train(ByVal anAnimal As Animal)
        anAnimal.Eat( )

        'Using Abstraction and Polymorphism

        anAnimal.MakeNoise( )
```

Example 6-3. Relying on abstraction and polymorphism (continued)

```
    End Sub
End Class
```

Now the Trainer class relies on the polymorphic behavior of the MakeNoise()
method. This code is far superior to using RTTI, as it's more extensible. It makes it
easier to add different domestic animals who might seek education from this Trainer.

Not all uses of RTTI are bad, though. For example, consider the case where an
Animal has a Play() method and a Dog decides that it only likes playing with other
Dogs. This code looks like Example 6-4.

Example 6-4. OK use of RTTI

✔ C# (RTTI)

```csharp
//Animal.cs
public abstract class Animal
{
    public void Eat()
    {
        Console.WriteLine("Animal eating");
    }

    public abstract void MakeNoise();

    public abstract bool Play(Animal other);
}

//Dog.cs
public class Dog : Animal
{
    public void Bark()
    {
        Console.WriteLine("Dog barking");
    }

    public override void MakeNoise()
    {
        Bark();
    }

    public override bool Play(Animal other)
    {
        if (other is Dog)
            return true;
        else
            return false;
    }

}
```

Example 6-4. OK use of RTTI (continued)

```
'Animal.vb
Public MustInherit Class Animal
    Public Sub Eat()
        Console.WriteLine("Animal eating")
    End Sub

    Public MustOverride Sub MakeNoise()

    Public MustOverride Function Play(ByVal other As Animal) As Boolean
End Class


'Dog.vb

Public Class Dog
    Inherits Animal

    Public Sub Bark()
        Console.WriteLine("Dog barking")
    End Sub


    Public Overrides Sub MakeNoise()
        Bark()
    End Sub

    Public Overrides Function Play(ByVal other As Animal) As Boolean
        If TypeOf other Is Dog Then
            Return True
        Else
            Return False
        End If
    End Function
End Class
```

The use of RTTI in the Play( ) method is benign. It checks to see if Other refers to an instance of its own type. At this point, there is no extensibility issue if a Dog never wants to play with any animals other than Dogs. Of course, if the Dog changes its mind, you'll have to externalize the rule (maybe in a configuration file), or apply a solution like the Visitor pattern. (Refer to [Freeman04, Gamma95] for more details on patterns.) Those would eliminate the use of RTTI here as well.

 **IN A NUTSHELL**

Use RTTI sparingly. Do not use it if you are checking against multiple types. Use it only if you do not violate the Open-Closed Principle.

SEE ALSO

Gotcha #23, "Copy Constructor hampers exensibility," Gotcha #43, "Using new/shadows causes "hideous hiding"," Gotcha #44, "Compilers are lenient toward forgotten override/overrides," Gotcha #45, "Compilers lean toward hiding virtual methods," Gotcha #46, "Exception handling can break polymorphism," and Gotcha #47, "Signature mismatches can lead to method hiding."

GOTCHA
#43 Using new/shadows causes "hideous hiding"

If a method is marked virtual/overridable, the base class tells the compiler not to bind to it statically at compile time, since a derived class may override that method. The method to be called is resolved at runtime. However, if a method is not marked virtual/overridable, then the compiler binds to it statically at compile time.

In C++, hiding occurs when a programmer writes a method in the derived class with the same name and signature as a method not marked virtual in the base class. Hiding can also result from virtual methods that differ in signature between base and derived classes (see Gotcha #47, "Signature mismatches can lead to method hiding"). Hiding of non-virtual methods in C++ is generally an accident and (hopefully) not the intent. Unfortunately, even though the managed compilers warn you against such mistakes, .NET gives you a legal way to violate the principles of good object-oriented programming—the new/shadows keyword. (The .NET approach to method hiding is like the laws in Las Vegas: "Oh yeah, that's illegal in most parts of the world, but here that's just fine and you are most welcome!")

 You may argue that hiding facilitates versioning—it allows a base class to introduce, in a later version, a method that is already present in the derived class. However, this facility leads to more trouble than it's worth, as discussed below. I prefer my code to behave consistently in an object-oriented manner (or fail compilation) than to quietly misbehave.

You should expect the same method to be executed on an object no matter how you invoke it—whether through a direct reference to its type, or through a reference to its base type. This is the essence of polymorphism, which says that the actual method invoked is based on the type of the object and not the type of the reference. Hiding works against this. It makes the method that is invoked dependent on the type of the reference and not on the real type of the object. Consider Example 6-5.

Example 6-5. Hiding methods

```csharp
//Base.cs
namespace Hiding
{
    public class Base
    {
        public virtual void Method1()
        {
            Console.WriteLine("Base.Method1 called");
        }
        public virtual void Method2()
        {
            Console.WriteLine("Base.Method2 called");
        }
    }
}

//Derived.cs
namespace Hiding
{
    public class Derived : Base
    {
        public override void Method1()
        {
            Console.WriteLine("Derived.Method1 called");
        }

        public new void Method2()
        {
            Console.WriteLine("Derived.Method2 called");
        }
    }
}

//Test.cs
namespace Hiding
{
    class Test
    {
        static void Main(string[] args)
        {
            Derived d = new Derived();
            Base b = d;

            d.Method1();
            d.Method2();

            b.Method1();
            b.Method2();
```

Example 6-5. Hiding methods (continued)

```
        }
    }
}
```

```vbnet
'Base.vb

Public Class Base
    Public Overridable Sub Method1()
        Console.WriteLine("Base.Method1 called")
    End Sub

    Public Overridable Sub Method2()
        Console.WriteLine("Base.Method2 called")
    End Sub
End Class


'Derived.vb

Public Class Derived
    Inherits Base

    Public Overrides Sub method1()
        Console.WriteLine("Derived.Method1 called")
    End Sub
    Public Shadows Sub method2()
        Console.WriteLine("Derived.Method2 called")
    End Sub
End Class


'Test.vb
 Module Test

    Sub Main()
        Dim d As New Derived
        Dim b As Base = d

        d.Method1()
        d.method2()

        b.Method1()
        b.Method2()
    End Sub

End Module
```

In this example, Method2( ) in Derived hides Method2( ) of Base, while Method1( ) in Derived overrides Method1( ) in Base. In Test, you have only one instance of Derived, but two references to it. One reference named d is of type Derived, and the other reference named b is of type Base. Regardless of how you invoke Method1( ), the same method Method1( ) in Derived is called, as shown in the output in Figure 6-3. However, the call to Method2( ) goes to Base.Method2( ) if called using b, and to Derived.Method2( ) if called using d. The method that is actually executed, in the latter case, depends on the type of the reference instead of the type of the object that it refers to; this is an example of hiding.

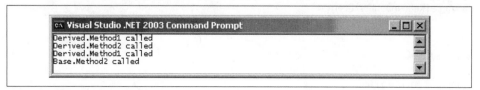

Figure 6-3. Output from Example 6-5

Hiding is very anti-object-oriented. After all, the reason you mark a method virtual/overridable is to allow derived classes to provide alternate implementations. If the base class uses virtual/overridable correctly, and the derived class uses override/overrides, a consistent method is invoked on that object without regard to how and where it is accessed. Hiding fundamentally breaks that tenet.

 **IN A NUTSHELL**

Do not mark a method as new/shadows. Avoid this insidious feature.

SEE ALSO

Gotcha #42, "Runtime Type Identification can hurt extensibility," Gotcha #44, "Compilers are lenient toward forgotten override/overrides," Gotcha #45, "Compilers lean toward hiding virtual methods," Gotcha #46, "Exception handling can break polymorphism," and Gotcha #47, "Signature mismatches can lead to method hiding."

GOTCHA
#44 Compilers are lenient toward forgotten override/overrides

Say a method in the base class is declared virtual/overridable, and you implement a method with the same name and signature in the derived class. What happens if you do not mark the method as override/overrides? When you compile the code and look at the output window in Visual Studio, you will not see any compilation error (see Gotcha #12, "Compiler warnings may not be benign"). However, a warning is generated. This warning tells you, very quietly, that the derived method has been assumed to hide the base class method (see Gotcha #43, "Using new/shadows causes "hideous hiding""). This is a serious warning that should not have been hidden in the output window. In fact, this should not be considered a warning at all, in my opinion. The compiler should jump out of the computer, grab the programmer by the collar, give him a smack, and demand that he fix the code. (Maybe I'm going a bit too far, but you get the point). Consider Example 6-6.

Example 6-6. Accidental hiding

✗ C# (RememberMarkOverride)

```
//Base.cs
using System;

namespace MarkOverride
{
    public class Base
    {
        public virtual void Method1()
        {
            Console.WriteLine("Base.Method1 called");
        }
    }
}

//Derived.cs
using System;

namespace MarkOverride
{
    public class Derived : Base
    {
        public void Method1()
        {
            Console.WriteLine("Derived.Method1 called");
        }
    }
}

//Test.cs
using System;

namespace MarkOverride
{
    class Test
    {
        [STAThread]
        static void Main(string[] args)
```

Example 6-6. Accidental hiding (continued)

```
    {
        Derived d = new Derived( );
        Base b = d;

        d.Method1( );
        b.Method1( );
    }
  }
}
```

✗ VB.NET (RememberMarkOverride)

```
'Base.vb
Public Class Base
    Public Overridable Sub Method1( )
        Console.WriteLine("Base.Method1 called")
    End Sub
End Class


'Derived.vb
Public Class Derived
    Inherits Base

    Public Sub Method1( )
        Console.WriteLine("Derived.Method1 called")
    End Sub
End Class


'Test.vb
Module Test

    Sub Main( )
        Dim d As New Derived
        Dim b As Base = d

        d.Method1( )
        b.Method1( )
    End Sub

End Module
```

In this example, Method1( ) is declared virtual/overridable in the Base class. However, in the Derived class Method1( ) has not been marked as override/overrides. This compiles OK, as you can see in Figure 6-4.

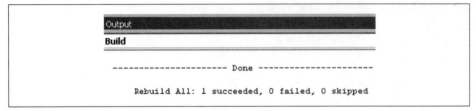

Figure 6-4. Visual Studio output window for Example 6-6

But this is misleading; a warning actually is printed, but it scrolls out of the output window. The message is:

```
warning CS0114: 'MarkOverride.Derived.Method1()' hides inherited member
'MarkOverride.Base.Method1()'. To make the current member override that
implementation, add the override keyword. Otherwise add the new keyword.
```

The output produced by the code is shown in Figure 6-5.

Figure 6-5. Output from Example 6-6

It would have been nice if the .NET compilers had erred on the side of caution. If a method is not marked override/overrides, why not assume that it overrides its base-class method, rather than assume that it hides it? Better still, shouldn't this have appeared as a fatal compilation error? Unfortunately it doesn't, so you need to pay attention to these warnings and treat them seriously. You can (and should) configure the compiler to treat warnings as errors. (See Gotcha #12, "Compiler warnings may not be benign.")

 IN A NUTSHELL

If you are overriding a method, always remember to mark the method as override/overrides. Otherwise, the compiler just gives you a polite warning and assumes the method is intended to be new/shadows.

SEE ALSO

Gotcha #12, "Compiler warnings may not be benign," Gotcha #42, "Runtime Type Identification can hurt extensibility," Gotcha #43, "Using new/shadows causes "hideous hiding"," Gotcha #45, "Compilers lean toward hiding virtual methods," Gotcha #46, "Exception handling can break polymorphism," and Gotcha #47, "Signature mismatches can lead to method hiding."

#45 Compilers lean toward hiding virtual methods

Programmers coming from C++ are used to marking methods as virtual in a derived class when overriding virtual methods of the base class. However, this habit should not be carried over to .NET. Let's see what happens if you mark a method in the derived class virtual/overridable when a virtual/overridable method with the same name and signature exists in the base class. Consider Example 6-7.

Example 6-7. Another accidental hiding

✗ C# (VirtualInDerived)

```csharp
//Base.cs
using System;

namespace DerivedMethod
{
    public class Base
    {
        public virtual void Method1()
        {
            Console.WriteLine("Base.Method1 called");
        }
    }
}

//Derived.cs
using System;

namespace DerivedMethod
{
    public class Derived : Base
    {
        public virtual void Method1()
        {
            Console.WriteLine("Derived.Method1 called");
        }
    }
}

//Test.cs
using System;

namespace DerivedMethod
{
    public class Test
```

Example 6-7. Another accidental hiding (continued)

```csharp
    {
        [STAThread]
        static void Main(string[] args)
        {
            Derived d = new Derived( );
            Base b = d;

            d.Method1( );
            b.Method1( );
        }
    }
}
```

✗ VB.NET (VirtualInDerived)

```vbnet
'Base.vb

Public Class Base
    Public Overridable Sub Method1( )
        Console.WriteLine("Base.Method1 called")
    End Sub
End Class


'Derived.vb

Public Class Derived
    Inherits Base

    Public Overridable Sub Method1( )
        Console.WriteLine("Derived.Method1 called")
    End Sub
End Class


'Test.vb

Public Class Test
    Shared Sub Main( )
        Dim d As New Derived
        Dim b As Base = d

        d.Method1( )
        b.Method1( )
    End Sub
End Class
```

Once again, as in Gotcha #44, "Compilers are lenient toward forgotten override/overrides," there is no compilation error. You only get a hidden warning message from the C# compiler:

```
warning CS0114: 'DerivedMethod.Derived.Method1()' hides inherited member
'DerivedMethod.Base.Method1()'. To make the current member override that
implementation, add the override keyword. Otherwise add the new keyword.
```

A similar message appears in the VB.NET version as well. The output from the program is shown in Figure 6-6.

Figure 6-6. Output from Example 6-7

 IN A NUTSHELL

Do not mark a method as virtual/overridable if your intent is to override a base method. Mark it as override/overrides.

SEE ALSO

Gotcha #42, "Runtime Type Identification can hurt extensibility," Gotcha #43, "Using new/shadows causes "hideous hiding"," Gotcha #44, "Compilers are lenient toward forgotten override/overrides," Gotcha #46, "Exception handling can break polymorphism," and Gotcha #47, "Signature mismatches can lead to method hiding."

GOTCHA
#46 Exception handling can break polymorphism

Liskov's Substitution Principle (LSP) [Martin03] is one of the cardinal tenets of inheritance and polymorphism. To quote Barbara Liskov:

> Any derived class object must be substitutable wherever a base class object is used, without the need for the user to know the difference.

Overridden methods in derived classes must appear to behave the same as their base-class version. After all, methods express a contract that users of a class must be able to rely on. While the number of parameters, their types, and the method return type can be verified syntactically, there are more subtle details not expressed through syntax. One is the exceptions that a method throws. Unlike Java, the .NET languages have no syntax to declare this, so it is often expressed using documentation. Consider Example 6-8.

Example 6-8. Expressing method exceptions

✔ **C# (ExceptionInDeriving)**

```csharp
//Base.cs
using System;

namespace ExceptionExample
{
    /// <summary>
    /// A class to illustrate exception when overriding
    /// </summary>
    public class Base
    {
        /// <summary>
        /// Method1 does some thing on input given.
        /// </summary>
        /// <param name="val">Input to work on</param>
        /// <exception
        /// cref="ExceptionExample.InvalidInputException">
        /// Thrown if parameter is less than 0.
        /// </exception>
        public virtual void Method1(int val)
        {
            if (val < 0)
                throw new InvalidInputException( );
            //... rest of the code goes here
        }
    }
}
```

✔ **VB.NET (ExceptionInDeriving)**

```vbnet
'Base.vb
''' <summary>
''' A class to illustrate exception when overriding
''' </summary>
Public Class Base

    ''' <summary>
    ''' Method1 does some thing on input given.
    ''' </summary>
    ''' <param name="val">Input to work on</param>
    ''' <exception
    ''' cref="ExceptionExample.InvalidInputException">
    ''' Thrown if parameter is less than 0.
    ''' </exception>
    Public Overridable Sub Method1(ByVal val As Integer)
        If val < 0 Then
            Throw New InvalidInputException
```

Example 6-8. Expressing method exceptions (continued)

```
        End If

        ' ... rest of the code goes here
    End Sub
End Class
```

The method Method1( ) of the Base class throws an exception if the parameter's value is less than zero. Looking at the NDoc-generated documentation, you see the details of Method1( ) as shown in Figure 6-7. (Third-party tools can be used to generate XML documentation for VB.NET code. VB.NET in VS 2005 will support XML comments directly.)

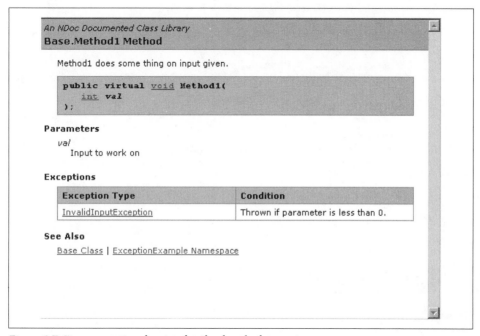

Figure 6-7. Documentation showing details of method exception

The documentation specifies that Method1( ) throws an InvalidInputException if the value of its val parameter is less than zero. If you are using an object of Base, then you can consult the documentation for the behavior of the methods. Based on that information, you write code that uses a Base object, as shown in Example 6-9. Notice that the Use( ) method, relying on the documentation of the Base class, handles the InvalidInputException.

Example 6-9. An example using a method that throws an exception

✔ **C# (ExceptionInDeriving)**

```
//Test.cs
using System;

namespace ExceptionExample
{
    class Test
    {
        private static void Use(Base baseObject, int theValue)
        {
            Console.WriteLine("Executing Use with {0}, {1}",
                baseObject.GetType( ).Name, theValue);

            try
            {
                baseObject.Method1(theValue);
            }
            catch(InvalidInputException e)
            {
                Console.WriteLine(
                    "{0} was thrown", e.GetType( ).FullName);
                // Handle the exception here
            }
        }

        //...
    }
}
```

✔ **VB.NET (ExceptionInDeriving)**

```
'Test.vb

Class Test
    Private Shared Sub Use(ByVal baseObject As Base, ByVal theValue As Integer)
        Console.WriteLine("Executing Use with {0}, {1}", _
            baseObject.GetType( ).Name, theValue)

        Try
            baseObject.Method1(theValue)
        Catch e As InvalidInputException
            Console.WriteLine( _
                "{0} was thrown", e.GetType( ).FullName)
            ' Handle the exception here
        End Try

    End Sub
```

Example 6-9. An example using a method that throws an exception (continued)

```
    '...


End Class
```

One implication of Liskov's Substitution Principle is that a derived class should not throw any exceptions that are not thrown by its base class in methods that it overrides. If it does so, then the base and derived classes have different behavior, and *the user needs to know the difference*. But suppose a programmer who has never heard of Liskov's Substitution Principle derives a class from Base, and in the course of his development decides he needs to throw a new type of exception. Example 6-10 shows the consequences.

Example 6-10. Improper overriding of a method that throws an exception

✗ C# (ExceptionInDeriving)

```csharp
using System;

namespace ExceptionExample
{
    /// <summary>
    /// A Derived class that violates LSP.
    /// </summary>
    public class Derived : Base
    {
        /// <summary>
        /// Method1 does something with input
        /// </summary>
        /// <param name="val">val to work with</param>
        /// <exception cref="InvalidInputException">
        /// thrown if parameter is 0
        /// </exception>
        /// <exception cref="InputMustBeEvenException">
        /// thrown if parameter is not even
        /// </exception>
        public override void Method1(int val)
        {
            if ((val % 2) != 0)
            {
                // Not an even number
                throw new InputMustBeEvenException();
            }

            base.Method1(val);
            //Continue with rest of the code
        }

    }
}
```

Example 6-10. Improper overriding of a method that throws an exception (continued)

✗ VB.NET (ExceptionInDeriving)

```
''' <summary>
''' A Derived class that violates LSP.
''' </summary>
Public Class Derived
    Inherits Base

    ''' <summary>
    ''' Method1 does something with input
    ''' </summary>
    ''' <param name="val">val to work with</param>
    ''' <exception cref="InvalidInputException">
    ''' thrown if parameter is 0
    ''' </exception>
    ''' <exception cref="InputMustBeEvenException">
    ''' thrown if parameter is not even
    ''' </exception>
    Public Overrides Sub Method1(ByVal val As Integer)
        If Not val Mod 2 = 0 Then
            'Not an even number
            Throw New InputMustBeEvenException
        End If


        MyBase.Method1(val)
        'Continue with rest of the code
    End Sub

End Class
```

In this example, Method1( ) of the Derived class violates LSP, because it throws an exception (InputMustBeEvenException) that differs from Method1( )'s behavior in Base. A method call through a reference to the base class must be able to target an object of any derived class without determining its type. Let's consider the code (as part of the Test class) in Example 6-11.

Example 6-11. Code that fails due to violation of LSP

✗ C# (ExceptionInDeriving)

```
//...

[STAThread]
static void Main(string[] args)
{
    Base object1 = new Base( );
    Use(object1, -1);
```

Example 6-11. Code that fails due to violation of LSP (continued)

```
        Use(object1, 3);

        Derived object2 = new Derived( );
        Use(object2, -1);
        //Use does not handle InputMustBeEvenException
        Use(object2, 3);
    }
```

✗ VB.NET (ExceptionInDeriving)

```
    '...

Shared Sub Main( )
    Dim object1 As New Base
    Use(object1, -1)
    Use(object1, 3)

    Dim object2 As New Derived
    Use(object2, -1)
    'Use does not handle InputMustBeEvenException
    Use(object2, 3)
End Sub
```

In the Main( ) method you create an instance of Base and call the Use( ) method with that object, first with a value of -1 and then with a value of 3. You then create an object of Derived and call the Use( ) method with this new instance and the same values as before. The output is shown in Figure 6-8.

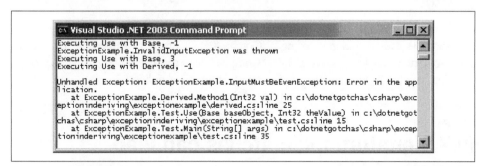

Figure 6-8. Output from Example 6-11

The program generates an unhandled exception when the Use( ) method is called with the Derived object as its first argument and -1 as its second, because Derived throws an InputMustBeEvenException. This is undesirable behavior and should be avoided.

If you do want to throw a new type of exception, how do you handle that? One possibility is for the InputMustBeEvenException to inherit from InvalidInputException. The output after this change is shown in Figure 6-9.

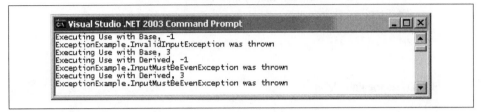

Figure 6-9. Output from Example 6-11 if InputMustBeEvenException derives from InvalidInputException

Note that in this case, the Use( ) method was able to catch the exception. Since the InputMustBeEvenException inherits from InvalidInputException, it is substitutable. This is still dangerous to a great extent. Why? You are still breaking the contract. Method1( ) in Base has promised to throw the InvalidInputException only when the parameter is less than zero. The derived class throws the exception (though of Derived type) even when its parameter is greater than zero. This again violates LSP.

 IN A NUTSHELL

The overriding method in a derived class should not throw an exception in a way that violates Liskov's Substitution Principle (LSP). An instance of the derived class must be substitutable wherever an instance of the base class is used.

SEE ALSO

Gotcha #42, "Runtime Type Identification can hurt extensibility," Gotcha #43, "Using new/shadows causes "hideous hiding"," Gotcha #44, "Compilers are lenient toward forgotten override/overrides," Gotcha #45, "Compilers lean toward hiding virtual methods," and Gotcha #47, "Signature mismatches can lead to method hiding."

GOTCHA
#47 Signature mismatches can lead to method hiding

The signature of a method is its parameter list: the number, order, and type of parameters it takes. When deriving from a class, you need to pay special attention to the signatures of its methods. If you want to introduce a method with a different signature in the derived class, it is not as simple as just writing the newer method. Going this route, you may end up hiding the base-class methods [Cline99]. This is demonstrated in Example 6-12.

Example 6-12. Hiding methods due to signature mismatch

✗ C# (MethodSignature)

```
//Base.cs
using System;

namespace MethodSignature
{
    public class Base
    {
        public virtual void Method1(double val)
        {
            Console.WriteLine("Base.Method1(double val) called");
        }
    }
}

//Derived.cs
using System;

namespace MethodSignature
{
    public class Derived : Base
    {
        public virtual void Method1(int val)
        {
            Console.WriteLine("Derived.Method1(int val) called");
        }
    }
}

//Test.cs
using System;

namespace MethodSignature
{
    class Test
    {
        [STAThread]
        static void Main(string[] args)
        {
            Derived d = new Derived();
            Base b = d;

            // b and d refer to the same object now.
            b.Method1(3);
            d.Method1(3);
        }
    }
}
```

Example 6-12. Hiding methods due to signature mismatch (continued)

✗ VB.NET (MethodSignature)

```
'Base.cs

Public Class Base
    Public Overridable Sub Method1(ByVal val As Double)
        Console.WriteLine("Base.Method1(double val) called")
    End Sub
End Class


'Derived.cs

Public Class Derived
    Inherits Base

    Public Overridable Sub Method1(ByVal val As Integer)
        Console.WriteLine("Derived.Method1(int val) called")
    End Sub
End Class


'Test.vb
Module Test

    Sub Main( )
        Dim d As New Derived
        Dim b As Base = d

        ' b and d refer to the same object now.
        b.Method1(3)
        d.Method1(3)
    End Sub

End Module
```

The VB.NET code generates a warning (not an error). The message is:

```
warning BC40003: sub 'Method1' shadows an overloadable member declared in the base
class 'Base'.
```

If you want to overload the base method, the derived method must be declared Overloads. However, adding the Overloads keyword to Derived.Method1( ) does not change the behavior; the output is still that shown in Figure 6-10.

The C# version does not even generate a warning.

In this example, a class Base has a virtual/overridable method Method1( ) that has one parameter of type double. In the class Derived, which inherits from Base, there is also a Method1( ), but its one parameter is of type int/Integer. Test.Main( ) creates an object of Derived and calls its Method1( ) using a reference of type Derived and then a reference of type Base. The output produced by this program is shown in Figure 6-10.

Figure 6-10. Output from Example 6-12

Even though you are dealing with one instance of Derived, you end up calling two different methods. What went wrong? When you call Method1(3) on the base reference, the compiler uses the base class's signature of the method to convert 3 to 3.0 at compile time. (You can see this clearly if you look at the MSIL for Test.Main( ) in *ildasm.exe*). However, when Method1(3) is called on the Derived reference, the value of 3 is sent as is. Both the calls are bound dynamically at runtime. Since the derived class has no overriding method that takes a double as a parameter, the call using the Base reference ends up in the Base method itself.

If you really want the method to have a different method signature in the derived class, it is better to overload and override at the same time, as shown in Example 6-13.

Example 6-13. Overriding and overloading to change signature

✔ C# (MethodSignature)

```
//Derived.cs
using System;

namespace MethodSignature
{
    public class Derived : Base
    {
        public override void Method1(double val)
        {
            Console.WriteLine(
                "Derived.Method1(double val) called");
        }

        public virtual void Method1(int val)
        {
            Console.WriteLine("Derived.Method1(int val) called");
            // You may call Method1((double) val) from here if
            // you want consistent behavior.
        }
    }
}
```

Example 6-13. Overriding and overloading to change signature (continued)

✔ VB.NET (MethodSignature)

```
'Derived.cs

Public Class Derived
    Inherits Base

    Public Overloads Overrides Sub Method1(ByVal val As Double)
        Console.WriteLine( _
                "Derived.Method1(double val) called")
    End Sub

    Public Overridable Overloads Sub Method1(ByVal val As Integer)
        Console.WriteLine("Derived.Method1(int val) called")
        ' You may call Method1((double) val) from here if
        ' you want consistent behavior.
    End Sub
End Class
```

As you can see, in this modified version of the Derived class, you override and overload Method1( ). The output is shown in Figure 6-11.

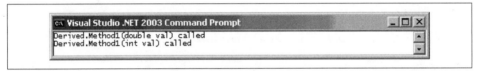

Figure 6-11. Output after modifications in Example 6-13

Now both the calls end up in Derived, though in two different methods. In the Derived class, you can take care of providing consistent and appropriate behavior for these two calls.

 IN A NUTSHELL

If you want to change the signature of a method in a derived class, then override and overload at the same time. This assures that all calls to a virtual/overridable method whose signature the derived class is changing consistently execute in that class, regardless of the type of reference used. Otherwise, you may end up hiding the method.

SEE ALSO

Gotcha #12, "Compiler warnings may not be benign" and Gotcha #13, "Ordering of catch processing isn't consist across languages."

CHAPTER 7

Multithreading Gotchas

Multithreading is a powerful tool. It is also complex—I have enjoyed many a pizza at the office during lengthy debugging sessions. There are methods and facilities that work well only when used in a certain way. It is like tightrope walking; you can't afford to slip to either side. Fully understand the capabilities, behavior, and limitations of the API before using it.

The Thread class provides a number of methods that are useful, a few that are not so useful, and some that are quite dangerous. Also, you have the options of creating a thread yourself, using one from the thread pool, or even using asynchronous features provided by the WinForms framework. Which one should you choose and why? What are the consequences of choosing one over the other? What happens if an exception is thrown from within a thread? How is this handled? Is it handled at all? What is the lifetime of a thread you create, and how can you control it? What happens when a thread is terminated? What about cleanup of resources? These are all questions you should ask before using the API.

In this chapter, I address these questions and provide answers that will steer you clear of the perils. I discuss general problems with threading, the thread pool, asynchronous calls using delegates, and threading problems related to Windows Forms [Griffiths03] and Web Services [Ballinger03, Ferrara02].

GOTCHA
#48 The Thread class supports some dangerous methods/properties

The Thread class provides a number of methods and properties to work with a specific thread. There are certain members in the Thread class, however, that you should not use, or use only with extreme caution. Here are some you should think twice about:

- The IsAlive property tells you if the thread represented by the Thread instance is alive or not. The problem is that the thread may die right after you call this method, but before you make a decision based on that information.

- The ThreadState property has the same drawbacks as IsAlive.

Now let's look at some potentially dangerous methods:

- The Suspend( ) method pauses, freezes, or suspends a thread of execution. But it is a blunt instrument. Any resources locked by the thread are held while it is blocked. This may easily result in a deadlock. Suspend( ) is not intended for normal day-to-day application programming. Do not use it, for example, to synchronize thread execution.

- The Resume( ) method reactivates a suspended thread. For the same reasons mentioned above in connection with Suspend( ), you should avoid it.

- The ResetAbort( ) method cancels an Abort( ) request on a thread. This may surprise a programmer who has called Abort( ) and has a reasonable expectation that the thread will go away.

If you think you need any of the methods mentioned above, you should revisit your design (For good discussions of multithreading issues, refer to [Lea00].) The most effective way to communicate between threads is to use what I call bait. Set some fields to a certain (boolean) value and let the other thread check for that value to take a particular action or terminate. You might also consider other facilities, such as Wait( ), Pulse( ), Join( ), and synchronizing on a wait handle.

 IN A NUTSHELL

Certain methods and properties of the Thread class have unpredictable behavior. Avoid them, or use them with extreme caution.

SEE ALSO

Gotcha #49, "Foreground threads may prevent a program from terminating," Gotcha #53, "Environment.Exit() brings down the CLR," and Gotcha #54, "ResetAbort() may lead to surprises."

GOTCHA
#49 Foreground threads may prevent a program from terminating

The IsBackground property on a Thread indicates whether the thread is a background (daemon) thread. The CLR quits executing if only background threads are running. In other words, in normal execution the CLR does not terminate as long as there is at least one non-background thread running.

In your application, if you start a thread and leave it running in the foreground (which is the default), then exit the program (by leaving Main( ) or by clicking on the close box in a Windows application), the program continues to run as long as that thread runs. But if you set the thread to background, the program will terminate when you expect it to. Consider Example 7-1.

Example 7-1. Thread behavior

✗ C# (IsBackground)

```
//Test.cs
using System;
using System.Threading;

namespace Background
{
    class Test
    {
        private static void Worker( )
        {
            // Some activity
            Thread.Sleep(5000);
            Console.WriteLine("worker done at {0}",
                DateTime.Now.ToLongTimeString( ));
        }
        [STAThread]
        static void Main(string[] args)
        {
            Thread workerThread
                = new Thread(new ThreadStart(Worker));
            //workerThread.IsBackground = true;
            workerThread.Start( );

            Console.WriteLine("Main done at {0}",
                DateTime.Now.ToLongTimeString( ));
        }
    }
}
```

✗ VB.NET (IsBackground)

```
Imports System.Threading

Module Test

    Private Sub Worker( )
        'Some activity
        Thread.Sleep(5000)
```

Example 7-1. Thread behavior (continued)

```
        Console.WriteLine("worker done at {0}", _
            DateTime.Now.ToLongTimeString( ))
    End Sub

    Sub Main( )
        Dim workerThread As New Thread(AddressOf Worker)
        'workerThread.IsBackground = true
        workerThread.Start( )

        Console.WriteLine("Main done at {0}", _
            DateTime.Now.ToLongTimeString( ))
    End Sub

End Module
```

In this example you create a Thread instance, assign it to execute the Worker( ) method, and start it. You print the message that Main( ) is done and leave the Main( ) method. When executed, the program will continue to run even after Main( ) completes. It terminates only after the Worker( ) method in the second thread completes, as shown in Figure 7-1.

Figure 7-1. Output from Example 7-1

If you uncomment the statement workerThread.IsBackground = true, the program terminates when it leaves the Main( ) method, as shown in Figure 7-2.

Figure 7-2. Output from Example 7-1 with IsBackground = true

By default, threads are created in the foreground. Should you set IsBackground to true or not? Say you are performing a search in another thread. If the user quits the application, you may want the program to terminate. In this case, you need to set the thread to a background thread. On the other hand, if the task the other thread is performing is critical, and should be carried out no matter what other threads are running, then you don't want to set it as background.

 ### IN A NUTSHELL

Before starting a Thread, ask yourself if you should be setting the IsBackground property to true.

Gotcha #50, "Background threads don't terminate gracefully," Gotcha #53, "Environment. Exit() brings down the CLR," and Gotcha #58, "Threads from the thread pool are scarce."

GOTCHA
#50 Background threads don't terminate gracefully

In Gotcha #49, "Foreground threads may prevent a program from terminating," you saw the advantage of setting a thread as background. Such a thread runs only as long as a foreground thread is running. But if your background thread uses critical resources, you want to make sure that it terminates gracefully.

The MSDN documentation says,

> Once all foreground threads belonging to a process have terminated, the common language runtime ends the process by invoking Abort on any background threads that are still alive.

If you write a method that executes in the background, you should expect its thread to terminate when all foreground threads quit. Unfortunately, contrary to what Microsoft's documentation might lead you to expect, the termination is not graceful. Let's look at Example 7-2.

Example 7-2. Abrupt termination of a background thread

✗ C# (BackgroundAbort)

```
using System;
using System.Threading;

namespace BackgroundThreadAndAbort
{
    class Test
    {
        private static void Worker()
        {
            Console.WriteLine(
                "Worker started... given chance to cleanup?");
            try
            {
                Thread.Sleep(5000);
            }
            catch(ThreadAbortException)
            {
                Console.WriteLine(
                    "Thread aborted exception received");
```

Example 7-2. Abrupt termination of a background thread (continued)

```
        }
    }

    [STAThread]
    static void Main(string[] args)
    {
        Thread workerThread
            = new Thread(new ThreadStart(Worker));
        workerThread.IsBackground = true;
        workerThread.Start( );

        Thread.Sleep(2000);
        Console.WriteLine("Main done");
    }
  }
}
```

✗ VB.NET (BackgroundAbort)

```
Imports System.Threading

Module Test

    Private Sub Worker( )
        Console.WriteLine( _
          "Worker started... given chance to cleanup?")
        Try
            Thread.Sleep(5000)
        Catch ex As ThreadAbortException
            Console.WriteLine("Thread aborted exception received")
        End Try
    End Sub

    Public Sub Main( )
        Dim workerThread As New Thread(AddressOf Worker)
        workerThread.IsBackground = True
        workerThread.Start( )

        Thread.Sleep(2000)
        Console.WriteLine("Main done")
    End Sub

End Module
```

In this program, you start a background thread that executes the Worker( ) method. In that method you anticipate the ThreadAbortException. When Main( ) terminates, the background thread executing the Worker( ) method is terminated. However, the

`ThreadAbortException` is not thrown on it. This is shown in the output in Figure 7-3. As a result, the background thread has no chance to clean up and exit gracefully. It just gets yanked.

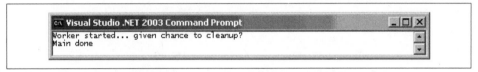

Figure 7-3. Output from Example 7-2

 IN A NUTSHELL

Remember that background threads are killed abruptly when the process terminates and do not have an opportunity to clean up gracefully.

SEE ALSO

Gotcha #49, "Foreground threads may prevent a program from terminating" and Gotcha #53, "Environment.Exit() brings down the CLR."

GOTCHA
#51 Interrupt ( ) kicks in only when a thread is blocked

When you invoke the `Interrupt()` method on a thread, the CLR throws a `ThreadInterruptedException` in the thread's context. However, this only happens when the thread is blocked—for instance, when it enters `Sleep()`, `Join()`, `Wait()`, or requests a lock. If the thread is busy executing, the exception is not received until the thread blocks. So if you call `Interrupt()` on a thread, the thread may not be interrupted for quite some time.

Furthermore, there is no guarantee that the thread will be interrupted at all. The thread may catch the `ThreadInterruptedException` and just ignore it. Consider Example 7-3.

Example 7-3. Interrupting a thread

✗ C# (Interrupt)

```
using System;
using System.Threading;

namespace Interrupting
{
```

Example 7-3. Interrupting a thread (continued)

```csharp
class Test
{
    public static void Worker()
    {
        try
        {
            Console.WriteLine("worker started at {0}",
                DateTime.Now.ToLongTimeString());

            string str = null;
            for(int i = 0; i < 30000; i++)
            {
                str += i.ToString();
                // Simulating some activity
            }

            Thread.Sleep(1000);
        }
        catch(ThreadInterruptedException)
        {
            Console.WriteLine("Thread interrupted at {0}",
                DateTime.Now.ToLongTimeString());
        }

        Console.WriteLine(
            "Continuing after Exception is caught");
    }

    [STAThread]
    static void Main(string[] args)
    {
        Thread workerThread = new Thread(
            new ThreadStart(Worker));
        //workerThread.IsBackground = true;
        workerThread.Start();
        Thread.Sleep(1000);

        Console.WriteLine("Interrupting worker at {0}",
            DateTime.Now.ToLongTimeString());

        workerThread.Interrupt();
    }
}
```

Example 7-3. Interrupting a thread (continued)

✗ VB.NET (Interrupt)

```
Imports System.Threading

Module Test
    Public Sub Worker()
        Try
            Dim str As String = Nothing

            Console.WriteLine("worker started at {0}", _
                DateTime.Now.ToLongTimeString())

            For i As Integer = 0 To 30000
                str += i.ToString()
                'Simulating some activity
            Next

            Thread.Sleep(1000)

        Catch ex As ThreadInterruptedException
            Console.WriteLine("Thread interrupted at {0}", _
                DateTime.Now.ToLongTimeString())
        End Try

        Console.WriteLine( _
            "Continuing after Exception is caught")
    End Sub

    Public Sub Main()
        Dim workerThread As New Thread(AddressOf Worker)

        'workerThread.IsBackground = True

        workerThread.Start()
        Thread.Sleep(1000)

        Console.WriteLine("Interrupting worker at {0}", _
            DateTime.Now.ToLongTimeString())

        workerThread.Interrupt()
    End Sub

End Module
```

The Main() method creates a thread to execute the Worker() method. Worker() enters a busy computation cycle concatenating strings. Then Main() interrupts the thread. However, the ThreadInterruptedException does not take effect until the thread finishes its computation and arrives at Sleep(). When you execute the program, you get the output shown in Figure 7-4.

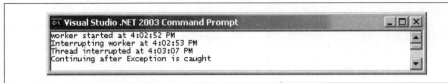

Figure 7-4. Output from Example 7-3

As you can see, even though the thread is interrupted one second after it was started, it did not receive the ThreadInterruptedException until fourteen seconds later.

 IN A NUTSHELL

Remember that a thread receives a ThreadInterruptedException only when it blocks, and that it is free to ignore the request.

SEE ALSO

Gotcha #52, "ThreadAbortException—a hot potato" and Gotcha #54, "ResetAbort( ) may lead to surprises."

GOTCHA
#52 ThreadAbortException—a hot potato

When you call Thread.Abort( ) to abort a thread, the CLR throws a ThreadAbortException on it. This allows the thread to clean up its resources and terminate gracefully. Unlike the ThreadInterruptedException, the thread receives the ThreadAbortException instantaneously. This can be dangerous at times. If you are in the middle of a call, or doing some important processing, it does not wait for you to finish. Of course, you can handle the ThreadAbortException and stabilize your code. The ThreadAbortException, however, is a special kind of exception. When you leave the catch block, the CLR automatically throws it again, thus terminating the thread. Let's take a look at this in Example 7-4.

Example 7-4. Behavior of Thread.Abort( )

✗ C# (Abort)

```
using System;
using System.Threading;

namespace ThreadAborting
{
    class Test
    {
```

Example 7-4. Behavior of Thread.Abort() (continued)

```csharp
        private static void Worker()
        {
            try
            {
                try
                {
                    Thread.Sleep(5000);
                }
                catch(ThreadAbortException)
                {
                    Console.WriteLine(
                        "ThreadAbortException caught");
                }

                Console.WriteLine(
                    "Let's leave the method now");
            }
            finally
            {
                Console.WriteLine("In the finally block");
            }
        }

        [STAThread]
        static void Main(string[] args)
        {
            Thread workerThread = new Thread(
                new ThreadStart(Worker));
            workerThread.Start();

            Thread.Sleep(1000);
            Console.WriteLine("Calling abort");
            workerThread.Abort();

            Thread.Sleep(1000);
            Console.WriteLine("Main done");
        }
    }
}
```

✗ VB.NET (Abort)

```vbnet
Imports System.Threading

Module Test

    Private Sub Worker()
        Try
            Try
```

Example 7-4. Behavior of Thread.Abort() (continued)

```
            Thread.Sleep(5000)
        Catch ex As ThreadAbortException
            Console.WriteLine("ThreadAbortException caught")
        End Try

        Console.WriteLine("Let's leave the method now")
    Finally
        Console.WriteLine("In the finally block")
    End Try
End Sub

Public Sub Main( )
    Dim workerThread As New Thread(AddressOf Worker)
    workerThread.Start( )

    Thread.Sleep(1000)
    Console.WriteLine("Calling abort")
    workerThread.Abort( )

    Thread.Sleep(1000)
    Console.WriteLine("Main done")
End Sub

End Module
```

In this example, Main( ) starts a thread to run the Worker( ) method. Then it invokes Abort( ) on that thread. The thread receives the ThreadAbortException right away. The exception is caught in the catch block. Note that there is no throw within the catch block; however, the exception is re-thrown automatically. As a result, instead of the "Let's leave the method now" message, the "In the finally block" message gets printed, as shown in the output in Figure 7-5.

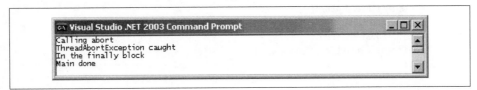

Figure 7-5. Output from Example 7-4

The ThreadAbortException is a hot potato. The CLR throws it automatically from the catch block in order to terminate the thread (Want to catch it again? No problem, it'll be re-thrown again). *There is no guarantee that any statements in your method will be executed.* However, all the finally blocks in the call stack are visited.

Write code defensively with the expectation that the thread may be aborted. Understand the special nature of the `ThreadAbortException`.

SEE ALSO

Gotcha #51, "Interrupt () kicks in only when a thread is blocked," Gotcha #54, "ResetAbort( ) may lead to surprises," and Gotcha #55, "Abort() takes time to clean up."

GOTCHA

#53 Environment.Exit( ) brings down the CLR

How do you exit from a thread? You do that by returning from its associated method. There is an `Environment.Exit( )` method, but it is somewhat more drastic: if you call the `Exit( )` method you terminate the process, no matter which thread you call it from. None of the application's other threads gets a chance to clean up gracefully. Consider the code in Example 7-5.

Example 7-5. Behavior of Exit( )

✗ C# (KnowTheExit)

```csharp
using System;
using System.Threading;

namespace Exit
{
    class Test
    {
        public static void Worker( )
        {
            Console.WriteLine("worker thread started");
            try
            {
                Thread.Sleep(5000);
            }
            catch(ThreadInterruptedException)
            {
                Console.WriteLine("worker interrupted");
            }
            catch(ThreadAbortException)
            {
                Console.WriteLine("worker aborted");
```

Example 7-5. Behavior of Exit( ) (continued)

```csharp
        }
    }

    [STAThread]
    static void Main(string[] args)
    {
        Thread workerThread1 = new Thread(
            new ThreadStart(Worker));
        workerThread1.Start( );
        Thread.Sleep(1000);

        Console.WriteLine("Interrupting worker1 at {0}",
            DateTime.Now.ToLongTimeString( ));

        workerThread1.Interrupt( );

        Thread workerThread2 = new Thread(
            new ThreadStart(Worker));
        workerThread2.Start( );
        Thread.Sleep(1000);

        Console.WriteLine("Calling Exit");

        Environment.Exit(0);
    }
  }
}
```

✘ VB.NET (KnowTheExit)

```vbnet
Imports System.Threading

Module Test

    Public Sub Worker( )
        Console.WriteLine("worker thread started")
        Try
            Thread.Sleep(5000)
        Catch ex As ThreadInterruptedException
            Console.WriteLine("worker interrupted")
        Catch ex As ThreadAbortException
            Console.WriteLine("worker aborted")
        End Try
    End Sub

    Public Sub Main( )
        Dim workerThread1 As New Thread(AddressOf Worker)
```

Example 7-5. Behavior of Exit( ) (continued)

```
        workerThread1.Start( )
        Thread.Sleep(1000)

        Console.WriteLine("Interrupting worker1 at {0}", _
         DateTime.Now.ToLongTimeString( ))

        workerThread1.Interrupt( )

        Dim workerThread2 As New Thread(AddressOf Worker)
        workerThread2.Start( )
        Thread.Sleep(1000)

        Console.WriteLine("Calling Exit")

        Environment.Exit(0)
    End Sub

End Module
```

You first create a thread and interrupt it after a one-second delay. From the output shown in Figure 7-6, you can see that the thread does get interrupted. Then you create another thread and after a one-second delay you call Exit( ). Note that the program terminates abruptly without giving the thread a chance to respond. The CLR terminates the process no matter which thread calls Exit( ). This is undesirable. You might consider using Exit( ) in your application under special conditions, such as after dealing with an unhandled fatal exception. However, you need to exercise extreme caution in using Exit( ).

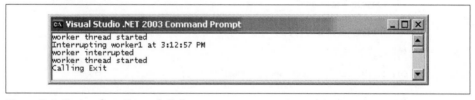

Figure 7-6. Output from Example 7-5

IN A NUTSHELL

Thoroughly understand the consequence of calling Exit( ) on a thread—you are bringing down the entire process.

SEE ALSO

Gotcha #49, "Foreground threads may prevent a program from terminating," Gotcha #50, "Background threads don't terminate gracefully," and Gotcha #58, "Threads from the thread pool are scarce."

#54 ResetAbort( ) may lead to surprises

In Gotcha #52, "ThreadAbortException—a hot potato," you saw the special nature of ThreadAbortException. The Thread class provides the interesting method ResetAbort( ) to overrule this exception. Let's start by reviewing the code in Example 7-6.

Example 7-6. ResetAbort() at work

✗ C# (ResetAbortMethod)

```csharp
using System;
using System.Threading;

namespace ResetAbort
{
    class Test
    {
        private static void Worker()
        {
            try
            {
                Thread.Sleep(5000);
            }
            catch(ThreadAbortException)
            {
                Console.WriteLine(
                    "ThreadAbortException caught");
                Thread.ResetAbort();
            }

            Console.WriteLine("Look where we are now!");

            Thread.Sleep(10000);
        }

        [STAThread]
        static void Main(string[] args)
        {
            Thread workerThread
                = new Thread(new ThreadStart(Worker));
            workerThread.Start();

            Thread.Sleep(1000);
            Console.WriteLine("Calling abort");
            workerThread.Abort();

            Thread.Sleep(2000);
```

Example 7-6. ResetAbort() at work (continued)

```
            Console.WriteLine("Main done");
        }
    }
}
```

✗ VB.NET (ResetAbortMethod)

```vb
Imports System.Threading

Module Test
    Private Sub Worker()
        Try
            Thread.Sleep(5000)
        Catch ex As ThreadAbortException

            Console.WriteLine("ThreadAbortException caught")
            Thread.ResetAbort()
        End Try

        Console.WriteLine("Look where we are now!")

        Thread.Sleep(10000)
    End Sub

    Public Sub Main()
        Dim workerThread As New Thread(AddressOf Worker)
        workerThread.Start()

        Thread.Sleep(1000)
        Console.WriteLine("Calling abort")
        workerThread.Abort()

        Thread.Sleep(2000)
        Console.WriteLine("Main done")
    End Sub

End Module
```

When the CLR throws the ThreadAbortException, within the catch block you call ResetAbort(). This cancels the Abort() and the method continues running, as you can see in Figure 7-7.

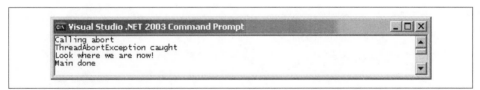

Figure 7-7. Output from Example 7-6

What's the issue here? The problem with ResetAbort( ) is that the code that calls Abort( ) won't know that the Thread has cancelled it. This can lead to unexpected (and unpredictable) behavior. If you find yourself doing something like this, you might need to redesign. Look at what you are trying to achieve and evaluate other ways to accomplish it (such as synchronization objects).

 IN A NUTSHELL

ResetAbort( ) cancels an Abort( ). This is counter to normal expectations. Avoid using it and find clearer ways to achieve your goal.

SEE ALSO

Gotcha #51, "Interrupt ( ) kicks in only when a thread is blocked" and Gotcha #52, "ThreadAbortException—a hot potato."

GOTCHA
#55 Abort( ) takes time to clean up

As you saw in Gotcha #52, "ThreadAbortException—a hot potato," when you abort a Thread, the CLR throws a ThreadAbortException on it. The thread can do whatever cleanup it needs to by handling the exception. The CLR then executes all the finally blocks in the thread's call stack before actually terminating it. So there might be a delay between the time you call Abort( ) and the time the thread quits. This is illustrated in Example 7-7.

Example 7-7. Delay during Abort

✔ **C# (JoinAbort)**

```
using System;
using System.Threading;

namespace AbortAndJoin
{
    class Test
    {
        private static void Worker( )
        {
            Console.WriteLine("Worker started");
            try
            {
                Thread.Sleep(5000);
            }
            finally
            {
                Console.WriteLine("Worker enters finally {0}",
```

Example 7-7. Delay during Abort (continued)

```csharp
                DateTime.Now.ToLongTimeString( ));
            Thread.Sleep(10000);
            // Simulates some cleanup activity
            Console.WriteLine("Cleanup done in Worker {0}",
                DateTime.Now.ToLongTimeString( ));
        }
    }

    [STAThread]
    static void Main(string[] args)
    {
        Thread workerThread
            = new Thread(new ThreadStart(Worker));
        workerThread.IsBackground = true;
        workerThread.Start( );
        Thread.Sleep(1000);

        Console.WriteLine("Aborting thread {0}",
            DateTime.Now.ToLongTimeString( ));
        workerThread.Abort( );

        workerThread.Join( );
        Console.WriteLine("Thread has aborted {0}",
            DateTime.Now.ToLongTimeString( ));
    }
  }
}
```

✔ **VB.NET (JoinAbort)**

```vbnet
Imports System.Threading

Module Test

    Private Sub Worker( )
        Console.WriteLine("Worker started")
        Try
            Thread.Sleep(5000)
        Finally
            Console.WriteLine("Worker enters finally {0}", _
                DateTime.Now.ToLongTimeString( ))
            Thread.Sleep(10000)
            ' Simulates some cleanup activity
            Console.WriteLine("Cleanup done in Worker {0}", _
                DateTime.Now.ToLongTimeString( ))
        End Try
    End Sub

    Public Sub Main( )
        Dim workerThread As New Thread(AddressOf Worker)
```

Example 7-7. Delay during Abort (continued)

```
        workerThread.IsBackground = True
        workerThread.Start( )
        Thread.Sleep(1000)

        Console.WriteLine("Aborting thread {0}", _
         DateTime.Now.ToLongTimeString( ))
        workerThread.Abort( )

        workerThread.Join( )
        Console.WriteLine("Thread has aborted {0}", _
         DateTime.Now.ToLongTimeString( ))
    End Sub

End Module
```

In this example, the Worker( ) method's finally block introduces a delay to simulate some activity. Main( ) first starts a thread to run the Worker( ) method. After a delay, it invokes Abort( ) on that thread. Then it calls Join( ) to wait for cleanup and completion. The output is shown in Figure 7-8.

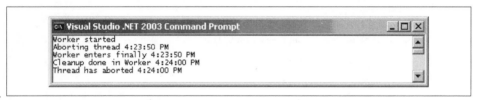

Figure 7-8. Output from Example 7-7

If your application requires you to Abort( ) a thread and perform some operation after that thread has quit, you should call Join( ) on the thread after calling Abort( ). This waits for the thread to clean up properly and exit gracefully before you continue processing.

 You may want to call the Join( ) method with a reasonable timeout to avoid any potential starvation or deadlock, as in:

```
    workerThread.Join(2000);  // Wait two seconds for
                              // the thread to complete
```

 **IN A NUTSHELL**

Ask yourself if you should call Join( ) after a call to Abort( ). That is, ask if you need to wait for the thread to actually quit.

SEE ALSO

Gotcha #52, "ThreadAbortException—a hot potato" and Gotcha #54, "ResetAbort( ) may lead to surprises."

#56 Calling Type.GetType( ) may not return what you expect

Say you have a static/Shared method and you want to make sure that only one thread at a time can perform that operation. Typically, you use lock/SyncLock on an object to define a critical section. However, this won't help if you are trying to synchronize within a static/Shared method or you're trying to synchronize access to a static/Shared field. Static/Shared members are, by definition, independent from any object of the type. Consider Example 7-8.

Example 7-8. Ineffective synchronization

✗ C# (Synchronizing)

```
//Bacteria.cs

using System;
using System.Threading;

namespace SynchOnType
{
    public class Bacteria
    {
        private static int bacteriaCount;

        private static void IncreaseCount()
        {
            Console.WriteLine(
                "IncreaseCount called by {0} at {1}",
                AppDomain.GetCurrentThreadId( ),
                DateTime.Now.ToLongTimeString( ));

            bacteriaCount++;

            Thread.Sleep(2000);
            // Used for illustration purpose
        }

        public Bacteria( )
        {
            lock(this)
            {
                IncreaseCount( );
            }
        }
    }
}
```

Example 7-8. Ineffective synchronization (continued)

```csharp
//Test.cs
using System;
using System.Threading;

namespace SynchOnType
{
    class Test
    {
        private static void Worker()
        {
            Console.WriteLine("In thread {0}",
                AppDomain.GetCurrentThreadId());

            Bacteria aBacteria = new Bacteria();
        }

        [STAThread]
        static void Main(string[] args)
        {
            Thread thread1 = new Thread(new ThreadStart(Worker));
            Thread thread2 = new Thread(new ThreadStart(Worker));

            thread1.Start();
            thread2.Start();
        }
    }
}
```

✗ VB.NET (Synchronizing)

```vbnet
'Bacteria.vb

Imports System.Threading

Public Class Bacteria
    Private Shared bacteriaCount As Integer

    Private Shared Sub IncreaseCount()
        Console.WriteLine( _
            "IncreaseCount called by {0} at {1}", _
            AppDomain.GetCurrentThreadId(), _
            DateTime.Now.ToLongTimeString())

        bacteriaCount += 1

        Thread.Sleep(2000)
        ' Used for illustration purpose
    End Sub
```

Example 7-8. Ineffective synchronization (continued)

```
    Public Sub New( )
        SyncLock Me
            IncreaseCount( )
        End SyncLock
    End Sub
End Class


'Test.vb

Imports System.Threading

Module Test

    Private Sub Worker( )
        Console.WriteLine("In thread {0}", _
            AppDomain.GetCurrentThreadId( ))

        Dim aBacteria As New Bacteria
    End Sub

    Public Sub Main( )
        Dim thread1 As New Thread(AddressOf Worker)
        Dim thread2 As New Thread(AddressOf Worker)

        thread1.Start( )
        thread2.Start( )
    End Sub
End Module
```

In this example, two threads create an object of the Bacteria class almost at the same time. Within the constructor of Bacteria you call a static/Shared method that requires synchronization, and you lock the instance before invoking the method.

The synchronization in the constructor is fundamentally flawed. The two threads in Test create one Bacteria object each. Each of the threads locks a different instance of Bacteria, and then calls the static method. When the program is executed, the output shown in Figure 7-9 is generated.

Figure 7-9. Output from Example 7-8

As you can see, the two threads execute the IncreaseCount( ) method at the same time, showing that neither is waiting the Sleep( ) time (2000 milliseconds) for the other as expected. The synchronization is ineffective.

For two threads to treat a code segment as a critical section, they need to synchronize on the same instance. What is common to both the instances of Bacteria? It's the Bacteria class itself, isn't it? So, why not synchronize on the Bacteria class, i.e., the metadata? The code that does just that is shown in Example 7-9.

Example 7-9. Synchronizing on the metadata

✗ C# (Synchronizing)

```
public Bacteria( )
{
    lock(GetType( ))
    {
        IncreaseCount( );
    }
}
```

✗ VB.NET (Synchronizing)

```
Public Sub New( )
    SyncLock Me.GetType( )
        IncreaseCount( )
    End SyncLock
End Sub
```

In the constructor of Bacteria you synchronize on the metadata of Bacteria. You obtain this object by calling the GetType( ) method on the instance. The output after the above change is shown in Figure 7-10.

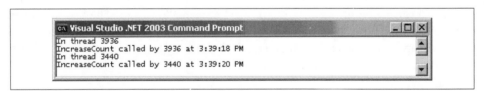

Figure 7-10. Output after change shown in Example 7-9

The two threads are executing the IncreaseCount( ) method two seconds apart, indicating that the calls to the method are being synchronized. It works, doesn't it? Are you done? Yep, let's ship it.

Well, sorry, the euphoria is short-lived. Let's write a new class and change the Test class, as in Example 7-10.

Example 7-10. Problem with instance's GetType( )

✗ C# (Synchronizing)

```
//SpecializedBacteria.cs
 using System;

namespace SynchOnType
{
    public class SpecializedBacteria : Bacteria
    {
    }
}



//Test.cs
using System;
using System.Threading;

namespace SynchOnType
{
    class Test
    {
        private static void Worker1( )
        {
            Console.WriteLine("In thread {0}",
                AppDomain.GetCurrentThreadId( ));

            Bacteria aBacteria = new Bacteria( );
        }

        private static void Worker2( )
        {
            Console.WriteLine("In thread {0}",
                AppDomain.GetCurrentThreadId( ));

            SpecializedBacteria aBacteria
                = new SpecializedBacteria( );
        }

        [STAThread]
        static void Main(string[] args)
        {
            Thread thread1
                = new Thread(new ThreadStart(Worker1));
            Thread thread2
                = new Thread(new ThreadStart(Worker2));

            thread1.Start( );
            thread2.Start( );
        }
```

Example 7-10. Problem with instance's GetType() (continued)

```
    }
}
```

✗ VB.NET (Synchronizing)

```vbnet
'SpecializedBacteria.vb

Public Class SpecializedBacteria
    Inherits Bacteria
End Class


'Test.vb

Imports System.Threading

Module Test

    Private Sub Worker1()
        Console.WriteLine("In thread {0}", _
            AppDomain.GetCurrentThreadId())

        Dim aBacteria As New Bacteria
    End Sub

    Private Sub Worker2()
        Console.WriteLine("In thread {0}", _
            AppDomain.GetCurrentThreadId())

        Dim aBacteria As New SpecializedBacteria
    End Sub


    Public Sub Main()
        Dim thread1 As New Thread(AddressOf Worker1)
        Dim thread2 As New Thread(AddressOf Worker2)

        thread1.Start()
        thread2.Start()
    End Sub
End Module
```

In this code, thread1 calls Worker1( ), which creates an instance of Bacteria. In the meantime, thread2 calls Worker2( ), which creates an instance of SpecializedBacteria. Recall that the constructor of Bacteria is called when you create an instance of SpecializedBacteria. Within the constructor, when you call GetType( ), which Type metadata is returned? Because the instance being created is SpecializedBacteria, GetType( ) returns the Type metadata for SpecializedBacteria, not that of Bacteria. Once again, the two threads end up locking different instances and get into the IncreaseCount( ) method at the same time, as shown in Figure 7-11.

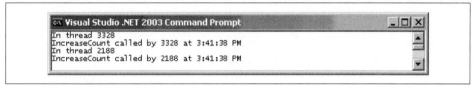

Figure 7-11. Output from Example 7-10

In this situation, locking on the metadata returned by GetType( ) has no effect. What can you do to solve this problem? You want to lock the Bacteria class. So, why not do that explicitly? Consider Example 7-11.

Example 7-11. Explicitly locking the right metadata

✗ C# (Synchronizing)

```csharp
public Bacteria( )
{
    lock(typeof(Bacteria))
    {
        IncreaseCount( );
    }
}
```

✗ VB.NET (Synchronizing)

```vbnet
Public Sub New( )
    SyncLock GetType(Bacteria)
        IncreaseCount( )
    End SyncLock
End Sub
```

Here you fetch the Bacteria's Type metadata by using the typeof operator in C# and the GetType( ) operator in VB.NET. This call returns a consistent metadata object regardless of the instance type. Now, when you execute the code, you get the desired output, as shown in Figure 7-12.

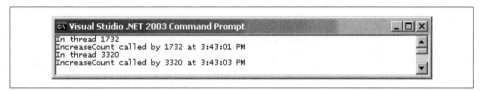

Figure 7-12. Output from Example 7-11

In this specific example, if your only objective is to synchronize the incrementing of the field, use `Interlocked.Increment( )`.

Are you done? Is this a solution you can be comfortable with? Well, not fully, but go with it for now while you look at more issues in the next gotcha.

 IN A NUTSHELL

If your intent is to fetch the metadata for a specific class, use the `typeof`/`GetType` operator instead of the `GetType( )` instance method.

SEE ALSO

Gotcha #20, "Singleton isn't guaranteed process-wide," Gotcha #57, "Locking on globally visible objects is too sweeping," Gotcha #62, "Accessing WinForm controls from arbitrary threads is dangerous," and Gotcha #64, "Raising events lacks thread-safety."

GOTCHA

#57 Locking on globally visible objects is too sweeping

In Gotcha #56, "Calling Type.GetType( ) may not return what you expect," I discussed options for synchronizing threads. While the last solution presented there seems to work for that specific example, there is still a problem. Locking the type metadata to define a critical section is much too sweeping. If all `static`/`Shared` methods synchronize on the type metadata, then all access to the class methods is one-at-a-time, even if it doesn't need to be. This certainly provides thread safety, but sacrifices concurrency in ways that are neither necessary nor desirable in most cases. Consider Example 7-12.

Example 7-12. Consequence of locking the Type metadata

✗ C# (SynchWithIntent)

```
//Bacteria.cs
using System;
using System.Threading;

namespace SynchOnType
{
    public class Bacteria
    {
```

Example 7-12. Consequence of locking the Type metadata (continued)

```csharp
        private static int bacteriaCount;

        private static void IncreaseCount()
        {
            Console.WriteLine(
                "IncreaseCount called by {0} at {1}",
                AppDomain.GetCurrentThreadId(),
                DateTime.Now.ToLongTimeString());

            bacteriaCount++;

            Thread.Sleep(2000);
            // Used for illustration purpose
        }

        public Bacteria()
        {
            lock(typeof(Bacteria))
            {
                IncreaseCount();
            }
        }
    }
}


//Test.cs
using System;
using System.Threading;

namespace SynchOnType
{
    class Test
    {
        private static void Worker()
        {
            Console.WriteLine("In thread {0}",
                AppDomain.GetCurrentThreadId());

            Bacteria aBacteria = new Bacteria();
        }

        [STAThread]
        static void Main(string[] args)
        {
            Thread thread1 = new Thread(new ThreadStart(Worker));
            Thread thread2 = new Thread(new ThreadStart(Worker));

            lock(typeof(Bacteria))
            {
```

Example 7-12. Consequence of locking the Type metadata (continued)

```
                Console.WriteLine("Starting threads at {0}",
                    DateTime.Now.ToLongTimeString( ));

                thread1.Start( );
                thread2.Start( );

                Thread.Sleep(3000);
            }
        }
    }
}
```

✘ VB.NET (SynchWithIntent)

```
Imports System.Threading

'Bacteria.vb
Public Class Bacteria

    Private Shared bacteriaCount As Integer

    Private Shared Sub IncreaseCount( )
        Console.WriteLine( _
          "IncreaseCount called by {0} at {1}", _
          AppDomain.GetCurrentThreadId( ), _
          DateTime.Now.ToLongTimeString( ))

        bacteriaCount += 1

        Thread.Sleep(2000)
        ' Used for illustration purpose
    End Sub

    Public Sub New( )
        SyncLock GetType(Bacteria)
            IncreaseCount( )
        End SyncLock
    End Sub

End Class


'Test.vb

Imports System.Threading

Module Test

    Private Sub Worker( )
        Console.WriteLine("In thread {0}", _
```

Example 7-12. Consequence of locking the Type metadata (continued)

```
            AppDomain.GetCurrentThreadId( ))

        Dim aBacteria As New Bacteria
    End Sub
    Public Sub Main( )
        Dim thread1 As New Thread(AddressOf Worker)
        Dim thread2 As New Thread(AddressOf Worker)

        SyncLock (GetType(Bacteria))
            Console.WriteLine("Starting threads at {0}", _
                DateTime.Now.ToLongTimeString( ))

            thread1.Start( )
            thread2.Start( )

            Thread.Sleep(3000)
        End SyncLock

    End Sub

End Module
```

When you execute the above program, since the Main( ) method holds a lock on the Bacteria type for 3 seconds, the creation of the Bacteria objects is delayed until Main( ) lets go of that lock. One reason why a client of the Bacteria class might hold a lock on its metadata is so it can call multiple static/Shared methods in a thread-safe way. For whatever reason, if Main( ) or any other method in the application grabs a lock on the Bacteria metadata, the execution of the constructors (and all other methods) is delayed. This is shown in the output in Figure 7-13.

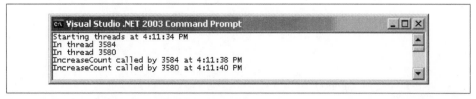

Figure 7-13. Output from Example 7-12

The problem here is that Bacteria's constructor claims a lock on the Bacteria type in order to synchronize the execution of its static/Shared method. The static/Shared method and the implementation of the constructor are purely private to the class. However, you rely on a publicly visible object (the metadata of Bacteria) to synchronize. You can lock much more locally and precisely. Let's look at a modified implementation in Example 7-13.

Example 7-13. Synchronizing locally and precisely

```csharp
//Bacteria.cs
using System;

namespace SynchOnType
{
    public class Bacteria
    {
        private static int bacteriaCount;
        private static object theIncrementCountLock = new Object();

        private static void IncreaseCount()
        {
            Console.WriteLine(
                "IncreaseCount called by {0} at {1}",
                AppDomain.GetCurrentThreadId(),
                DateTime.Now.ToLongTimeString());

            bacteriaCount++;

            System.Threading.Thread.Sleep(2000);
            // Used for illustration purpose
        }

        public Bacteria()
        {
            lock(theIncrementCountLock)
            {
                IncreaseCount();
            }
        }
    }
}
```

```vbnet
Imports System.Threading

'Bacteria.vb
Public Class Bacteria

    Private Shared bacteriaCount As Integer
```

Example 7-13. Synchronizing locally and precisely (continued)

```
Private Shared theIncrementCountLock As New Object

Private Shared Sub IncreaseCount( )
    Console.WriteLine( _
     "IncreaseCount called by {0} at {1}", _
     AppDomain.GetCurrentThreadId( ), _
     DateTime.Now.ToLongTimeString( ))

    bacteriaCount += 1

    Thread.Sleep(2000)
    ' Used for illustration purpose
End Sub

Public Sub New( )
    SyncLock theIncrementCountLock
        IncreaseCount( )
    End SyncLock
End Sub

End Class
```

In this case, you have created a dummy object (theIncrementCountLock refers to it) within the Bacteria class. In the constructor, you lock this object. Note that the dummy lock-facilitator object is private, so no method outside the class can claim a lock with it.

There are two advantages to this approach. One, code in other classes can't affect the concurrency of the constructor, because they can't see theIncrementCountLock. Second, suppose you have two different tasks, call them Task A and Task B. Each of these tasks must be executed one-at-a-time. But if Task A doesn't access any resources that Task B needs, and Task B touches none of Task A's resources, there is no problem with their running concurrently. You can realize this most effectively using two private dummy-lock objects. The output after this change is shown in Figure 7-14.

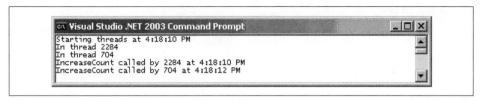

Figure 7-14. Output after change in Example 7-13

For a great discussion on possible deadlock consequences, refer to the article "Don't Lock Type Objects!" in the "On the Web" section of the Appendix.

 **IN A NUTSHELL**

Do not synchronize within your class on publicly visible objects. Synchronize precisely by synchronizing locally.

SEE ALSO

Gotcha #20, "Singleton isn't guaranteed process-wide," Gotcha #56, "Calling Type. GetType() may not return what you expect," Gotcha #62, "Accessing WinForm controls from arbitrary threads is dangerous," and Gotcha #64, "Raising events lacks thread-safety."

GOTCHA
#58 Threads from the thread pool are scarce

Should you create a thread or use a thread from the thread pool? There are several considerations here.

First, if you create a Thread object, it will start to execute the method of interest within a fairly brief interval (subject to system limitations). In the case of the thread pool, however, you are using shared resources in your process. If another task that uses the thread pool is taking a little longer, your task may get delayed because there is no available thread in the thread pool.

At any given time up to twenty five threads are available per process per processor. You can change this default value at the system level. What does that mean to your application? If your tasks take a short amount of time and you have only a few of them, it is efficient to use the thread pool. However, if your tasks may take an arbitrary amount of time, then using the thread pool may not be a good idea.

Let's get a better understanding of these issues from Example 7-14.

Example 7-14. Using your own thread versus one from thread pool

✗ C# (ThreadFromPool)

```
using System;
using System.Threading;

namespace ThreadPool
{
    class Test
    {
        private static void Method1()
        {
```

Example 7-14. Using your own thread versus one from thread pool (continued)

```csharp
        Console.Write("Executed by Thread {0} which is ",
            AppDomain.GetCurrentThreadId( ));

        if (!Thread.CurrentThread.IsThreadPoolThread)
            Console.Write("not ");

        Console.WriteLine("from the thread pool at {0}",
            DateTime.Now.ToLongTimeString( ));

        //Thread.Sleep(10000);
    }

    [STAThread]
    static void Main(string[] args)
    {
        Console.WriteLine("Using our own thread");
        for(int i = 0; i < 5; i++)
        {
            new Thread(new ThreadStart(Method1)).Start( );
            Thread.Sleep(1000);
        }

        Console.WriteLine("Press any key to use timer");
        Console.ReadLine( );
        Console.WriteLine("Using timer");
        System.Timers.Timer theTimer
            = new System.Timers.Timer(1000);
        theTimer.Elapsed
            += new System.Timers.ElapsedEventHandler(
                    theTimer_Elapsed);
        theTimer.Start( );
        Thread.Sleep(6000);
        theTimer.Stop( );
    }

    private static void theTimer_Elapsed(
        object sender, System.Timers.ElapsedEventArgs e)
    {
        Method1( );
    }
    }
}
```

✗ VB.NET (ThreadFromPool)

```vbnet
Imports System.Threading

Module Test

  Private Sub Method1( )
```

Example 7-14. Using your own thread versus one from thread pool (continued)

```
Console.Write("Executed by Thread {0} which is ", _
AppDomain.GetCurrentThreadId())

If Not Thread.CurrentThread.IsThreadPoolThread Then
Console.Write("not ")
End If

Console.WriteLine("from the thread pool at {0}", _
DateTime.Now.ToLongTimeString())

'Thread.Sleep(10000)
End Sub

Public Sub Main()
Console.WriteLine("Using our own thread")
For i As Integer = 0 To 4

Dim aThread As New Thread(AddressOf Method1)
aThread.Start()
Thread.Sleep(1000)
Next

Console.WriteLine("Press any key to use timer")
Console.ReadLine()
Console.WriteLine("Using timer")
Dim theTimer As New System.Timers.Timer(1000)
AddHandler theTimer.Elapsed, _
New System.Timers.ElapsedEventHandler( _
AddressOf theTimer_Elapsed)

theTimer.Start()
Thread.Sleep(6000)
theTimer.Stop()
End Sub

Private Sub theTimer_Elapsed( _
ByVal sender As Object, ByVal e As System.Timers.ElapsedEventArgs)
Method1()
End Sub
```

End Module

In the previous example, you first run Method1() using threads you create. Then you run the method using a System.Timers.Timer object, which uses a thread from the thread pool. The output from the program is shown in Figure 7-15.

Notice that all the calls to Method1() using the timer were executed by the same thread from the thread pool. Now, what happens if you put a delay in the method? Executing the code after uncommenting Thread.Sleep(10000), you get the output shown in Figure 7-16.

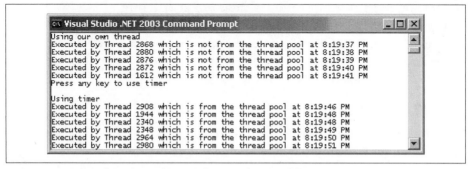

Figure 7-15. Output from Example 7-14

Figure 7-16. Output from Example 7-14 after introducing a delay

Different threads from the thread pool now execute the method. However, the calls to the method using the thread pool are not distributed evenly once per second (note that two calls to Method1( ) were made at 8:19:48 PM).

Furthermore, let's see what happens if you change Thread.Sleep(10000) to Thread. Sleep(35000) and let the Timer run for more than 35 seconds. Partial output from this change is shown in Example 7-15.

Example 7-15. Partial output upon increasing the delay in Method1( )

```
Using timer
Executed by Thread 2864 which is from the thread pool at 8:21:55 PM
Executed by Thread 2196 which is from the thread pool at 8:21:57 PM
Executed by Thread 4064 which is from the thread pool at 8:21:57 PM
Executed by Thread 1536 which is from the thread pool at 8:21:58 PM
Executed by Thread 2492 which is from the thread pool at 8:21:59 PM
Executed by Thread 3024 which is from the thread pool at 8:22:00 PM
Executed by Thread 2588 which is from the thread pool at 8:22:01 PM
Executed by Thread 3000 which is from the thread pool at 8:22:02 PM
Executed by Thread 2932 which is from the thread pool at 8:22:03 PM
Executed by Thread 3952 which is from the thread pool at 8:22:04 PM
Executed by Thread 3004 which is from the thread pool at 8:22:05 PM
...
```

Example 7-15. Partial output upon increasing the delay in Method1() (continued)

```
Executed by Thread 2524 which is from the thread pool at 8:22:11 PM
Executed by Thread 3016 which is from the thread pool at 8:22:12 PM
Executed by Thread 3012 which is from the thread pool at 8:22:13 PM
Executed by Thread 3160 which is from the thread pool at 8:22:14 PM
Executed by Thread 3156 which is from the thread pool at 8:22:15 PM
Executed by Thread 2992 which is from the thread pool at 8:22:16 PM
Executed by Thread 3008 which is from the thread pool at 8:22:17 PM
Executed by Thread 2984 which is from the thread pool at 8:22:18 PM
Executed by Thread 3040 which is from the thread pool at 8:22:19 PM
Executed by Thread 2864 which is from the thread pool at 8:22:30 PM
Executed by Thread 2196 which is from the thread pool at 8:22:32 PM
Executed by Thread 4064 which is from the thread pool at 8:22:32 PM
Executed by Thread 1536 which is from the thread pool at 8:22:33 PM
Executed by Thread 2492 which is from the thread pool at 8:22:34 PM
```

The threads in the thread pool are reused once they become available. This is of course good news. However, notice the lag time between the method executions when all the threads in the thread pool are busy.

 IN A NUTSHELL

The thread pool offers a very efficient use of resources, but it should only be used for tasks that are quick and short-lived.

SEE ALSO

Gotcha #50, "Background threads don't terminate gracefully," Gotcha #53, "Environment. Exit() brings down the CLR," Gotcha #59, "Threads invoked using delegates behave like background threads," Gotcha #61, "Exceptions thrown from threads in the pool are lost," and Gotcha #62, "Accessing WinForm controls from arbitrary threads is dangerous."

GOTCHA
#59 Threads invoked using delegates behave like background threads

If you want a method to be executed from another thread, you can create a thread, set it to background, and then start it. That is three lines of code at least, isn't it? What if your method takes parameters? That is even more work. This is where the Delegate class's BeginInvoke() and EndInvoke() methods look very enticing. Delegates provide BeginInvoke() and EndInvoke() to call a method asynchronously. The intended method is invoked from another thread, and the code is pretty easy to write.

Let's see how you can do just that in Example 7-16.

Example 7-16. Using Delegate to call methods in another thread

```csharp
using System;

namespace DelegateThread
{
    class Test
    {
        private static void Method1(int val)
        {
            Console.Write("Method 1 called from Thread {0}",
                AppDomain.GetCurrentThreadId( ));
            Console.WriteLine(" with value {0}", val);
        }

        delegate void Method1Delegate(int val);

        [STAThread]
        static void Main(string[] args)
        {
            // It is not so easy to call Method1 from
            // another thread using the Thread class.

            Method1Delegate dlg = new Method1Delegate(Method1);
            dlg.BeginInvoke(2, null, null);

            Console.ReadLine( );
        }
    }
}
```

```vbnet
Module Test

    Private Sub Method1(ByVal val As Integer)
        Console.Write("Method 1 called from Thread {0}", _
            AppDomain.GetCurrentThreadId( ))

        Console.WriteLine(" with value {0}", val)
    End Sub

    Delegate Sub Method1Delegate(ByVal val As Integer)

    Public Sub Main( )
        ' It is not so easy to call Method1 from
        ' another thread using the Thread class.
```

Example 7-16. Using Delegate to call methods in another thread (continued)

```
        Dim dlg As New Method1Delegate(AddressOf Method1)
        dlg.BeginInvoke(2, Nothing, Nothing)

        Console.ReadLine( )

    End Sub

End Module
```

In this example, you simply create an object of the delegate Method1Delegate and call its BeginInvoke( ) method, passing the desired value for its first argument. The two null/Nothing arguments indicate that you are not passing a callback method or AsyncState object. The output is shown in Figure 7-17.

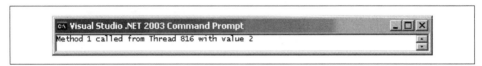

Figure 7-17. Output from Example 7-16

If you are able to execute the method in another thread so easily, why would you do it any other way? Well, this is perfectly OK, but you need to understand the benefits and drawbacks:

- The method is executed by a thread from the thread pool.
- The method is executed by a thread that is marked as a background thread.
- Exceptions thrown from the method are lost unless you call EndInvoke( ), even for methods that do not return any results.

What do these considerations imply? Since you use a thread from the thread pool, its execution depends on the availability of a thread (see "Gotcha #58, "Threads from the thread pool are scarce). Since it is a background thread, it will be terminated if all foreground threads terminate (see Gotcha #49, "Foreground threads may prevent a program from terminating" and Gotcha #50, "Background threads don't terminate gracefully"). Also, since it is from the thread pool, any exceptions thrown in it are handled by the pool. As a result you may not even realize that an exception occurred until you call EndInvoke( ) (see Gotcha #61, "Exceptions thrown from threads in the pool are lost"). With a C# void method, or a VB.NET Sub, you normally have no reason to call EndInvoke( ). But you have to if you want to know if the method completed successfully. Finally, you don't want to synchronize with any other threads while running in the context of a thread-pool thread. If you do, it may delay the start of other tasks that need a thread from the thread pool.

 **IN A NUTSHELL**

Fully understand the behavior and limitations of using `Delegate.BeginInvoke()`. It has all the advantages and limitations of using a background thread and a thread from the thread pool.

SEE ALSO

Gotcha #49, "Foreground threads may prevent a program from terminating," Gotcha #50, "Background threads don't terminate gracefully," Gotcha #58, "Threads from the thread pool are scarce," and Gotcha #61, "Exceptions thrown from threads in the pool are lost."

GOTCHA
#60 Passing parameters to threads is tricky

Say you want to call a method of your class in a separate thread of execution. To start a new thread, you create a `Thread` object, provide it with a `ThreadStart` delegate, and call the `Start()` method on the `Thread` instance. The `ThreadStart` delegate, however, only accepts methods that take no parameters. So how can you pass parameters to the thread?

One option is to use a different `Delegate` (as discussed in Gotcha #59, "Threads invoked using delegates behave like background threads") and call the method asynchronously using the `Delegate.BeginInvoke()` method. This is by far the most convenient option. However, this executes the method in a thread from the thread pool. Therefore, its time of execution has to stay pretty short. Otherwise you end up holding resources from the thread pool and may slow down the start of other tasks.

Let's consider Example 7-17, in which you want to start a thread and pass it an integer parameter.

Example 7-17. Calling method with parameter from another thread

✗ C# (ParamThreadSafety)

```
//SomeClass.cs part of ALib.dll
using System;
using System.Threading;

namespace ALib
{
    public class SomeClass
    {
        private void Method1(int val)
```

Example 7-17. Calling method with parameter from another thread (continued)

```csharp
    {
        // Some operation takes place here
        Console.WriteLine(
            "Method1 runs on Thread {0} with {1}",
            AppDomain.GetCurrentThreadId( ), val);
    }

    public void DoSomething(int val)
    {
        // Some operation...

        // Want to call Method1 in different thread
        // from here?

        // Some operation...
    }
  }
}


//Test.cs part of TestApp.exe
using System;
using ALib;

namespace TestApp
{
    class Test
    {
        [STAThread]
        static void Main(string[] args)
        {
            Console.WriteLine("Main running in Thread {0}",
                AppDomain.GetCurrentThreadId( ));
            SomeClass anObject = new SomeClass( );
            anObject.DoSomething(5);
        }
    }
}
```

✗ VB.NET (ParamThreadSafety)

```vbnet
'SomeClass.vb part of ALib.dll
Imports System.Threading

Public Class SomeClass

    Private Sub Method1(ByVal val As Integer)
        Console.WriteLine( _
            "Method1 runs on Thread {0} with {1}", _
```

Example 7-17. Calling method with parameter from another thread (continued)

```
            AppDomain.GetCurrentThreadId( ), val)

        ' Some operation takes place here
    End Sub

    Public Sub DoSomething(ByVal val As Integer)
        ' Some operation...

        ' Want to call Method1 in different thread
        ' from here?

        ' Some operation...
    End Sub
End Class


'Test.vb

Imports ALib

Module Test
    Public Sub Main( )
        Console.WriteLine("Main running in Thread {0}", _
            AppDomain.GetCurrentThreadId( ))
        Dim anObject As New SomeClass
        anObject.DoSomething(5)
    End Sub
End Module
```

In this example, SomeClass.DoSomething( ) wants to call Method1( ) in a different thread. Unfortunately, you can't just create a new Thread instance and pass a ThreadStart delegate with the address of Method1( ). How can you invoke Method1( ) from here? One approach is shown in Example 7-18.

Example 7-18. One approach to invoking method with parameter

✗ C# (ParamThreadSafety)

```
//SomeClass.cs part of ALib.dll
using System;
using System.Threading;

namespace ALib
{
    public class SomeClass
    {
        private void Method1(int val)
        {
            // Some operation takes place here
```

Example 7-18. One approach to invoking method with parameter (continued)

```
        Console.WriteLine(
            "Method1 runs on Thread {0} with {1}",
            AppDomain.GetCurrentThreadId( ), val);
    }

    private int theValToUseByCallMethod1;

    private void CallMethod1( )
    {
        Method1(theValToUseByCallMethod1);
    }

    public void DoSomething(int val)
    {
        // Some operation...

        // Want to call Method1 in different thread
        // from here?
        theValToUseByCallMethod1 = val;
        new Thread(new ThreadStart(CallMethod1)).Start( );

        // Some operation...
    }
  }
}
```

✗ VB.NET (ParamThreadSafety)

```
'SomeClass.vb part of ALib.dll
Imports System.Threading

Public Class SomeClass

    Private Sub Method1(ByVal val As Integer)
        Console.WriteLine( _
            "Method1 runs on Thread {0} with {1}", _
            AppDomain.GetCurrentThreadId( ), val)

        ' Some operation takes place here
    End Sub

    Private theValToUseByCallMethod1 As Integer

    Private Sub CallMethod1( )
        Method1(theValToUseByCallMethod1)
    End Sub
```

Example 7-18. One approach to invoking method with parameter (continued)

```
    Public Sub DoSomething(ByVal val As Integer)
        ' Some operation...

        ' Want to call Method1 in different thread
        ' from here?
        theValToUseByCallMethod1 = val
        Dim aThread As New Thread(AddressOf CallMethod1)
        aThread.Start( )

        ' Some operation...
    End Sub
End Class
```

In the DoSomething( ) method, you first store the argument you want to pass to the thread in the private field theValToUseByCallMethod1. Then you call a no-parameter method CallMethod1( ) in a different thread. CallMethod1( ), executing in this new thread, picks up the private field set by the main thread and calls Method1( ) with it. The output from the above code is shown in Figure 7-18.

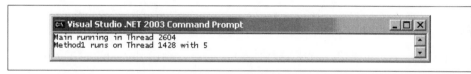

Figure 7-18. Output from Example 7-18

See, it works! Well, yes, if a click of a button is going to call DoSomething( ), then the chances of DoSomething( ) being called more than once before Method1( ) has had a chance to execute are slim. But if this is invoked from a class library, or from multiple threads in the UI itself, how thread-safe is the code? Not very.

Let's add a line to the Main( ) method as shown in Example 7-19.

Example 7-19. Testing thread safety of approach in Example 7-18

✗ C# (ParamThreadSafety)

```
    static void Main(string[] args)
    {
        Console.WriteLine("Main running in Thread {0}",
            AppDomain.GetCurrentThreadId( ));
        SomeClass anObject = new SomeClass( );
        anObject.DoSomething(5);
        anObject.DoSomething(6);
    }
```

Example 7-19. Testing thread safety of approach in Example 7-18 (continued)

✗ VB.NET (ParamThreadSafety)

```
Public Sub Main( )
    Console.WriteLine("Main running in Thread {0}", _
        AppDomain.GetCurrentThreadId( ))
    Dim anObject As New SomeClass
    anObject.DoSomething(5)
    anObject.DoSomething(6)
End Sub
```

Here, you invoke the DoSomething( ) method with a value of 6 immediately after calling it with a value of 5. Let's look at the output from the program after this change, shown in Figure 7-19.

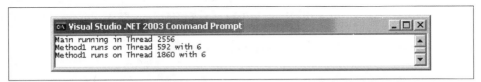

Figure 7-19. Output from Example 7-19

As you can see, both calls to DoSomething( ) pass Method1( ) the value 6. The value of 5 you send in the first invocation is simply overwritten.

One way to attain thread safety in this situation is to isolate the value in a different object. This is shown in Example 7-20.

Example 7-20. Providing thread safety of parameter

✔ C# (ParamThreadSafety)

```
//...
class CallMethod1Helper
{
    private SomeClass theTarget;
    private int theValue;
    public CallMethod1Helper(int val, SomeClass target)
    {
        theValue = val;
        theTarget = target;
    }

    private void CallMethod1( )
    {
        theTarget.Method1(theValue);
    }
```

Example 7-20. Providing thread safety of parameter (continued)

```
        public void Run( )
        {
            new Thread(
                new ThreadStart(CallMethod1)).Start( );
        }
    }

    public void DoSomething(int val)
    {
        // Some operation...

        // Want to call Method1 in different thread
        // from here?
        CallMethod1Helper helper = new CallMethod1Helper(
            val, this);
        helper.Run( );

        // Some operation...
    }
```

✔ VB.NET (ParamThreadSafety)

```
'...
Class CallMethod1Helper
    Private theTarget As SomeClass
    Private theValue As Integer

    Public Sub New(ByVal val As Integer, ByVal target As SomeClass)
        theValue = val
        theTarget = target
    End Sub

    Private Sub CallMethod1( )
        theTarget.Method1(theValue)
    End Sub

    Public Sub Run( )
        Dim theThread As New Thread(AddressOf CallMethod1)
        theThread.Start( )
    End Sub
End Class

Public Sub DoSomething(ByVal val As Integer)
    ' Some operation...

    ' Want to call Method1 in different thread
    ' from here?
```

Example 7-20. Providing thread safety of parameter (continued)

```
        Dim helper As New CallMethod1Helper(val, Me)
        helper.Run()

        ' Some operation...
    End Sub
```

In this case, you create a nested helper class ClassMethod1Helper that holds the val and a reference to the object of SomeClass. You invoke the Run() method on an instance of the helper in the original thread. Run() in turn invokes CallMethod1() of the helper in a separate thread. This method calls Method1(). Since the instance of helper is created within the DoSomething() method, multiple calls to DoSomething() will result in multiple helper objects being created on the heap. They are isolated from one another and provide thread safety for the parameter. The output from the program is shown in Figure 7-20.

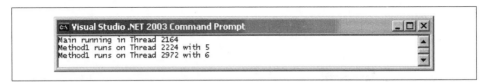

Figure 7-20. Output from Example 7-20

In this example, it took over 20 lines of code (with proper indentation, that is) to create a thread-safe start of Method1(). If you need to invoke another method with parameters, you will have to write almost the same amount of code. You will end up writing a class for each method you want to call. This is quite a bit of redundant coding.

Why not write your own thread-safe thread starter? The code to start the thread might look like Example 7-21 (using the ThreadRunner class, which you'll see shortly).

Example 7-21. Using ThreadRunner

✔ C# (ParamThreadSafety)

```
//SomeClass.cs part of ALib.dll
using System;
using System.Threading;

namespace ALib
{
    public class SomeClass
    {
        private void Method1(int val)
```

Example 7-21. Using ThreadRunner (continued)

```
        {
            // Some operation takes place here
            Console.WriteLine(
                "Method1 runs on Thread {0} with {1}",
                AppDomain.GetCurrentThreadId(), val);
        }

        private delegate void CallMethod1Delegate(int val);

        public void DoSomething(int val)
        {
            // Some operation...

            // Want to call Method1 in different thread
            // from here?
            ThreadRunner theRunner
                = new ThreadRunner(
                    new CallMethod1Delegate(Method1), val);

            theRunner.Start();

            // Some operation...
        }
    }
}
```

✔ VB.NET (ParamThreadSafety)

```
'SomeClass.vb part of ALib.dll
Imports System.Threading

Public Class SomeClass

    Private Sub Method1(ByVal val As Integer)
        Console.WriteLine( _
            "Method1 runs on Thread {0} with {1}", _
            AppDomain.GetCurrentThreadId(), val)

        ' Some operation takes place here
    End Sub

    Private Delegate Sub CallMethod1Delegate(ByVal val As Integer)


    Public Sub DoSomething(ByVal val As Integer)
        ' Some operation...

        ' Want to call Method1 in different thread
        ' from here?
```

Example 7-21. Using ThreadRunner (continued)

```
        Dim theRunner As New ThreadRunner( _
            New CallMethod1Delegate(AddressOf Method1), val)

        theRunner.Start( )

        ' Some operation...
    End Sub
End Class
```

That is sweet and simple. You create a ThreadRunner object and send it a delegate with the same signature as the method you're going to call. You also send it the parameters you want to pass. The ThreadRunner launches a new thread to execute the method that is referred to by the given delegate.

The code for ThreadRunner is shown in Example 7-22. Note that you do not write a ThreadRunner for each method you want to call. Unlike the CallMethod1Helper, this is a class written once and used over and over.

Example 7-22. ThreadRunner class

✔ C# (ParamThreadSafety)

```
//ThreadRunner.cs
using System;
using System.Threading;

namespace ALib
{
    public class ThreadRunner
    {
        private Delegate toRunDelegate;
        private object[] toRunParameters;
        private Thread theThread;

        public bool IsBackground
        {
            get { return theThread.IsBackground; }
            set { theThread.IsBackground = value; }
        }

        public ThreadRunner(Delegate theDelegate,
            params object[] theParameters)
        {
            toRunDelegate = theDelegate;
            toRunParameters = theParameters;

            theThread = new Thread(new ThreadStart(Run));
        }
```

Example 7-22. ThreadRunner class (continued)

```
        public void Start( )
        {
            theThread.Start( );
        }

        private void Run( )
        {
            toRunDelegate.DynamicInvoke(toRunParameters);
        }
    }
}
```

✔ **VB.NET (ParamThreadSafety)**

```
'ThreadRunner.vb

Imports System.Threading

Public Class ThreadRunner
    Private toRunDelegate As System.Delegate

    Private toRunParameters( ) As Object

    Private theThread As Thread

    Public Property IsBackground( ) As Boolean
        Get
            Return theThread.IsBackground
        End Get
        Set(ByVal Value As Boolean)
            theThread.IsBackground = Value
        End Set
    End Property

    Public Sub New(ByVal theDelegate As System.Delegate, _
                ByVal ParamArray theParameters( ) As Object)
        toRunDelegate = theDelegate
        toRunParameters = theParameters

        theThread = New Thread(AddressOf Run)
    End Sub

    Public Sub Start( )
        theThread.Start( )
    End Sub

    Private Sub Run( )
        toRunDelegate.DynamicInvoke(toRunParameters)
    End Sub
End Class
```

Because ThreadRunner exposes the IsBackground property of its underlying Thread object, a user of ThreadRunner can set IsBackground to true if desired. To start the target method in a separate thread, the user of this class calls ThreadRunner.Start( ).

How does this differ in .NET 2.0 Beta 1? A new delegate named ParameterizedThreadStart is introduced. Using this new delegate, you may invoke methods that take one parameter by passing the argument to the Thread class's Start( ) method.

 IN A NUTSHELL

When you start a thread with a method that requires parameters, wrapper classes like ThreadRunner (see Example 7-22) can help ensure thread safety.

SEE ALSO

Gotcha #59, "Threads invoked using delegates behave like background threads."

GOTCHA

#61 Exceptions thrown from threads in the pool are lost

If any exceptions are thrown from a thread you create and you don't handle them, the CLR reports them to the user. In a console application, a message is printed on the console. In a Windows application, a dialog appears with the details of the exception. Of course, a program that displays such unhandled exceptions is undesirable. However, you might also agree that such a program is better than a program that continues to execute and quietly misbehaves after things go wrong. Let's look at Example 7-23.

Example 7-23. Unhandled exception

✗ C# (ExceptionInThread)

```
using System;
using System.Threading;

namespace DelegateThread
{
    class Test
    {
        private static void Method1( )
        {
            Console.WriteLine("Method1 is throwing exception");
            throw new ApplicationException("**** oops ****");
        }
```

Example 7-23. Unhandled exception (continued)

```
delegate void Method1Delegate( );

[STAThread]
static void Main(string[] args)
{
    Console.WriteLine("We first use a thread");
    Thread aThread
        = new Thread(new ThreadStart(Method1));
    aThread.Start( );

    Console.WriteLine("press return");
    Console.ReadLine( );

    Console.WriteLine("We will use a Delegate now");
    Method1Delegate dlg = new Method1Delegate(Method1);
    IAsyncResult handle = dlg.BeginInvoke(null, null);

    Thread.Sleep(1000);

    Console.WriteLine("Was the exception reported so far?");

    try
    {
        Console.WriteLine("Let's call EndInvoke");
        dlg.EndInvoke(handle);
    }
    catch(Exception ex)
    {
        Console.WriteLine("Exception: {0}", ex.Message);
    }

    Console.WriteLine("press return");
    Console.ReadLine( );

    Console.WriteLine("We will use a timer now");

    System.Timers.Timer theTimer
        = new System.Timers.Timer(1000);
    theTimer.Elapsed
        += new System.Timers.ElapsedEventHandler(
            theTimer_Elapsed);
    theTimer.Start( );

    Thread.Sleep(3000);
    theTimer.Stop( );

    Console.WriteLine("press return");
    Console.ReadLine( );
}
```

Example 7-23. Unhandled exception (continued)

```
        private static void theTimer_Elapsed(
            object sender, System.Timers.ElapsedEventArgs e)
        {
            Method1();
        }
    }
}
```

✗ VB.NET (ExceptionInThread)

```
Imports System.Threading

Module Test

 Private Sub Method1()
 Console.WriteLine("Method1 is throwing exception")
 Throw New ApplicationException("**** oops ****")
 End Sub

 Delegate Sub Method1Delegate()

 Public Sub Main()
 Console.WriteLine("We first use a thread")
 Dim aThread As New Thread(AddressOf Method1)
 aThread.Start()

 Console.WriteLine("press return")
 Console.ReadLine()

 Console.WriteLine("We will use a Delegate now")
 Dim dlg As New Method1Delegate(AddressOf Method1)

 Dim handle As IAsyncResult = dlg.BeginInvoke(Nothing, Nothing)

 Thread.Sleep(1000)

 Console.WriteLine("Was the exception reported so far?")

 Try
 Console.WriteLine("Let's call EndInvoke")
 dlg.EndInvoke(handle)
 Catch ex As Exception
 Console.WriteLine("Exception: {0}", ex.Message)
 End Try

 Console.WriteLine("press return")
 Console.ReadLine()

 Console.WriteLine("We will use a timer now")
```

Example 7-23. Unhandled exception (continued)

```
Dim theTimer As New System.Timers.Timer(1000)

AddHandler theTimer.Elapsed, _
New System.Timers.ElapsedEventHandler( _
AddressOf theTimer_Elapsed)

theTimer.Start()

Thread.Sleep(3000)
theTimer.Stop()

Console.WriteLine("press return")
Console.ReadLine()
End Sub

Private Sub theTimer_Elapsed( _
ByVal sender As Object, ByVal e As System.Timers.ElapsedEventArgs)

Method1()
End Sub
End Module
VB.NET (ExceptionInThread)
```

In this example, you have a method Method1( ) that throws an exception. You first call this method from our own thread. The CLR reports this exception by displaying a message on the console. Then you invoke the method using Method1Delegate. BeginInvoke( ). The exception is not caught or reported when it is thrown. It does surface eventually when you call the delegate's EndInvoke( ). The worst offender is the Timer, where the exception simply goes unnoticed. The output from the above program is shown in Figure 7-21.

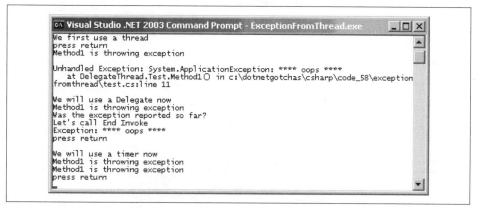

Figure 7-21. Output from Example 7-23

Why is this important to know? Consider invoking a web service asynchronously. You set up a delegate to it and in the callback, you call EndInvoke(). The problem is that the callback itself is called from a thread in the thread pool. If an exception is raised in the callback, it is never seen. This is illustrated in Examples 7-24 through 7-27, and in Figures 7-22 and 7-23.

Example 7-24. Lost exception in asynchronous call, Web service (C#)

✗ C# (ExceptionInThread), server-side code

```
//MyService.asmx.cs part of ACSWebService.dll (Web Service)
using System;
using System.Collections;
using System.ComponentModel;
using System.Data;
using System.Diagnostics;
using System.Web;
using System.Web.Services;

namespace ACSWebService
{
    [WebService(Namespace="MyServiceNameSpace")]
    public class MyService : System.Web.Services.WebService
    {
        // ...

        [WebMethod]
        public int Method1(int val)
        {
            if (val == 0)
                throw new ApplicationException(
                    "Do not like the input");

            return val;
        }
    }
}
```

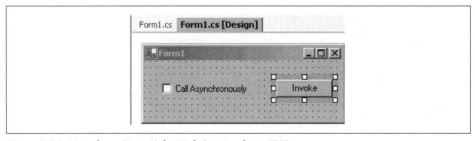

Figure 7-22. Main form (Form1) for Web Service client (C#)

Example 7-25. Lost exception in asynchronous call, Web service client (C#)

✗ C# (ExceptionInThread), client-side code

```
///Form1.cs part of AWSClient
using System;
using System.Drawing;
using System.Collections;
using System.ComponentModel;
using System.Windows.Forms;
using System.Data;
using System.Threading;
using AWSClient.ACSWebService;

namespace AWSClient
{
    public class Form1 : System.Windows.Forms.Form
    {
        private static MyService service;

        // Parts of this file not shown...

        private void InvokeButton_Click(
            object sender, System.EventArgs e)
        {

            service = new MyService( );
            service.Credentials =
                System.Net.CredentialCache.DefaultCredentials;

            if (AsynchCheckBox.Checked)
            {
                CallAsynch( );
            }
            else
            {
                CallSynch( );
            }

        }

        private static void CallSynch( )
        {
            int result = service.Method1(1);
            MessageBox.Show("Result received: " + result);

            result = service.Method1(0);
            MessageBox.Show("Result received: " + result);
        }

        private static void CallAsynch( )
```

Example 7-25. Lost exception in asynchronous call, Web service client (C#) (continued)

```
    {
        service.BeginMethod1(1,
            new AsyncCallback(response), service);

        Thread.Sleep(1000);

        service.BeginMethod1(0,
            new AsyncCallback(response), service);

        Thread.Sleep(1000);
    }

    private static void response(IAsyncResult handle)
    {
        MyService theService = handle.AsyncState as MyService;

        int result = theService.EndMethod1(handle);
        MessageBox.Show("Result received asynchronously " +
            result);
    }
    }
}
```

Example 7-26. Lost exception in asynchronous call, Web service (VB.NET)

✗ VB.NET (ExceptionInThread), server-side code

```
'MyService.asmx.vb part of AVBWebService.dll (Web Service)
Imports System.Web.Services

<System.Web.Services.WebService(Namespace:="MyServiceNameSpace")> _
Public Class MyService
    Inherits System.Web.Services.WebService

    '...

    <WebMethod( )> _
    Public Function Method1(ByVal val As Integer) As Integer
        If val = 0 Then
            Throw New ApplicationException("Do not like the input")
        End If

        Return val
    End Function
```

Example 7-26. Lost exception in asynchronous call, Web service (VB.NET) (continued)

End Class

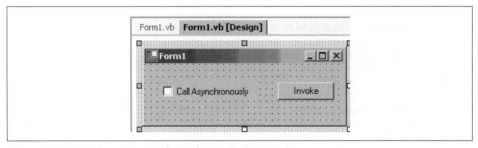

Figure 7-23. Main form (Form1) for Web Service (VB.NET)

Example 7-27. Lost exception in asynchronous call, Web service client (VB.NET)

✗ VB.NET (ExceptionInThread), client-side code

```
'Form1.vb part of AWSClient

Imports System.Threading
Imports AWSClient.AVBWebService

Public Class Form1
    Inherits System.Windows.Forms.Form

    Private Shared service As MyService

    'Parts of this file not shown...

    Private Sub InvokeButton_Click(ByVal sender As System.Object, _
        ByVal e As System.EventArgs) Handles InvokeButton.Click

        service = New MyService
        service.Credentials = _
         System.Net.CredentialCache.DefaultCredentials

        If AsynchCheckBox.Checked Then
            CallAsynch()
        Else
            CallSynch()
        End If

    End Sub

    Private Shared Sub CallSynch()
        Dim result As Integer = service.Method1(1)
        MessageBox.Show("Result received: " & result)
```

```
    result = service.Method1(0)
    MessageBox.Show("Result received: " & result)
End Sub

Private Shared Sub CallAsynch()
    service.BeginMethod1(1, _
    New AsyncCallback(AddressOf response), service)

    Thread.Sleep(1000)

    service.BeginMethod1(0, _
    New AsyncCallback(AddressOf response), service)

    Thread.Sleep(1000)
End Sub

Private Shared Sub response(ByVal handle As IAsyncResult)
    Dim theService As MyService = _
        CType(handle.AsyncState, MyService)

    Dim result As Integer = theService.EndMethod1(handle)
    MessageBox.Show("Result received asynchronously " & _
        result)
End Sub

End Class
```

The web service throws an exception if the parameter to Method1( ) is zero. From a Windows application, you invoke the web service, first sending a value of 1 and then a value of 0. When you invoke the method synchronously with an argument of zero, the CLR displays an exception, as shown in Figure 7-24.

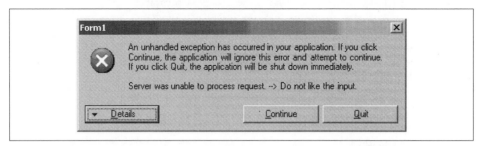

Figure 7-24. Output from Example 7-24 for a synchronous call with a parameter of zero

However, if you call it asynchronously, no exception is reported. This is because the callback itself executes on a thread pool thread. You might expect the exception to be received when you call EndInvoke( ) in the response( ) method. Yes, an exception is raised (a System.Web.Services.Protocols.SoapException, to be precise). But it isn't propagated to you; the CLR suppresses any exception raised from a thread in the thread pool. You can verify this by adding a try/catch block around the EndInvoke( ) call, as shown in Example 7-28.

Example 7-28. Catching exception after call to EndInvoke( )

✔ C# (ExceptionInThread), client-side code

```csharp
private static void response(IAsyncResult handle)
{
    MyService theService
        = handle.AsyncState as MyService;

    try
    {
        int result = theService.EndMethod1(handle);
        MessageBox.Show("Result received asynchronously " +
            result);
    }
    catch(System.Web.Services.Protocols.SoapException ex)
    {
        MessageBox.Show("Now I got " + ex);
    }
}
```

✔ VB.NET (ExceptionInThread), client-side code

```vbnet
Private Shared Sub response(ByVal handle As IAsyncResult)
    Dim theService As MyService = _
        CType(handle.AsyncState, MyService)

    Try
        Dim result As Integer = theService.EndMethod1(handle)
        MessageBox.Show("Result received asynchronously " & _
            result)
    Catch ex As System.Web.Services.Protocols.SoapException
        MessageBox.Show("Now I got " & ex.ToString( ))
    End Try
End Sub
```

Now when you make the call asynchronously, you get the message shown in Figure 7-25.

Figure 7-25. Exception reported after change shown in Example 7-28

 IN A NUTSHELL

When using threads from the thread pool, pay extra attention to exception handling. Exceptions may not be reported, depending on what type of object you use: Delegate or Timer.

SEE ALSO

Gotcha #6, "Exceptions may go unhandled" and Gotcha #58, "Threads from the thread pool are scarce."

GOTCHA

#62 Accessing WinForm controls from arbitrary threads is dangerous

Typically, you execute a task in a thread other than the main thread if that task might take a long time, but meanwhile you want your application to be responsive, plus you want to be able to preempt the task. Once it has completed, how do you display the results in the form's control? Keep in mind that the form's controls are not thread-safe. The only methods and properties of a control that are thread-safe are BeginInvoke( ), EndInvoke( ), Invoke( ), InvokeRequired, and CreateGraphics( ). This is not a flaw. It was done by design to improve performance by eliminating thread-synchronization overhead. If you want to access any other methods or properties of a control, you should do so only from the thread that owns the control's underlying window handle. This is typically the thread that created the control, which generally is the main thread in your application.

What happens if you access the non-thread-safe methods of a control from another thread? Unfortunately, the program may appear to work fine on several occasions. But just because the program runs, it does not mean it has no problems. In this case it is not a question of *if*, but of *when* the program will misbehave. These kinds of problems are difficult to predict and often may not be easily reproduced.

How can you call a method on a control from within another thread? You can do that using the System.Windows.Forms.Control.Invoke() method on the control. This method executes a delegate on the thread that owns the control's window handle. The call to Invoke() blocks until that method completes.

Say you create a System.Windows.Forms.Timer in a Form. Should you access the controls of a Form from within the Timer's callback method? What about from the callback of an asynchronous method call to a web service? The answers depend on understanding the thread in which each of these executes. Things become clearer when you examine the details.

An example will clarify this. Figure 7-26 shows a WinForm application with three buttons and a couple of labels.

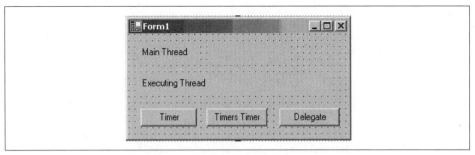

Figure 7-26. A WinForm application to understand threads

The Timer button is linked to code that creates a System.Windows.Forms.Timer. It in turn executes a method, SetExecutingThreadLabel(), that provides some details on the executing thread.

 It is important to distinguish this Timer, which resides in the System.Windows.Forms namespace, from the Timer class you've already seen, which is in System.Timers.Timers. (See Gotcha #58, "Threads from the thread pool are scarce" and Gotcha #61, "Exceptions thrown from threads in the pool are lost.")

The Timers Timer button is linked to a handler that creates a System.Timers.Timer object. It raises an event that also executes SetExecutingThreadLabel(). Finally, the Delegate button is tied to a handler that creates a Delegate. It then calls its BeginInvoke(), which also executes SetExecutingThreadLabel(). The code is shown in Examples 7-29 and 7-30.

Example 7-29. Executing thread for different Timers and Delegate (C#)

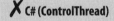 **C# (ControlThread)**

```
private void Form1_Load(object sender, System.EventArgs e)
```

```csharp
    {
        MainThreadLabel.Text
            = AppDomain.GetCurrentThreadId( ).ToString( );
    }

    private delegate void SetLabelDelegate(string message);

    private void SetExecutingThreadLabel(string message)
    {
        ExecutingThreadLabel.Text = message;
    }

    private void TimerButton_Click(
        object sender, System.EventArgs e)
    {
        Timer theTimer = new Timer( );
        theTimer.Interval = 1000;
        theTimer.Tick += new EventHandler(Timer_Tick);
        theTimer.Start( );
    }

    private void Timer_Tick(object sender, EventArgs e)
    {
        Invoke(new SetLabelDelegate(SetExecutingThreadLabel),
            new object[] {
                "Timer : "
                + AppDomain.GetCurrentThreadId( ) + ": "
                + InvokeRequired });
        (sender as Timer).Stop( );
    }

    private void TimersTimerButton_Click(
        object sender, System.EventArgs e)
    {
        System.Timers.Timer theTimer
            = new System.Timers.Timer(1000);
        theTimer.Elapsed
            += new System.Timers.ElapsedEventHandler(
                Timer_Elapsed);
        theTimer.Start( );
    }

    private void Timer_Elapsed(
        object sender, System.Timers.ElapsedEventArgs e)
    {
        Invoke(new SetLabelDelegate(SetExecutingThreadLabel),
            new object[] {
                "Timers.Timer : "
                + AppDomain.GetCurrentThreadId( ) + ": "
                + InvokeRequired });
```

```csharp
        (sender as System.Timers.Timer).Stop();
    }

    private delegate void AsynchDelegate();

    private void DelegateButton_Click(
        object sender, System.EventArgs e)
    {
        AsynchDelegate dlg
            = new AsynchDelegate(AsynchExecuted);
        dlg.BeginInvoke(null, null);
    }

    private void AsynchExecuted()
    {
        Invoke(new SetLabelDelegate(SetExecutingThreadLabel),
            new object[] {
                "Delegate : "
                + AppDomain.GetCurrentThreadId() + ": "
                + InvokeRequired });
    }
```

Example 7-30. Executing thread for different Timers and Delegate (VB.NET)

✗ VB.NET (ControlThread)

```vbnet
Private Sub Form1_Load(ByVal sender As System.Object, _
        ByVal e As System.EventArgs) Handles MyBase.Load
    MainThreadLabel.Text _
        = AppDomain.GetCurrentThreadId().ToString()
End Sub

Private Delegate Sub SetLabelDelegate(ByVal message As String)

Private Sub SetExecutingThreadLabel(ByVal message As String)
    ExecutingThreadLabel.Text = message
End Sub

Private Sub TimerButton_Click( _
        ByVal sender As System.Object, _
        ByVal e As System.EventArgs) _
        Handles TimerButton.Click
    Dim theTimer As Timer = New Timer
    theTimer.Interval = 1000
    AddHandler theTimer.Tick, _
        New EventHandler(AddressOf Timer_Tick)
    theTimer.Start()
End Sub
```

```
Private Sub Timer_Tick(ByVal sender As Object, _
        ByVal e As EventArgs)
    Invoke(New SetLabelDelegate( _
        AddressOf SetExecutingThreadLabel), _
     New Object() { _
      "Timer : " _
      & AppDomain.GetCurrentThreadId( ) & ": " _
      & InvokeRequired})
    CType(sender, Timer).Stop( )
End Sub

Private Sub TimersTimerButton_Click( _
        ByVal sender As System.Object, _
        ByVal e As System.EventArgs) Handles TimersTimerButton.Click
    Dim theTimer As System.Timers.Timer = _
        New System.Timers.Timer(1000)

    AddHandler theTimer.Elapsed, _
        New System.Timers.ElapsedEventHandler( _
            AddressOf Timer_Elapsed)

    theTimer.Start( )
End Sub

Private Sub Timer_Elapsed( _
        ByVal sender As Object, _
        ByVal e As System.Timers.ElapsedEventArgs)
    Invoke(New SetLabelDelegate( _
        AddressOf SetExecutingThreadLabel), _
     New Object() { _
      "Timers.Timer : " _
      & AppDomain.GetCurrentThreadId( ) & ": " _
      & InvokeRequired})

    CType(sender, System.Timers.Timer).Stop( )
End Sub

Private Delegate Sub AsynchDelegate( )

Private Sub DelegateButton_Click(ByVal sender As System.Object, _
        ByVal e As System.EventArgs) Handles DelegateButton.Click
    Dim dlg As AsynchDelegate _
        = New AsynchDelegate(AddressOf AsynchExecuted)
    dlg.BeginInvoke(Nothing, Nothing)
End Sub

Private Sub AsynchExecuted( )
    Invoke(New SetLabelDelegate( _
        AddressOf SetExecutingThreadLabel), _
```

Example 7-30. Executing thread for different Timers and Delegate (VB.NET) (continued)

```
        New Object() { _
          "Delegate : " _
          & AppDomain.GetCurrentThreadId( ) & ": " _
          & InvokeRequired})
    End Sub
```

Running the program and clicking on the buttons produces the results shown in Figures 7-27 through 7-29.

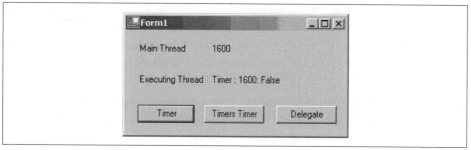

Figure 7-27. Output from Example 7-29 clicking Timer button

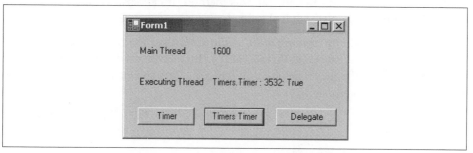

Figure 7-28. Output from Example 7-29 clicking Timers Timer button

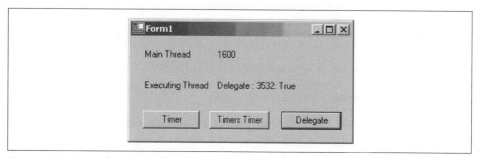

Figure 7-29. Output from Example 7-29 clicking Delegate button

A few observations can be made from the above example and the related output:

- The event executed by the `System.Windows.Forms.Timer` runs in the main thread. So it is perfectly safe to access the controls directly from within this `Timer`'s event handler. Be careful not to put any long-running code in this method. Otherwise, you will be holding up the main event-dispatch thread, and the performance and responsiveness of your application will suffer.

- The `System.Timers.Timer`'s event handler executes in a thread from the thread pool. From this thread, you should not interact with the controls directly, as it is not the thread that owns them. You have to use the `System.Windows.Forms.Control.Invoke()` method.

- The `Delegate`'s `BeginInvoke()` method calls the method from a thread pool thread as well. You should not access the controls directly from the invoked method either. Here, too, you have to call `Invoke()`.

If you write an application that involves several threads, you can see how the above details can complicate your efforts. Further, forgetting them may lead to programs that misbehave. How can you ease these concerns?

One good way is to write a method that talks to the controls. Instead of accessing the controls from any random thread, call this method. It can easily check if it's OK to access the controls directly, or if it should go through a delegate.

Let's modify the code in Example 7-29 to illustrate this. From the three event-handler methods, call `SetExecutingThreadLabel()`. In this method, check to see if the executing thread is the one that owns the control. This can be done using the control's `InvokeRequired` property.*

If the executing thread does own the control (`InvokeRequired` is `false`), then access it directly. Otherwise, `SetExecutingThreadLabel()` uses the `Invoke()` method to call itself, as shown in Example 7-31.

Example 7-31. Effectively addressing InvokeRequired issue

✔ C# (ControlThread)

```
private void SetExecutingThreadLabel(string message)
{
    if(ExecutingThreadLabel.InvokeRequired)
    {
        Invoke(new SetLabelDelegate(SetExecutingThreadLabel),
            new object[] {message});
    }
    else
    {
```

---

* Thanks to Naresh Chaudhary for refactoring this code.

Example 7-31. Effectively addressing InvokeRequired issue (continued)

```csharp
            ExecutingThreadLabel.Text = message;
        }
    }

    private void Timer_Tick(object sender, EventArgs e)
    {
        (sender as Timer).Stop( );

        SetExecutingThreadLabel(
                "Timer : "
                + AppDomain.GetCurrentThreadId( ) + ": "
                + InvokeRequired);
    }

    private void Timer_Elapsed(
        object sender, System.Timers.ElapsedEventArgs e)
    {
        (sender as System.Timers.Timer).Stop( );

        SetExecutingThreadLabel(
            "Timer : "
            + AppDomain.GetCurrentThreadId( ) + ": "
            + InvokeRequired);
    }

    private void AsynchExecuted( )
    {
        SetExecutingThreadLabel(
            "Delegate : "
            + AppDomain.GetCurrentThreadId( ) + ": "
            + InvokeRequired);
    }
```

✔ **VB.NET (ControlThread)**

```vbnet
Private Sub SetExecutingThreadLabel(ByVal message As String)
    If ExecutingThreadLabel.InvokeRequired Then
        Invoke(New SetLabelDelegate( _
                AddressOf SetExecutingThreadLabel), _
                New Object( ) {message})
    Else
        ExecutingThreadLabel.Text = message
    End If

Private Sub Timer_Tick(ByVal sender As Object, _
        ByVal e As EventArgs)
    CType(sender, Timer).Stop( )

    SetExecutingThreadLabel( _
```

Example 7-31. Effectively addressing InvokeRequired issue (continued)

```
            "Timer : " _
            & AppDomain.GetCurrentThreadId( ) & ": " _
            & InvokeRequired)
    End Sub

    Private Sub Timer_Elapsed( _
            ByVal sender As Object, _
            ByVal e As System.Timers.ElapsedEventArgs)
        CType(sender, System.Timers.Timer).Stop( )

        SetExecutingThreadLabel( _
            "Timer : " _
            & AppDomain.GetCurrentThreadId( ) & ": " _
            & InvokeRequired)

    End Sub

    Private Sub AsynchExecuted( )
        SetExecutingThreadLabel( _
            "Delegate : " _
            & AppDomain.GetCurrentThreadId( ) & ": " _
            & InvokeRequired)
    End Sub
```

As you can see from this example, the methods executed by the various threads don't have to worry about Invoke( ). They can simply call a method (SetExecutingThreadLabel( ) in this case) to communicate with the control, and that method determines if it has to use Invoke( ). This approach not only makes it easier, it also helps deal with situations where you may inadvertently access controls from the wrong thread.

(The output screens are not shown here, because the change in the code does not affect them, except that the thread IDs are different.)

 IN A NUTSHELL

Understand which thread is executing your code. This is critical to decide if you can communicate with your controls directly, or if you should use the System.Windows. Forms.Control.Invoke( ) method instead.

SEE ALSO

Gotcha #58, "Threads from the thread pool are scarce" and Gotcha #61, "Exceptions thrown from threads in the pool are lost."

#63 Web-service proxy may fail when used for multiple asynchronous calls

Say you are interested in making multiple independent requests to a web service that has a method with a delayed response. You can certainly take advantage of the asynchronous access that the service proxy generated by *wsdl.exe*/Visual Studio provides. However, if you want to make more than one request at the same time, should you use the same proxy instance or different instances?

Taking a closer look at the `BeginInvoke( )` and `EndInvoke( )` methods of the proxy, it is clear that when you call `BeginInvoke( )`, you are given an `IAsyncResult` handle. When you call `EndInvoke( )`, you send this handle to it and get the result for that specific invocation. Doesn't that suggest that you can make multiple asynchronous requests using a single instance of the proxy?

As it turns out, you can. However, you need to understand some issues from the web server's point of view.

I have been asked this question quite a few times. I even ran into this situation inadvertently, and came to the realization illustrated in Examples 7-32 through 7-35.

Example 7-32. Multiple calls on a web service (C# server side)

✗ C# (MultipleWSCalls), server side

```
//MyService.asmx.cs part of ACSWSForMultiRequest.dll (Web Service)
using System;
using System.Collections;
using System.ComponentModel;
using System.Data;
using System.Diagnostics;
using System.Web;
using System.Web.Services;

namespace ACSWSForMultiRequest
{
    [WebService(Namespace="http://www.ACSWSForMultiRequest.com")]
    public class MyService : System.Web.Services.WebService
    {
        /// ...

        [WebMethod]
        public string Method1(int val)
        {
            System.Threading.Thread.Sleep(5000);
```

Example 7-32. Multiple calls on a web service (C# server side) (continued)

```
            return val.ToString( );
        }
    }
}
```

Example 7-33. Multiple calls on a web service (C# client side)

✗ C# (MultipleWSCalls), client side

```csharp
///Test.cs part of AClient.exe
using System;
using AClient.ACSWSForMultiRequest;

namespace AClient
{
    class Test
    {
        [STAThread]
        static void Main(string[] args)
        {
            MyService service = new MyService( );
            service.Credentials =
                System.Net.CredentialCache.DefaultCredentials;

            Console.WriteLine(
                "Making synchronous request at {0}",
                DateTime.Now.ToLongTimeString( ));

            Console.WriteLine("Recevied {0} at {1}",
                service.Method1(0),
                DateTime.Now.ToLongTimeString( ));

            Console.WriteLine("Making two requests at {0}",
                DateTime.Now.ToLongTimeString( ));

            service.BeginMethod1(1, new AsyncCallback(display),
                service);

            service.BeginMethod1(2, new AsyncCallback(display),
                service);

            Console.ReadLine( );
        }

        private static void display(IAsyncResult handle)
        {
            MyService theService =
                handle.AsyncState as MyService;
```

Example 7-33. Multiple calls on a web service (C# client side) (continued)

```
        string result = theService.EndMethod1(handle);

        Console.WriteLine("Result {0} received {1}",
            result, DateTime.Now.ToLongTimeString());
    }
  }
}
```

Example 7-34. Multiple calls on a web service (VB.NET server side)

✗ VB.NET (MultipleWSCalls), server side

```
'MyService.asmx.vb part of AVBWSForMultiRequest.dll (Web Service)
Imports System.Web.Services

<System.Web.Services.WebService(Namespace := _
    "http://tempuri.org/AVBWSForMultiRequest/MyService")> _
Public Class MyService
    Inherits System.Web.Services.WebService

        '...

    <WebMethod()> _
    Public Function Method1(ByVal val As Integer) As String
        System.Threading.Thread.Sleep(5000)
        Return val.ToString()
    End Function
End Class
```

Example 7-35. Multiple calls on a web service (VB.NET client side)

✗ VB.NET (MultipleWSCalls), client side

```
''Test.vb part of AClient.exe
Imports AClient.AVSWSForMultiRequest

Module Test

    Sub Main()
        Dim service As New MyService
        service.Credentials = _
         System.Net.CredentialCache.DefaultCredentials

        Console.WriteLine( _
            "Making synchronous request at {0}", _
            DateTime.Now.ToLongTimeString())
```

Example 7-35. Multiple calls on a web service (VB.NET client side) (continued)

```
        Console.WriteLine("Recevied {0} at {1}", _
          service.Method1(0), _
          DateTime.Now.ToLongTimeString( ))

        Console.WriteLine("Making two requests at {0}", _
          DateTime.Now.ToLongTimeString( ))

        service.BeginMethod1(1, _
            New AsyncCallback(AddressOf display), service)

        service.BeginMethod1(2, _
            New AsyncCallback(AddressOf display), service)

        Console.ReadLine( )
    End Sub

    Private Sub display(ByVal handle As IAsyncResult)
        Dim theService As MyService = _
          CType(handle.AsyncState, MyService)

        Dim result As String = theService.EndMethod1(handle)

        Console.WriteLine("Result {0} received {1}", _
          result, DateTime.Now.ToLongTimeString( ))
    End Sub

End Module
```

In this example, the web service has a method Method1( ) that has an artificial delay to simulate some activity. The client first makes one synchronous call, to which it gets a response after five seconds. (The reason you see an additional two-second delay on the first call is that the web service warms up when it receives the first request.) Then the client makes two asynchronous calls, one right after the other. The output from the above program is shown in Figure 7-30.

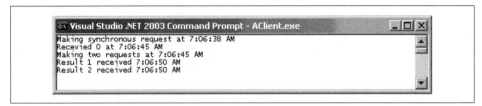

Figure 7-30. Output from Example 7-32

No problem—so far. Now, let's say the service maintains state and expects the client code to set the proxy's CookieContainer property, as shown in Example 7-36.

Example 7-36. Making multiple calls when session is maintained

✗ C# (MultipleWSCalls)

```csharp
//MyService.asmx.cs part of ACSWSForMultiRequest.dll (Web Service)

...
        [WebMethod(true)]
        public string Method1(int val)
        {
            System.Threading.Thread.Sleep(5000);
            return val.ToString();
        }
...


//Test.cs. part of AClient.exe

...

            MyService service = new MyService();
            service.CookieContainer =
                new System.Net.CookieContainer();

            service.Credentials =
                System.Net.CredentialCache.DefaultCredentials;

...
```

✗ VB.NET (MultipleWSCalls)

```vbnet
'MyService.asmx.vb part of AVBWSForMultiRequest.dll (Web Service)
...
    <WebMethod(True)> _
    Public Function Method1(ByVal val As Integer) As String
        System.Threading.Thread.Sleep(5000)
        Return val.ToString()
    End Function
...


'Test.vb part of AClient.exe

...

        Dim service As New MyService
        service.CookieContainer = _
         New System.Net.CookieContainer

        service.Credentials = _
```

Example 7-36. Making multiple calls when session is maintained (continued)

```
System.Net.CredentialCache.DefaultCredentials
```

...

In this code you have made one change to the web service. In the `WebMethod` attribute, you have set the parameter (true) to enable session management. You have also set the `CookieContainer` property on the client proxy to a non-null reference. Let's run the application now and see what the response is. The output is shown in Figure 7-31.

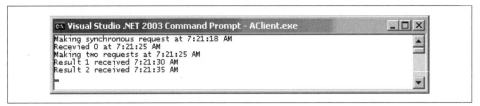

Figure 7-31. Output from Example 7-36

Even though the two asynchronous requests are made simultaneously, the responses are separated by a five-second delay. This is because on the server side the requests get serialized. The web service recognizes the session id from the cookie that the proxy transmits and determines that the two requests belong to the same session. As a result, in order to avoid any threading conflicts, it serializes the requests, allowing only one request belonging to a session to execute at a time.

 IN A NUTSHELL

When you send multiple concurrent requests to a web service, do not use the same proxy instance if you set the `CookieContainer` property on the proxy, or if session state is supported by the web service. Doing so causes the requests to execute consecutively on the server, rather than concurrently. If consecutive behavior is what you want, then this is a good approach.

SEE ALSO

Gotcha #58, "Threads from the thread pool are scarce" and Gotcha #61, "Exceptions thrown from threads in the pool are lost."

#64 Raising events lacks thread-safety

When you are about to raise an event, what happens if all handlers for that event are suddenly removed by other threads? What you don't want is for your program to crash with a `NullReferenceException`, which it may well do if you aren't careful. In Gotcha #7, "Uninitialized event handlers aren't treated gracefully," I discussed the issues with raising events. At the end of that gotcha I raised a concern about thread safety. In this gotcha I address that.

Unfortunately, this problem manifests itself slightly differently in C# than it does in VB.NET. First, I'll discuss the problem with raising events in VB.NET. Then I'll discuss the same problem in C#. The discussion regarding VB.NET is relevant for C# programmers as I build on it.

First, RaiseEvent() in VB.NET is not thread-safe. Consider the example in Example 7-37.

Example 7-37. Example of RaiseEvent in VB.NET

✗ VB.NET (RaisingEventThreadSafety)

```vb
Imports System.Threading

Public Class AComponent
    Public Event myEvent As EventHandler

    Private Sub DoWork()
        Thread.Sleep(5) ' Simulate some work delay
        RaiseEvent myEvent(Me, New EventArgs)
    End Sub
    Public Sub Work()
        Dim aThread As New Thread(AddressOf DoWork)
        aThread.Start()
    End Sub
End Class

'Test.vb
Imports System.Threading

Module Test

    Private Sub TestHandler(ByVal sender As Object, ByVal e As EventArgs)
        Console.WriteLine("TestHandler called")
    End Sub
```

Example 7-37. Example of RaiseEvent in VB.NET (continued)

```
Sub Main()
    Dim obj As New AComponent

    AddHandler obj.myEvent, AddressOf TestHandler

    obj.Work()

    Thread.Sleep(5)

    RemoveHandler obj.myEvent, AddressOf TestHandler
End Sub

End Module
```

In the Work( ) method of the AComponent class, you call the DoWork( ) method in a separate thread. In the DoWork( ) method you raise an event after a small delay (5ms). In the Main( ) method of the Test class you create an instance of AComponent, register a handler with it, then call its Work( ) method. You then quickly (after a delay of 5 ms) remove the handler you registered. A quick run of this program produces the output in Figure 7-32.

Figure 7-32. Output from AComponent.vb

It worked this time, but you just got lucky—lucky that the thread executing DoWork( ) got to its RaiseEvent( ) before Main( ) got to its RemoveHandler( ). With the code the way it is, though, there's no guarantee things will always turn out so well.

There's good news and there's bad news. First, let's look at the good news. AddHandler and RemoveHandler are thread-safe. The VB.NET compiler translates them into calls to special hidden thread-safe add and remove methods (add_myEvent( ) and remove_myEvent( ) in this case). You can verify this by observing the MSIL code for Example 7-37 in Figure 7-33.

Notice that AddHandler( ) is translated to a call to the add_myEvent( ) method. add_myEvent( ) is marked synchronized (as you can see at the top of Figure 7-34). What does that mean? When add_myEvent( ) is called, it gains a lock on the AComponent instance that myEvent belongs to. Within the method, the registration of the handler (by the call to the Combine( ) method on the delegate) is done with thread safety. The code for remove_myEvent( ) method is similarly thread-safe. You can see this by examining the MSIL (not shown here) using ildasm.exe.

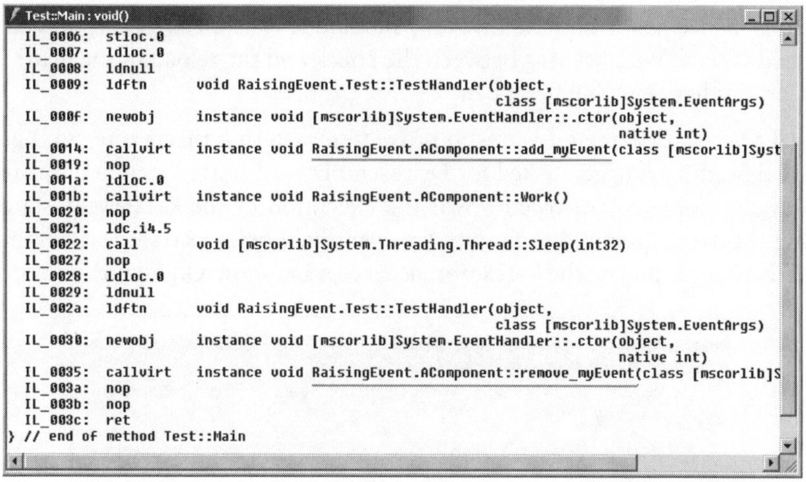

```
Test::Main : void()
  IL_0006:  stloc.0
  IL_0007:  ldloc.0
  IL_0008:  ldnull
  IL_0009:  ldftn      void RaisingEvent.Test::TestHandler(object,
                                                        class [mscorlib]System.EventArgs)
  IL_000f:  newobj     instance void [mscorlib]System.EventHandler::.ctor(object,
                                                                      native int)
  IL_0014:  callvirt   instance void RaisingEvent.AComponent::add_myEvent(class [mscorlib]Syst
  IL_0019:  nop
  IL_001a:  ldloc.0
  IL_001b:  callvirt   instance void RaisingEvent.AComponent::Work()
  IL_0020:  nop
  IL_0021:  ldc.i4.5
  IL_0022:  call       void [mscorlib]System.Threading.Thread::Sleep(int32)
  IL_0027:  nop
  IL_0028:  ldloc.0
  IL_0029:  ldnull
  IL_002a:  ldftn      void RaisingEvent.Test::TestHandler(object,
                                                        class [mscorlib]System.EventArgs)
  IL_0030:  newobj     instance void [mscorlib]System.EventHandler::.ctor(object,
                                                                      native int)
  IL_0035:  callvirt   instance void RaisingEvent.AComponent::remove_myEvent(class [mscorlib]S
  IL_003a:  nop
  IL_003b:  nop
  IL_003c:  ret
} // end of method Test::Main
```

Figure 7-33. MSIL for AddHandler and RemoveHandler calls in Example 7-37

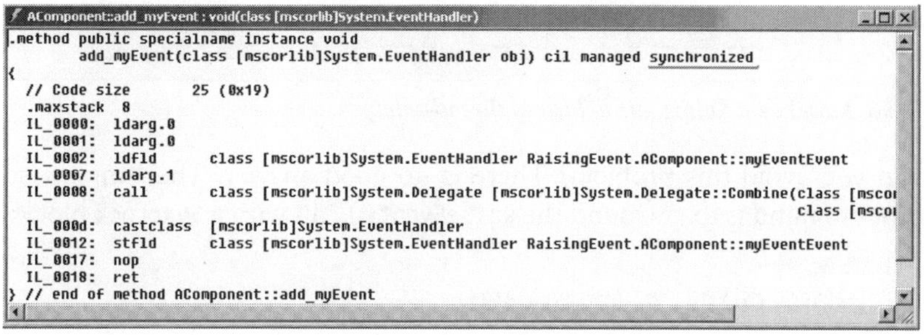

```
AComponent::add_myEvent : void(class [mscorlib]System.EventHandler)
.method public specialname instance void
        add_myEvent(class [mscorlib]System.EventHandler obj) cil managed synchronized
{
  // Code size       25 (0x19)
  .maxstack  8
  IL_0000:  ldarg.0
  IL_0001:  ldarg.0
  IL_0002:  ldfld      class [mscorlib]System.EventHandler RaisingEvent.AComponent::myEventEvent
  IL_0007:  ldarg.1
  IL_0008:  call       class [mscorlib]System.Delegate [mscorlib]System.Delegate::Combine(class [msco
                                                                                         class [msco
  IL_000d:  castclass  [mscorlib]System.EventHandler
  IL_0012:  stfld      class [mscorlib]System.EventHandler RaisingEvent.AComponent::myEventEvent
  IL_0017:  nop
  IL_0018:  ret
} // end of method AComponent::add_myEvent
```

Figure 7-34. Auto-generated hidden special thread-safe add_myEvent() method

Unfortunately, `RaiseEvent` is not thread-safe, as you can see from the MSIL in Figure 7-35.

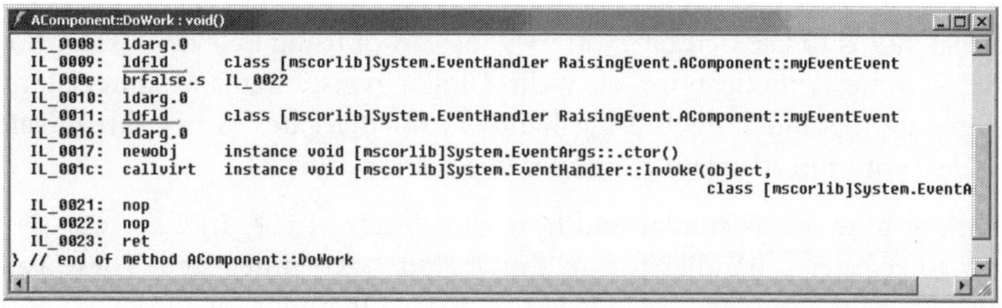

```
AComponent::DoWork : void()
  IL_0008:  ldarg.0
  IL_0009:  ldfld      class [mscorlib]System.EventHandler RaisingEvent.AComponent::myEventEvent
  IL_000e:  brfalse.s  IL_0022
  IL_0010:  ldarg.0
  IL_0011:  ldfld      class [mscorlib]System.EventHandler RaisingEvent.AComponent::myEventEvent
  IL_0016:  ldarg.0
  IL_0017:  newobj     instance void [mscorlib]System.EventArgs::.ctor()
  IL_001c:  callvirt   instance void [mscorlib]System.EventHandler::Invoke(object,
                                                                  class [mscorlib]System.EventA
  IL_0021:  nop
  IL_0022:  nop
  IL_0023:  ret
} // end of method AComponent::DoWork
```

Figure 7-35. MSIL for RaiseEvent that shows lack of thread-safety

The event field is first loaded and verified to be not Nothing. If the test succeeds, then the field is loaded again, and the Invoke( ) method is called. Here is the gotcha: what if the field is set to null/Nothing between the check and the reload of the field? Tough luck. Can this happen? You bet it can.

I wanted to go to extreme measures to prove to myself that this is true. So, I got into the Visual Studio debugger, asked for Disassembly, and started stepping through the assembly. By doing so, I slowed down the execution of the RaiseEvent statement, allowing the Main( ) method to modify the event field before RaiseEvent completes. I had no trouble producing the NullReferenceException shown in Figure 7-36

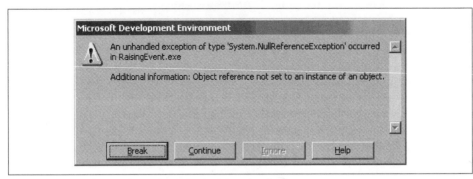

Figure 7-36. RaiseEvent failing due to lack of thread-safety

How can you avoid this problem? There is no good answer. The simplest solution that comes to mind is to surround the RaiseEvent( ) call with a SyncLock block:

```
SyncLock Me
    RaiseEvent myEvent(Me, New EventArgs)
End SyncLock
```

While this certainly provides thread safety from concurrent AddHandler and RemoveHandler calls, it may also delay the registration and unregistration of handlers if the event-handler list is large. It would be nice if you could get the list of delegates from the event. Unfortunately, the VB.NET compiler does not allow you to access the underlying delegate (the C# compiler does).

One possibility is to use delegates directly instead of using an event. This, however, introduces some complications as well. Unlike registering and unregistering for events, registering and unregistering handlers for delegates is not thread-safe; you have to deal with thread safety yourself if you go this route.

Let's look at how this is similar and how this differs in C#. In C#, you use the += operator to register a handler for an event, and -= to unregister. These two calls become calls to the hidden special add and remove methods, as discussed above for VB.NET. Providing thread safety while raising events in C# is pretty easy. The code in Example 7-38 shows how to do that.

Example 7-38. C# example to raise event with thread-safety

✔ **C# (RaisingEventThreadSafety)**

```csharp
//AComponent.cs

using System;
using System.Threading;

namespace RaisingEvent
{
    public class AComponent
    {
        public event EventHandler myEvent;

        private void DoWork()
        {
            EventHandler localHandler = null;
            lock(this)
            {
                if (myEvent != null)
                {
                    Console.WriteLine("myEvent is not null");
                    Thread.Sleep(2000);
                    // Intentional delay to illustrate

                    localHandler = myEvent;
                    Console.WriteLine("Got a safe copy");
                }
            }

            if (localHandler != null)
            {
                localHandler(this, new EventArgs());
            }
            else
            {
                Console.WriteLine("localHandler is null!!!!!!!!!!!!");
            }
        }

        public void Work()
        {
            Thread aThread = new Thread(
                new ThreadStart(DoWork));

            aThread.Start();
        }
    }
}

//Test.cs
```

Example 7-38. C# example to raise event with thread-safety (continued)

```
using System;
using System.Threading;

namespace RaisingEvent
{
    public class Test
    {
        private static void TestHandler(
            object sender, EventArgs e)
        {
            Console.WriteLine("Handler called");
        }

        public static void TestIt()
        {
            AComponent obj = new AComponent();
            obj.myEvent += new EventHandler(TestHandler);

            obj.Work();

            Thread.Sleep(1000);

            Console.WriteLine("Trying to unregister handler");
            obj.myEvent -= new EventHandler(TestHandler);
            Console.WriteLine("handler unregistered");
        }

        public static void Main()
        {
            TestIt();
        }
    }
}
```

The output from this example is shown in Figure 7-37. You can see that the remove-handler code (the -= operator) in the TestIt( ) method blocks while a copy of the *reference* to myEvent is made in DoWork( ).

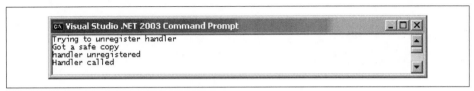

Figure 7-37. Output from Example 7-38 illustrates thread-safety

Well, that looks good. Are you done? I wish. For its share, C# has made a mess with the thread safety of events when the registration and unregistration of handlers is done inside the class owning the event. But first, let's quickly take a look at the MSIL for the TestIt( ) method as shown in Figure 7-38.

Figure 7-38. MSIL for the Test.TestIt() method in Example 7-38

As you can see, the call to += in the source code of Testit( ) method uses the thread-safe add_myEvent( ) method at the MSIL level. This is good news.

Now, copy the TestIt( ) method and the TestHandler( ) method from the Test class to the AComponent class, compile the code and take a look at the MSIL (shown in Figure 7-39).

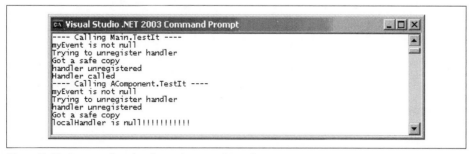

Figure 7-39. MSIL for AComponent.Testit() method

Unfortunately, this version uses the Combine( ) method directly instead of the thread-safe add_myEvent( ) method. Let's make a small change to Main( ) as shown below. The output after this change is shown in Figure 7-40.

Figure 7-40. Output after the above change to Main()

```csharp
public static void Main()
{
    Console.WriteLine("---- Calling Main.TestIt ----");
    TestIt();
    Thread.Sleep(5000);
    Console.WriteLine("---- Calling AComponent.TestIt ----");
    AComponent.TestIt();
}
```

You would expect the result of the calls to Test.TestIt( ) and AComponent.TestIt( ) to be identical, but they're not. This is because event registration and unregistration are not thread-safe within the class that contains the event.

While this gotcha is a problem in C#, it does not exist in VB.NET. AddHandler( ) and RemoveHandler( ) are consistently thread-safe no matter where they're called from.

🥜 IN A NUTSHELL

- Calls to register and unregister events are thread-safe in VB.NET.
- In C#, they are thread-safe only if called from outside the class with the event. For calls within the class, you must provide thread safety yourself by calling += or -= within a lock(this) statement.
- The thread-safe calls to register and unregister events rely on the special hidden thread-safe add and remove methods, respectively.
- Calls to RaiseEvent in VB.NET are inherently not thread-safe. You need to take care of thread-safety for these calls.
- You can use the underlying delegate to raise the event in a thread-safe manner in C#. You achieve this by getting a local reference to the delegate within a lock(this) statement and then using the local reference (if not null) to raise the event.

SEE ALSO

Gotcha #7, "Uninitialized event handlers aren't treated gracefully," Gotcha #56, "Calling Type.GetType() may not return what you expect," Gotcha #57, "Locking on globally visible objects is too sweeping," and Gotcha #62, "Accessing WinForm controls from arbitrary threads is dangerous."

CHAPTER 8

COM-Interop and Enterprise Services Gotchas

COM-Interop in .NET allows a .NET component to communicate with a COM component using a Runtime Callable Wrapper. It also makes it possible for unmanaged code to talk to a .NET component as if it's a COM component by way of a COM Callable Wrapper. These facilities and the related API make it easier to interoperate. However, you need to give due consideration to the object life cycle and threading issues to get the most out of interoperability. Furthermore, the quickest way to expose a .NET object for COM interoperability is to set the project settings to Register for COM interop. While this may be the "it's that simple" approach, you need to watch out for a number of things. In this chapter I focus on details you should be aware of to make interoperability work for you. I also delve into issues related to Enterprise Services, a set of classes that allows you to programmatically utilize the COM+ services in the .NET Framework.

I assume that you are fairly familiar with COM [Box98]. The discussions in this chapter are intended for programmers with COM knowledge (aCOMplished programmers?!) and interested in .NET to COM interoperability. The gotchas are organized as follows:

- Gotchas 65–70 discuss issues with using COM components in .NET.
- Gotchas 71–73 are about using .NET classes from unmanaged code through COM.
- Gotchas 74–75 deal with Enterprise Services.

GOTCHA

#65 Release of COM object is confusing

Programming with COM in C++ has always been quite a task. You can recognize C++ COM programmers by the scars on their bodies. By comparison, VB6 COM programming is easier. I have heard that one of Microsoft's goals for .NET is to make

COM interoperability as simple as possible. Unfortunately, they have reached something of a middle ground, and even VB.NET programmers have to do some extra work now to clean up COM objects.

In C++, you have to call Release( ) on an interface pointer when you are done with the COM object. Forgetting to call Release( ) leaves the COM component stuck in memory. In VB6, setting the reference to Nothing is sufficient; the call to Release( ) is done automatically.

In .NET, you use a Runtime Callable Wrapper (RCW) to communicate with the COM component. As you would guess, the RCW takes care of releasing the component when it is cleaned up. However, you don't have much control over the timing of the garbage collection. So, the logical thought is to Dispose( ) the RCW when you're done with it. Sorry, the RCW doesn't implement the IDisposable interface. It would be easier if it did, wouldn't it? So what should you do?

Suppose you have a COM component (not shown here) which pops up a message box (just for demo purposes) when an object is created and also when it's destroyed. Look at the .NET code that communicates with this component in Example 8-1.

Example 8-1. Problem releasing the COM object

✗ C# (ThouShaltReleaseObject)

```
using System;

namespace COMCompUser
{
    class Test
    {
        [STAThread]
        static void Main(string[] args)
        {
            Console.WriteLine("Creating object");
            MyCOMCompLib.IMyComp theMyComp
                = new MyCOMCompLib.MyCompClass( );

            Console.WriteLine("Calling Method1");
            theMyComp.Method1( );

            //Console.WriteLine("Releasing the object");
            //System.Runtime.InteropServices.Marshal.ReleaseComObject(
            //    theMyComp);

            Console.WriteLine("Setting reference to null");
            theMyComp = null;

            Console.WriteLine("Has the Object been destroyed?");
            Console.ReadLine( );
```

Example 8-1. Problem releasing the COM object (continued)

```
        }
    }
}
```

✗ VB.NET (ThouShaltReleaseObject)

```
Module Test

    Sub Main( )
        Console.WriteLine("Creating object")
        Dim theMyComp As MyCOMCompLib.IMyComp _
            = New MyCOMCompLib.MyCompClass

        Console.WriteLine("Calling Method1")
        theMyComp.Method1( )

        'Console.WriteLine("Releasing the object")
        'System.Runtime.InteropServices.Marshal.ReleaseComObject( _
        '    theMyComp)

        Console.WriteLine("Setting reference to null")
        theMyComp = Nothing

        Console.WriteLine("Has the Object been destroyed?")
        Console.ReadLine( )
    End Sub

End Module
```

In this example you create an RCW for the COM component. You call Method1( ) on it, then set the reference to the RCW to null/Nothing. As the above code executes, you get the output shown in Figures 8-1 through 8-3.

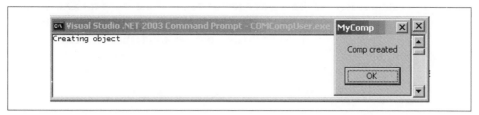

Figure 8-1. Object created

The object is created (Figure 8-1) and Method1( ) is called (Figure 8-2). However, the object has not been destroyed yet (Figure 8-3). Pressing Return now, in response to Console.ReadLine( ), will pop up the message box showing that the object has been destroyed. As you can see, setting the reference to null/Nothing does not release the object, a departure from COM component interaction in VB6.

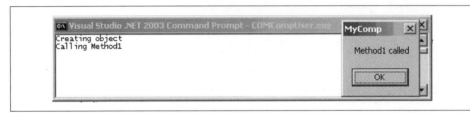

Figure 8-2. Calling Method1( )

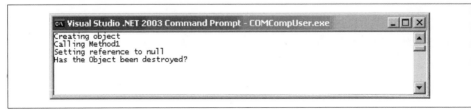

Figure 8-3. Has the object been destroyed?

How can you clean up the object? As I mentioned, there is no Dispose( ) method you can call using the RCW reference. To properly release the object in Example 8-1, uncomment the two commented-out statements in the Main( ) method. This gives you:

```
Console.WriteLine("Releasing the object");
System.Runtime.InteropServices.Marshal.ReleaseComObject(
    theMyComp);
```

When you are done using the component, you invoke the System.Runtime. InteropServices.Marshal.ReleaseComObject( ) static/Shared method. This releases the COM component at that very moment without waiting for the garbage collector. (It's better to call ReleaseComObject( ) from a finally block to make sure the object is released even if an exception occurs.)

Should you call ReleaseComObject( ) as soon as you're done using a COM component? Well, if you don't call it, the object is held until the garbage collector eventually (and much later than you might desire), decides to clean it up. The program could end up holding critical resources for an extended period of time, and this might also affect the overall performance of the system.

However, calling ReleaseComObject( ) has risks. (The next gotcha discusses one of them.) If you are not worried about resources being held for too long, then do not bother using ReleaseComObject( ). This is especially true for client applications. If, on the other hand, you are concerned about out-of-process unmanaged resources being held (especially in a server application), then you need to use ReleaseComObject( ).

For insight into other problems with ReleaseComObject( ), see the blogs referenced in "ReleaseComObject( ) issues" in the "On the Web" section of the Appendix.

IN A NUTSHELL

When you are done using a COM component, if you want any critical resources to be cleaned up right away, release it using the `ReleaseComObject( )` static/Shared method of the `System.Runtime.InteropServices.Marshal` class. Do so in a `finally` block. Note the risks with `ReleaseComObject( )`, however.

SEE ALSO

Gotcha #66, "Using interface pointers after calling ReleaseComObject() will fail" and Gotcha #70, "Spattering access to COM components makes code hard to maintain."

GOTCHA

#66 Using interface pointers after calling ReleaseComObject( ) will fail

As I mentioned in Gotcha #65, "Release of COM object is confusing," there are a few problems with using the `ReleaseComObject( )` method. In this gotcha I discuss one of those issues—dealing with multiple interfaces.

When working with COM components you often use more than one interface. For instance, say you have a component that exposes two interfaces, `IMyComp` and `IMyComp2`. When using these two interfaces, which one should you release? Those of you who have worked with COM in C++ or VB6 are probably saying, "Both of them, of course." But in .NET, that is not the case. You can't continue to use a COM component after you have called `ReleaseComObject( )` on *any* of the interface references to that component.

Let's pursue an example where a COM component supports the two interfaces `IMyComp` and `IMyComp2`, with one method in each, `Method1( )` and `Method2( )`. Example 8-2 shows the .NET code to access it.

Example 8-2. Working with multiple interfaces of a COM component

✗ C# (COMInterfaces)

```
using System;

namespace COMCompUser
{
    class Test
    {
        [STAThread]
        static void Main(string[] args)
        {
```

Example 8-2. Working with multiple interfaces of a COM component (continued)

```
        Console.WriteLine("Creating object");
        MyCOMCompLib.IMyComp theMyComp
            = new MyCOMCompLib.MyCompClass( );

        MyCOMCompLib.IMyComp2 theMyComp2
            = (MyCOMCompLib.IMyComp2) theMyComp;

        Console.WriteLine("Calling Method1");
        theMyComp.Method1( );

        Console.WriteLine("Releasing the object");
        System.Runtime.InteropServices.Marshal.ReleaseComObject(
            theMyComp);

        Console.WriteLine("Calling Method2");
        theMyComp2.Method2( );
        Console.ReadLine( );
    }
  }
}
```

✗ VB.NET (COMInterfaces)

```
Module Test

    Sub Main( )
        Console.WriteLine("Creating object")
        Dim theMyComp As MyCOMCompLib.IMyComp _
            = New MyCOMCompLib.MyCompClass

        Dim theMyComp2 As MyCOMCompLib.IMyComp2 _
            = CType(theMyComp, MyCOMCompLib.IMyComp2)

        Console.WriteLine("Calling Method1")
        theMyComp.Method1( )

        Console.WriteLine("Releasing the object")
            System.Runtime.InteropServices.Marshal.ReleaseComObject( _
                theMyComp)

        Console.WriteLine("Calling Method2")
        theMyComp2.Method2( )
        Console.ReadLine( )
    End Sub

End Module
```

In this example, you obtain two references to the COM component, one for each of its interfaces. You then release the first reference using ReleaseComObject( ). When

---

you invoke Method2() using the IMyComp2 interface reference, you get a NullReferenceException, as shown in Figure 8-4.

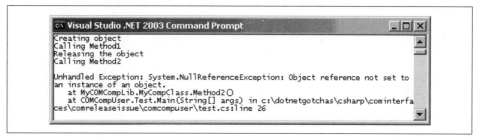

```
Creating object
Calling Method1
Releasing the object
Calling Method2

Unhandled Exception: System.NullReferenceException: Object reference not set to
an instance of an object.
    at MyCOMCompLib.MyCompClass.Method2()
    at COMCompUser.Test.Main(String[] args) in c:\dotnetgotchas\csharp\cominterfa
ces\comreleaseissue\comcompuser\test.cs:line 26
```

Figure 8-4. Output from Example 8-2

The exception is raised from the RCW because, as its name implies, ReleaseComObject() has released the object. Working with a COM component using the interface reference in .NET is different from C++ and VB6.

Understand the issues related to proper cleanup and the state of the RCW. This is another reason to isolate the interaction with the component as discussed in Gotcha #70, "Spattering access to COM components makes code hard to maintain."

 IN A NUTSHELL

If you have obtained multiple interfaces on a COM component, do not use any of the references after calling ReleaseComObject. The RCW disconnects from the COM object when you call ReleaseComObject(). Understand that calling ReleaseComObject() is not the same as calling IUnknown's Release() method.

SEE ALSO

Gotcha #65, "Release of COM object is confusing" and Gotcha #70, "Spattering access to COM components makes code hard to maintain."

GOTCHA
#67 Cross-apartment calls are expensive

One of the goals of COM is to make it easier to substitute one component for another. You should be able to swap out a component that supports a set of interfaces and replace it with another one that supports the same set of interfaces and abides by their implied contract. The client must be able to interchange multiple components that satisfy a set of interface contracts, and interact with all of them in the same way.

What is the purpose of an *apartment* [Box98]? It is to make the component substitutable while having different threading needs. Say a component A takes care of thread safety. It is meant to be invoked from multiple threads simultaneously. Say another component B, which fulfills the same interface contract as component A, doesn't deal with thread safety. It is meant to be invoked from a single thread. How can a client swap these two components seamlessly?

The purpose of an apartment is to provide a logical thread isolation boundary in COM. A client thread executes in an apartment. The object may be created in the same or a different apartment. If the object is in the same apartment as the client, the calls to its methods are executed directly by the client thread. If they are in different apartments, then the client communicates using a proxy, and a method call request is sent to the other apartment. One of the threads in the other apartment picks up the request and executes it. An object that is not thread-safe is created in a Single Threaded Apartment (STA) while an object that can handle multiple threads is created in a Multithreaded Apartment (MTA). Once the apartment in which a thread will execute is decided, it is pretty much set.

While multiple threads may execute in an MTA, only one thread ever executes in an STA. What is the effect of multiple threads invoking a method on an object at the same time? If the object is in an STA, then the method calls are queued and the single thread that resides in the object's STA picks one call at a time and executes it. This guarantees that only one thread calls the object's methods at any time. If the object, however, is in an MTA, then multiple threads in the MTA will pick up requests from the queue and execute them simultaneously. Of course, if any of the calling threads are in the same apartment as the object, then the call will be direct and not go through a proxy, stub, and call message queue.

So, now that I have reviewed what apartments in COM are, what is the significance of this when it comes to .NET code that interacts with a COM component? If the component and client are in the same apartment, you have no COM overhead. You incur only the marshalling overhead (to go from .NET through an RCW to COM). However, if the client and the component are in different apartments, then you incur overhead at both levels. This is shown in Figure 8-5 and demonstrated in Example 8-3.

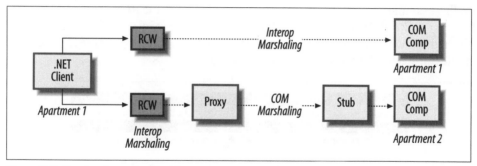

Figure 8-5. Overhead associated with cross-apartment invocation

Example 8-3. Effect of apartment-related attributes

✗ C# (Apartment)

```csharp
using System;

namespace COMCompUser
{
    class Test
    {
        [STAThread] // You will see the effect of this attribute
        static void Main(string[] args)
        {
            MyCOMCompLib.IMyComp theMyComp
                = new MyCOMCompLib.MyCompClass();

            theMyComp.Method1();
        }
    }
}
```

✗ VB.NET (Apartment)

```vbnet
Module Test

    'You will see the effect of this attribute
    <STAThread()> _
    Sub Main()
        Dim theMyComp as MyCOMCompLib.IMyComp _
                = new MyCOMCompLib.MyCompClass()

        theMyComp.Method1()
    End Sub

End Module
```

In this example, you create a COM component (actually the RCW of the COM component) and call Method1( ) on it. You place the STAThread attribute on the Main( ) method. Now, let's put a breakpoint in the COM component's Method1( ) and look at the call stack. The stack trace is shown in Figure 8-6.

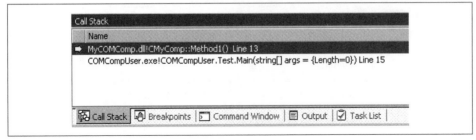

Figure 8-6. Stack trace of Method1 of COM component in Example 8-3

You are only two levels deep in the call stack in this case. Now, change the STAThread attribute in the Main( ) method to MTAThread, as shown in Example 8-4, and rerun the program.

Example 8-4. Changing the apartment of Main() method

✗ C# (Apartment)

```
//...
[MTAThread] // You will see the effect of this attribute
static void Main(string[] args)
//...
```

✗ VB.NET (Apartment)

```
'...
'You will see the effect of this attribute
<MTAThread( )> _
Sub Main( )
    '...
```

Figure 8-7 shows the new call stack (or as much of it as will fit).

The call stack is 59 levels deep. What made the difference? The client code is running in an MTA while the component resides in a STA. The call to the method now has to go through a proxy and a stub. It is better to avoid this overhead when invoking COM components. While in principle COM isolates the threading needs of a component from its client, you still need to be sensitive to the impact on performance.

So how do you interact efficiently with two components that have different threading models? You might consider creating two different threads in your .NET applica-

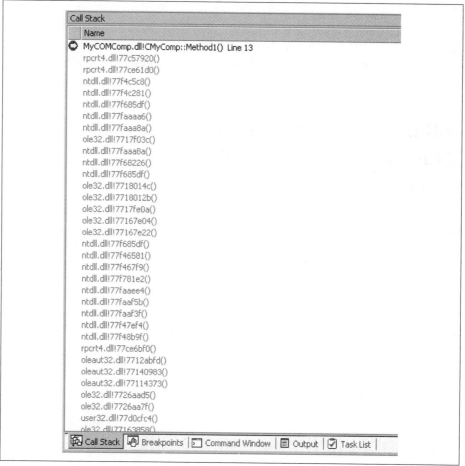

Figure 8-7. COM component's Method1() call stack for Example 8-4

tion, one in an STA and the other in an MTA, then interact with the COM components from the appropriate threads, based on the COM component's apartment. This is another reason to isolate the interaction with the component as discussed in Gotcha #70, "Spattering access to COM components makes code hard to maintain." You can find the apartment of the COM object by looking at the ThreadingModel in its Registry settings, or by reading its documentation. Details of setting the apartment of a thread are presented later in Example 8-7.

IN A NUTSHELL

Understand the apartment of your thread to get the best performance when interacting with COM components. If possible, invoke methods on a COM component from the same apartment as the component.

SEE ALSO

Gotcha #68, "Default apartment of main thread is inconsistent across languages," Gotcha #69, "STAThread attribute may have no effect on your methods," and Gotcha #70, "Spattering access to COM components makes code hard to maintain."

GOTCHA

#68 Default apartment of main thread is inconsistent across languages

In Example 8-3 you first marked the Main( ) method with the STAThread attribute, then in Example 8-4 changed it to MTAThread. What is the apartment if you do not mark Main( ) with either attribute? The answer, unfortunately, depends on which language you are using. Consider Example 8-5.

Example 8-5. Default apartment

✗ C# (DefaultApartment)

```csharp
using System;
using System.Threading;

namespace COMCompUser
{
    class Test
    {
        static void Worker( )
        {
            Thread currentThread = Thread.CurrentThread;
            Console.WriteLine("In worker thread");

            Console.WriteLine("Apartment in worker is {0}",
                currentThread.ApartmentState.ToString( ));

            Console.WriteLine("Creating COM object");
            MyCOMCompLib.IMyComp theMyComp
                = new MyCOMCompLib.MyCompClass( );

            Console.WriteLine("Apartment in worker is {0}",
                currentThread.ApartmentState.ToString( ));
        }

        static void Main(string[] args)
        {
            Thread currentThread = Thread.CurrentThread;
```

Example 8-5. Default apartment (continued)

```
            Console.WriteLine("Apartment in main is {0}",
                currentThread.ApartmentState.ToString());

            Console.WriteLine("Creating COM object");
            MyCOMCompLib.IMyComp theMyComp
                = new MyCOMCompLib.MyCompClass();

            Console.WriteLine("Apartment in main is {0}",
                currentThread.ApartmentState.ToString());

            Thread workerThread = new Thread(
                new ThreadStart(Worker));
            //Not setting IsBackground on thread intentionally
            workerThread.Start();
        }
    }
}
```

✘ VB.NET (DefaultApartment)

```
Imports System.Threading

Module Test

    Private Sub Worker()
        Dim currentThread As Thread = Thread.CurrentThread
        Console.WriteLine("In worker thread")

        Console.WriteLine("Apartment in worker is {0}", _
                    currentThread.ApartmentState.ToString())

        Console.WriteLine("Creating COM object")
        Dim theMyComp as MyCOMCompLib.IMyComp _
                = new MyCOMCompLib.MyCompClass()

        Console.WriteLine("Apartment in worker is {0}", _
            currentThread.ApartmentState.ToString())
    End Sub

    Public Sub Main()
        Dim currentThread As Thread = Thread.CurrentThread

        Console.WriteLine("Apartment in main is {0}", _
            currentThread.ApartmentState.ToString())

        Console.WriteLine("Creating COM object")
        Dim theMyComp as MyCOMCompLib.IMyComp _
                = new MyCOMCompLib.MyCompClass()

        Console.WriteLine("Apartment in main is {0}", _
```

Example 8-5. Default apartment (continued)

```
        currentThread.ApartmentState.ToString())

        Dim workerThread As New Thread(AddressOf Worker)
        'Not setting IsBackground on thread intentionally
        workerThread.Start()
    End Sub
End Module
```

In this example, the apartment attribute is not set on the Main() and Worker() methods. When you execute the code, the output differs between the languages. The output from the C# version is shown in Figure 8-8; the VB.NET output appears in Figure 8-9.

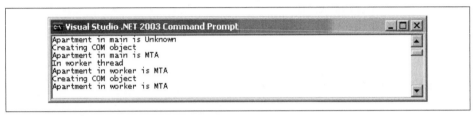

Figure 8-8. Output from the C# version of Example 8-5

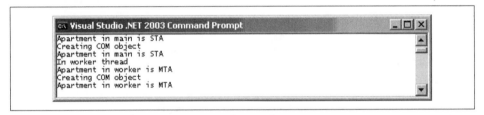

Figure 8-9. Output from the VB.NET version of Example 8-5

As you can see, the apartment of Main() is different between the C# and VB.NET versions. This is because in C#, if you don't set either STAThread or MTAThread, the apartment is first unknown. Once you access the COM component, it is set to MTA. In VB.NET, however, if you don't set either of the attributes, the compiler sets the STAThread automatically for Main(). (You'll see this if you view the MSIL for Main() with *ildasm.exe*.) But the apartment of the worker thread, i.e., the apartment within the Worker() method, is MTA for both languages. So the apartment of the Main() thread defaults to different values depending on the language used. This can be troublesome to programmers who have to maintain code in both languages.

 IN A NUTSHELL

Understand the apartment in which your thread is running. Don't assume or depend on the defaults. Set it explicitly to the desired value.

Gotcha #67, "Cross-apartment calls are expensive," Gotcha #69, "STAThread attribute may have no effect on your methods," and Gotcha #70, "Spattering access to COM components makes code hard to maintain."

GOTCHA

#69 STAThread attribute may have no effect on your methods

Let's continue with the discussions from Gotcha #68, "Default apartment of main thread is inconsistent across languages" You may think, "Well, I want my worker thread to be in an STA, so let me mark the method with the STAThread attribute just like it's done in Main( )." Is that a good idea? Let's find out. Consider Example 8-6.

Example 8-6. Effect of using the STAThreadAttribute

✗ C# (SettingApartment)

```
using System;
using System.Threading;

namespace COMCompUser
{
    class Test
    {
        [STAThread]
        static void Worker()
        {
            Thread currentThread = Thread.CurrentThread;
            Console.WriteLine("In worker thread");

            Console.WriteLine("Apartment in worker is {0}",
                currentThread.ApartmentState.ToString());

            Console.WriteLine("Creating COM object");
            MyCOMCompLib.IMyComp theMyComp
                = new MyCOMCompLib.MyCompClass();

            Console.WriteLine("Apartment in worker is {0}",
                currentThread.ApartmentState.ToString());
        }

        [STAThread]
        static void Main(string[] args)
        {
            Thread currentThread = Thread.CurrentThread;
```

Example 8-6. Effect of using the STAThreadAttribute (continued)

```csharp
            Console.WriteLine("Apartment in main is {0}",
                currentThread.ApartmentState.ToString());

            Console.WriteLine("Creating COM object");
            MyCOMCompLib.IMyComp theMyComp
                = new MyCOMCompLib.MyCompClass();

            Console.WriteLine("Apartment in main is {0}",
                currentThread.ApartmentState.ToString());

            Thread workerThread = new Thread(
                new ThreadStart(Worker));
            //Not setting IsBackground on thread intentionally
            workerThread.Start();
        }
    }
}
```

✗ VB.NET (SettingApartment)

```vbnet
Imports System.Threading

Module Test

    <STAThread()> _
    Private Sub Worker()

        Dim currentThread As Thread = Thread.CurrentThread

        Console.WriteLine("In worker thread")


        Console.WriteLine("Apartment in worker is {0}", _
                    currentThread.ApartmentState.ToString())

        Console.WriteLine("Creating COM object")
        Dim theMyComp As MyCOMCompLib.IMyComp _
         = New MyCOMCompLib.MyCompClass

        Console.WriteLine("Apartment in worker is {0}", _
         currentThread.ApartmentState.ToString())
    End Sub

    <STAThread()> _
    Public Sub Main()

        Dim currentThread As Thread = Thread.CurrentThread
        Console.WriteLine("Apartment in main is {0}", _
         currentThread.ApartmentState.ToString())
```

Example 8-6. Effect of using the STAThreadAttribute (continued)

```
        Console.WriteLine("Creating COM object")

        dim theMyComp as MyCOMCompLib.IMyComp _
                = new MyCOMCompLib.MyCompClass()

        Console.WriteLine("Apartment in main is {0}", _
         currentThread.ApartmentState.ToString())

        Dim workerThread As New Thread(AddressOf Worker)

        'Not setting IsBackground on thread intentionally
        workerThread.Start()
    End Sub

End Module
```

In this example, you have set the STAThread attribute on the Worker() method, which is called from a separate thread. If you expect the apartment of the thread within the Worker() method to be STA, you're in for a surprise. The output from the program is shown in Figure 8-10.

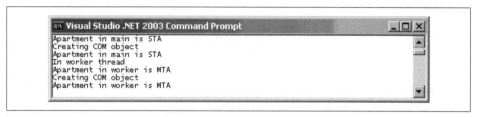

Figure 8-10. Output from Example 8-6

Even though you have set the STAThread attribute on the Worker() method, it is running in an MTA thread. How do you make Worker() run in an STA thread? The code that does that is shown in Example 8-7.

Example 8-7. Correct way to set apartment for a thread

✗ C# (SettingApartment)

```
//...
class Test
{
    //[STAThread]
    static void Worker()
    {
        //...
    }

    [STAThread]
```

Example 8-7. Correct way to set apartment for a thread (continued)

```
static void Main(string[] args)
{
    //...

    Thread workerThread = new Thread(
        new ThreadStart(Worker));
    //Not setting IsBackground on thread intentionally

    workerThread.ApartmentState = ApartmentState.STA;

    workerThread.Start();
}
}
}
```

✗ VB.NET (SettingApartment)

```
'...
Module Test

    '<STAThread()> _
    Private Sub Worker()
        '...

    End Sub

    <STAThread()> _
    Public Sub Main()

        '...

        Dim workerThread As New Thread(AddressOf Worker)

        workerThread.ApartmentState = ApartmentState.STA

        'Not setting IsBackground on thread intentionally
        workerThread.Start()
    End Sub

End Module
```

As soon as you create the thread, set the ApartmentState property on it. Don't set the STAThread attribute (or the MTAThread attribute) on methods like the Worker() method. The output from this modified version is shown in Figure 8-11.

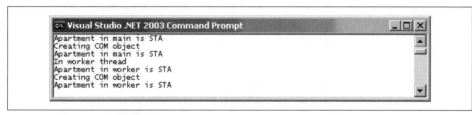

Figure 8-11. Output from Example 8-7

 IN A NUTSHELL

For threads that interact with COM components, set the apartment of the thread yourself; don't use method attributes to do so.

SEE ALSO

Gotcha #67, "Cross-apartment calls are expensive," Gotcha #68, "Default apartment of main thread is inconsistent across languages," and Gotcha #70, "Spattering access to COM components makes code hard to maintain."

GOTCHA

#70 Spattering access to COM components makes code hard to maintain

After reviewing the gotchas in communicating from .NET to COM, you might sit back with a deep breath and say, "Hmm, what a mess. How am I going to use all these correctly in my application?"

Well, let's start with how you use them incorrectly. The easiest way to fail at it is to call COM components from all over your code, as shown in Figure 8-12 (this diagram shows classes and not instances; instances of your .NET classes will talk to different instances of RCW during execution). In this figure, a number of .NET classes want to utilize a COM component. Each one of them creates an instance of RCW and interacts with it. The complexity of the application goes up in this approach for reasons mentioned below.

There are several things that you need to do when interacting with COM:

- Decide if you must release COM components when you no longer need them, or if you're content to let garbage collection take care of them.
- Communicate with COM components from the proper apartment.

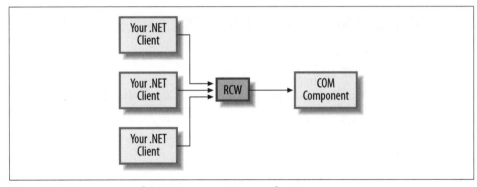

Figure 8-12. Improper use of COM component in an application

- Set the apartment of your .NET threads correctly.

- Don't use any interface on the COM component once you have called `ReleaseComObject()` on it.

How can you verify that your application follows these guidelines?

One easy way to manage this complexity is to isolate access to COM components in logical wrapper classes, as shown in Figure 8-13. First, build a .NET class that exposes the intended interface(s) of the COM component to the rest of the application. From within this wrapper class, you will interact with the COM Component(s). You can carefully manage the access and lifetime of the component(s) based on their apartment, state, and resource utilization. For example, by implementing the `IDisposable` interface and calling `ReleaseComObject()` in the `Dispose()` method, you can take care of proper cleanup of the COM component. Likewise, you can determine the apartment needs of the COM component and launch a thread with proper apartment settings to interact with it if required. The rest of your application does not have to worry about these details.

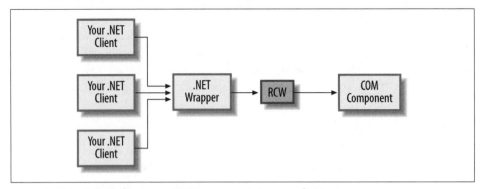

Figure 8-13. Isolation of access to COM components in an application

This isolation confers several benefits:

- It reduces the coupling of your code to the COM component.

- You can better manage the lifetime of the COM component.

- You can tailor the performance to take advantage of specific threading needs based on the apartment of the COM component.

- The rest of your system does not have to deal with the complexity of correctly interacting with COM components.

- You can focus on supporting the functionality of your application and map its implementation to the appropriate COM components.

- You can replace or substitute the COM component easily without affecting the rest of your application.

- In the future, if so desired, you can trade the COM component for an alternate .NET implementation with minimal impact on the code.

 IN A NUTSHELL

Route all interaction to the RCW of a COM component through a .NET wrapper class. This isolates the problems related to interoperability and makes your code easier to maintain.

SEE ALSO

Gotcha #65, "Release of COM object is confusing," Gotcha #66, "Using interface pointers after calling ReleaseComObject( ) will fail," Gotcha #67, "Cross-apartment calls are expensive," Gotcha #68, "Default apartment of main thread is inconsistent across languages," and Gotcha #69, "STAThread attribute may have no effect on your methods."

GOTCHA

#71 Auto-generating GUID for your classes leads to versioning woes

Let's switch focus to accessing your .NET classes from unmanaged code using COM.

How can you do that? You can use COM to achieve this—Microsoft has done something smart here. You can associate a GUID with a .NET component and register its assembly as if it were a COM component. In the Registry, the name and location of the assembly are stored under the key

```
HKEY_CLASSES_ROOT\CLSID\{...GUID...}\InprocServer32
```

(where ...GUID... is the GUID given to the .NET class) as shown in Figure 8-14.

The InprocServer32's Default key entry refers to the host component DLL as mscoree.dll, the primary DLL that initializes the CLR. Remember that when a

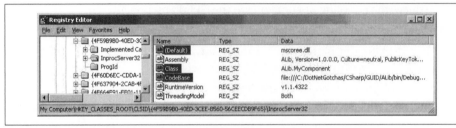

Figure 8-14. Registration of .NET class for access from COM

client activates a COM object, the component's DLL is loaded and the
`DllGetClassObject()` method is invoked with the CLSID/GUID for the component
as its parameter (again refer to [Box98]). If the CLSID/GUID is related to a .NET
class, the component DLL that's loaded is the CLR's `mscoree.dll`. It then finds the
name of the .NET class and the location of the assembly from the `Class` and
`CodeBase` entries in the Registry key. The CLR then creates a COM Callable Wrapper (CCW) object as a proxy for the client to interact with. This CCW manages and
properly routes the calls from the COM client to the .NET component. So.NET
classes can easily pretend to be COM components.

You know that every COM component has a Class ID or CLSID that is a Globally
Unique ID (GUID). In exposing a .NET class for COM interoperability, if you do not
specify a `GUID` attribute for the class, then a new GUID is created. According to the
documentation, the GUID that is automatically generated uniquely identifies the
combination of the namespace name and the class name. This is to guarantee that no
two classes will have the same GUID.

In practice though, the generated GUID is unique to the assembly version as well; i.e.,
the GUID generation scheme uses the namespace name, the class name, and the
assembly version number. This may actually be good in a lot of ways. However, what
if you change nothing but the revision number part of the four-part version number,
and the newer version is compatible with the older version? Say your intent is for clients that use the older version to use this newer version, which has a different revision
number, maybe because of a small bug fix. Consider Example 8-8.

 By default, the assembly version in your project is set to `1.0.*`. This
ends up generating a new version number each time you build your
project. That's trouble from the point of view of GUID generation.
Give a proper assembly version number for your projects.

Example 8-8. Problem with automatic GUID generation

 C# (GUID)

```
//MyComponent.cs
using System;
```

Example 8-8. Problem with automatic GUID generation (continued)

```csharp
namespace ALib
{
    public class MyComponent
    {
        public void Method1( )
        {
            //... whatever code goes here
        }
    }
}

//AssemblyInfo.cs
using System.Reflection;
using System.Runtime.CompilerServices;

//... (not shown)

//
// Version information for an assembly consists of the following four values:
//
//      Major Version
//      Minor Version
//      Build Number
//      Revision
//
// You can specify all the values or you can default the Revision and Build Numbers
// by using the '*' as shown below:

[assembly: AssemblyVersion("1.0.0.0")]
```

✗ VB.NET (GUID)

```vbnet
'MyComponent.vb

Public Class MyComponent
    Public Sub Method1( )
        '... whatever code goes here
    End Sub
End Class


'AssemblyInfo.vb
Imports System
Imports System.Reflection
Imports System.Runtime.InteropServices

' ... (Not shown)
```

Example 8-8. Problem with automatic GUID generation (continued)

```
' Version information for an assembly consists of the following four values:
'
'       Major Version
'       Minor Version
'       Build Number
'       Revision
'
' You can specify all the values or you can default the Build and Revision Numbers
' by using the '*' as shown below:
```

<Assembly: AssemblyVersion("1.0.0.0")>

For the above assembly, the version number is 1.0.0.0. You have selected Register for COM Interop in the project settings. Part of the registration information created from this assembly is shown in Example 8-9.

Example 8-9. COM Registration information for .NET component

```
REGEDIT4

[HKEY_CLASSES_ROOT\ALib.MyComponent]
@="ALib.MyComponent"

[HKEY_CLASSES_ROOT\ALib.MyComponent\CLSID]
@="{4F59B9B0-40ED-3CEE-B560-56CEECDB9F65}"

[HKEY_CLASSES_ROOT\CLSID\{4F59B9B0-40ED-3CEE-B560-56CEECDB9F65}]
@="ALib.MyComponent"

[HKEY_CLASSES_ROOT\CLSID\{4F59B9B0-40ED-3CEE-B560-56CEECDB9F65}\InprocServer32]
@="mscoree.dll"
"ThreadingModel"="Both"
"Class"="ALib.MyComponent"
"Assembly"="ALib, Version=1.0.0.0, Culture=neutral, PublicKeyToken=null"
"RuntimeVersion"="v1.1.4322"
...
```

The GUID created for class MyComponent is 4F59B9B0-40ED-3CEE-B560-56CEECDB9F65. Now let's modify the version number in the AssemblyInfo file from 1.0.0.0 to 1.0.0. 1 (changing only the revision number).

When you recompile and regenerate the registration, you will find the information shown in Example 8-10.

Example 8-10. Effect of change in version number on generated GUID

```
REGEDIT4

[HKEY_CLASSES_ROOT\ALib.MyComponent]
```

```
@="ALib.MyComponent"

[HKEY_CLASSES_ROOT\ALib.MyComponent\CLSID]
@="{D0190E9A-AD60-3EA2-B268-2C5D96507F21}"

[HKEY_CLASSES_ROOT\CLSID\{D0190E9A-AD60-3EA2-B268-2C5D96507F21}]
@="ALib.MyComponent"

[HKEY_CLASSES_ROOT\CLSID\{D0190E9A-AD60-3EA2-B268-2C5D96507F21}\InprocServer32]
@="mscoree.dll"
"ThreadingModel"="Both"
"Class"="ALib.MyComponent"
"Assembly"="ALib, Version=1.0.0.1, Culture=neutral, PublicKeyToken=null"
"RuntimeVersion"="v1.1.4322"
...
```

The GUID value is now D0190E9A-AD60-3EA2-B268-2C5D96507F21, which is different from the one generated earlier. This might not be desirable if you have changed only the revision number and still want existing COM clients to use this updated component, because they won't be able to. The intent of changing the revision number may be a minor bug fix, or a very small change. The disadvantage of generating the GUID automatically is that it becomes harder to manage the versioning of components. This problem can be easily avoided by providing the GUID attribute for classes you want to expose for COM interoperability, as shown in Example 8-11.

Example 8-11. Exposing .NET component using GUID attribute

✗ C# (ClassInterfaceType)

```csharp
using System;
using System.Runtime.InteropServices;

namespace ALib
{
    [Guid("53DEF193-D7A4-4ce3-938E-A7A35B5F7AB7"),
        ClassInterface(ClassInterfaceType.AutoDispatch)]
    public class MyComponent
    {
        public void Method1( )
        {
            //...
        }
    }
}
```

Example 8-11. Exposing .NET component using GUID attribute (continued)

```
Imports System.Runtime.InteropServices

<Guid("53DEF193-D7A4-4ce3-938E-A7A35B5F7AB7"), _
  ClassInterface(ClassInterfaceType.AutoDispatch)> _
Public Class MyComponent
    Public Sub Method1()
        '...
    End Sub
End Class
```

By default, all public classes are exposed for COM interoperability. You must set the COMVisible attribute on the class (or the assembly to affect all classes in it) to false if you don't want to expose the class(es).

 IN A NUTSHELL

Set the GUID attribute on your class if you intend to make it available for COM interoperability. To prevent COM access, use the COMVisible(false) attribute.

SEE ALSO

Gotcha #72, "All but one of the ClassInterface options are ineffective" and Gotcha #73, "Simply turning the switch for COM interop is dangerous."

GOTCHA

#72 All but one of the ClassInterface options are ineffective

COM clients interact with a component through its supported interfaces. There are three ways to expose a .NET class for COM interoperability. The options are specified through the ClassInterfaceType enumeration's values of AutoDispatch, AutoDual, and None. What is the consequence of choosing one option over another? Understand this to avoid some common mistakes in enabling COM interoperability for your .NET classes. In this gotcha I will discuss each of these approaches. First, consider using AutoDispatch, as shown in Example 8-12 (which is the same as Example 8-11 but has different lines highlighted).

Example 8-12. Exposing .NET component using AutoDispatch

```
using System;
using System.Runtime.InteropServices;
```

Example 8-12. Exposing .NET component using AutoDispatch (continued)

```
namespace ALib
{
    [Guid("53DEF193-D7A4-4ce3-938E-A7A35B5F7AB7"),
        ClassInterface(ClassInterfaceType.AutoDispatch)]
    public class MyComponent
    {
        public void Method1( )
        {
            //...
        }
    }
}
```

✗ VB.NET (ClassInterfaceType)

```
Imports System.Runtime.InteropServices

<Guid("53DEF193-D7A4-4ce3-938E-A7A35B5F7AB7"), _
  ClassInterface(ClassInterfaceType.AutoDispatch)> _
Public Class MyComponent
    Public Sub Method1( )
        '...
    End Sub
End Class
```

In this case, you have set the ClassInterface attribute on the class to ClassInterfaceType.AutoDispatch, which is the default value for that attribute. What is the consequence of this setting? What's exposed for the client is affected by this setting and is shown in Figure 8-15.

```
interface _MyComponent : IDispatch {}

coclass MyComponent
{
        [default] interface _MyComponent
}
```

Figure 8-15. Effect of ClassInterfaceType.AutoDispatch

The class implements only the IDispatch interface. The methods of the class are not exposed directly, so the only way for a client to access this component is using automation. While this is great for scripting clients and VB6 using automation, it is not desirable from the point of view of C++ clients and VB6 in early binding mode.

In the second approach, let's modify the code to use AutoDual as in Example 8-13. The change from AutoDispatch to AutoDual results in a change to what the client sees, as shown in Figure 8-16.

Example 8-13. Exposing .NET component using AutoDual

✗ C# (ClassInterfaceType)

```csharp
using System;
using System.Runtime.InteropServices;

namespace ALib
{
    [Guid("53DEF193-D7A4-4ce3-938E-A7A35B5F7AB7"),
        ClassInterface(ClassInterfaceType.AutoDual)]
    public class MyComponent
    {
        public void Method1()
        {
            //...
        }
    }
}
```

✗ VB.NET (ClassInterfaceType)

```vbnet
Imports System.Runtime.InteropServices

<Guid("53DEF193-D7A4-4ce3-938E-A7A35B5F7AB7"), _
  ClassInterface(ClassInterfaceType.AutoDual)> _
Public Class MyComponent
    Public Sub Method1()
        '...
    End Sub
End Class
```

There is good news and bad news. The good news is that you are exposing Method1( ) of the component for clients to use. This means that strongly typed languages such as C++ can use your component easily. However, in addition to Method1( ), methods of the Object base class are exposed. Second, remember that in COM, interfaces are immutable. Unfortunately, if you add methods, or just move them around, the interface generated will be different. This violates interface immutability, and forces client applications to be recompiled.

A third approach, and the most effective one, is to have the class expose no COM interface at all. Rather, it exposes .NET interfaces separately to COM clients. This is shown in Example 8-14.

```
        interface _MyComponent : IDispatch
        {
            //
            // Property data
            //

            __declspec(property(get=GetToString))
            _bstr_t ToString;

            //
            // Wrapper methods for error-handling
            //

            _bstr_t GetToString ( );
            VARIANT_BOOL Equals (
                const _variant_t & obj );
            long GetHashCode ( );
            _TypePtr GetType ( );
            HRESULT Method1 ( );

            //
            // Raw methods provided by interface
            //
            ...
        }

        coclass MyComponent
        {
                [default] interface _MyComponent
                interface _Object
        }
```

Figure 8-16. Effect of ClassInterfaceType.AutoDual

Example 8-14. The only option that works

✔ C# (ClassInterfaceType)

```
using System;
using System.Runtime.InteropServices;

namespace ALib
{
    [Guid("74555C62-75CD-4c87-940A-4AE8A69FFCB2"),
        InterfaceType(ComInterfaceType.InterfaceIsDual)]
    public interface IMy
    {
        void Method1( );
    }

    [Guid("53DEF193-D7A4-4ce3-938E-A7A35B5F7AB7"),
        ClassInterface(ClassInterfaceType.None)]
    public class MyComponent : IMy
    {
```

Example 8-14. The only option that works (continued)

```
        public void Method1( )
        {
            //...
        }
    }
}
```

✔ VB.NET (ClassInterfaceType)

```
Imports System.Runtime.InteropServices

<Guid("74555C62-75CD-4c87-940A-4AE8A69FFCB2"), _
  InterfaceType(ComInterfaceType.InterfaceIsDual)> _
Public Interface IMy
    Sub Method1( )
End Interface

<Guid("53DEF193-D7A4-4ce3-938E-A7A35B5F7AB7"), _
  ClassInterface(ClassInterfaceType.None)> _
Public Class MyComponent
    Implements IMy

    Public Sub Method1( ) Implements IMy.Method1

    End Sub
End Class
```

In this example, you have an interface IMy with Method1( ) that you intend to expose
to the client. For the IMy interface you have declared its InterfaceType attribute as
ComInterfaceType.InterfaceIsDual. This makes the methods of the interface available for both scripting and strongly typed clients. The class MyComponent implements
that interface. Furthermore, you have declared its ClassInterface attribute as
ClassInterfaceType.None. The types exposed to a COM client are shown in
Figure 8-17.

```
        interface _MyComponent : IDispatch
        {
            HRESULT Method1 ( );

        }

        coclass MyComponent
        {
                [default] interface _MyComponent
                interface _Object
        }
```

Figure 8-17. Effect of ClassInterfaceType.None

The use of `ClassInterfaceType.None` brings a .NET component back to how a real COM component should behave—it supports interfaces and does not expose anything to the client on its own. While there are three options to expose a .NET class for COM interoperability, only this last one is meaningful to use.

 IN A NUTSHELL

Set the `ClassInterface` attribute to `ClassInterfaceType.None` on .NET components you want to expose for COM interoperability; do not use the default. Expose the desired methods to the COM clients through a .NET interface by setting its `InterfaceType` attribute to `ComInterfaceType.InterfaceIsDual`.

SEE ALSO

Gotcha #71, "Auto-generating GUID for your classes leads to versioning woes" and Gotcha #73, "Simply turning the switch for COM interop is dangerous."

GOTCHA
#73 Simply turning the switch for COM interop is dangerous

Checking the project setting `Register for COM Interop` prepares your assembly for COM interoperability. When your code is compiled, Visual Studio invokes regasm to place the codebase entry details for the assembly into the Registry at `HKEY_CLASSES_ROOT\CLSID\...\InprocServer32`. When things are that easy, you probably wonder "what's the catch?" There are several things to ponder. First, consider some of the .NET capabilities that are not quite supported in COM, or must not be used with COM:

- COM doesn't support method overloading.
- COM doesn't handle static variables well.
- `CoCreateInstance( )` expects a no-parameter constructor.
- You may not intend to expose all of your public classes for COM interoperability (the `COMVisible` attribute affects this) .
- It is better to define a GUID for the classes you wish to expose.
- It is better to expose functionality through interfaces instead of classes.

Say you are working on your code one afternoon and someone walks in saying, "Hey I need to access this class through COM, can I?" You say "Sure, all I need to do is turn on the settings to register the assembly for COM interop." This will result in the COM clients talking to your assembly in the manner shown in Figure 8-18.

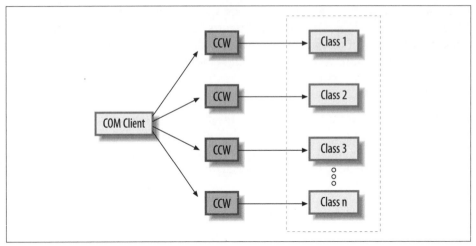

Figure 8-18. Improperly exposing an assembly for COM Interop

Ask the questions:

- Do you want every public class in your assembly to be visible for COM interop?
- Do you want to control which methods of your class are available for COM clients?
- Should you rethink what the COM client wants to do with your assembly?
- Should you provide a more coarsely grained object for COM clients to inter-act with? That is, should you provide one class with the functionality the COM client actually needs, rather than just exposing a number of your . NET classes?

Most likely, you wrote your assembly with .NET clients in mind. When you are approached with a request to expose your classes for COM interoperability, it may be better to write a separate façade assembly that the COM client will interact with, as shown in Figure 8-19.

You provide a wrapper or façade that takes requests from COM clients and routes them to one or more .NET classes. The wrapper classes do not expose any COM interfaces directly to the COM client; instead they implement .NET interfaces that are available and accessible to those clients (see Gotcha #72, "All but one of the ClassInterface options are ineffective").

Why should you do this? The wrapper or façade approach gives you a number of advantages:

- You can control what a COM client actually sees.
- You don't expose all public classes in your assembly.
- The façade is written with interoperability in mind and hence is more cohesive.

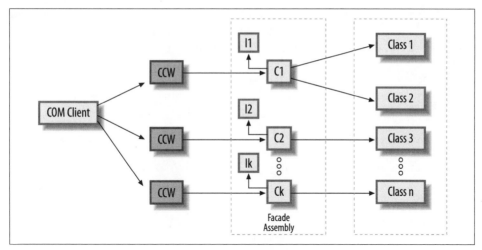

Figure 8-19. Exposing .NET components for COM interop using Wrappers

- It is easier to deal with changes from the COM client point of view.
- Over time, if applications that use COM are upgraded to use .NET, this is easier to manage—the wrapper simply goes away without affecting anything else.

 IN A NUTSHELL

Do not open up an assembly for arbitrary COM access. Instead provide a façade for the COM clients to interact through.

SEE ALSO

Gotcha #71, "Auto-generating GUID for your classes leads to versioning woes" and Gotcha #72, "All but one of the ClassInterface options are ineffective."

GOTCHA

#74 ServicedComponents implemented inconsistently on XP and 2003

Enterprise Services in .NET provide ServicedComponents, which give you COM+ features like object pooling, just-in-time activation, and transactions. I learned a few lessons when I ran into this gotcha. Enterprise Services don't behave the same on different versions of Windows. If you are using transactions and expect your application to run on Windows 2000, XP, and 2003, there are things that you need to be aware of.

Say you want to perform an operation on some objects, and when it completes you may decide to commit or abort the transaction. You would expect this to be pretty straightforward. Consider Examples 8-15 and 8-16.

Example 8-15. Using Transactions in Enterprise Services (C#)

✗ C# (ES)

```csharp
// Factory.cs part of ESLib.dll
using System;
using System.EnterpriseServices;

namespace ESLib
{
    [Transaction(TransactionOption.Required), JustInTimeActivation]
    public class Factory : ServicedComponent
    {
        public Comp CreateComp(int key)
        {
            ContextUtil.MyTransactionVote
                = TransactionVote.Abort;

            Comp theComp = new Comp( );
            theComp.init(key);

            ContextUtil.MyTransactionVote
                = TransactionVote.Commit;

            return theComp;
        }

        protected override void Dispose(bool disposing)
        {
            if (disposing)
            {
                ContextUtil.DeactivateOnReturn = true;
            }
            base.Dispose (disposing);
        }

    }
}


// Comp.cs part of ESLib.dll
using System;
using System.EnterpriseServices;

namespace ESLib
{
```

Example 8-15. Using Transactions in Enterprise Services (C#) (continued)

```csharp
[Transaction(TransactionOption.Required), JustInTimeActivation]
public class Comp : ServicedComponent
{
    private int theKey;
    private int theVal;

    internal void init(int key)
    {
        ContextUtil.MyTransactionVote
            = TransactionVote.Abort;

        theKey = key;
        theVal = key * 10;

        ContextUtil.MyTransactionVote
            = TransactionVote.Commit;
    }

    public int GetValue()
    {
        return theVal;
    }

    public void SetValue(int val)
    {
        ContextUtil.MyTransactionVote
            = TransactionVote.Abort;

        theVal = val;

        if (val < 0)
        {
            ContextUtil.DeactivateOnReturn = true;
            throw new ApplicationException(
                    "Invalid value");
        }

        ContextUtil.MyTransactionVote
            = TransactionVote.Commit;
    }
}
}


//Test.cs part of ESUser.exe
using System;
using ESLib;

namespace ESUser
```

Example 8-15. Using Transactions in Enterprise Services (C#) (continued)

```csharp
{
    class Test
    {
        public static void Work()
        {
            using(Factory theFactory = new Factory())
            {

                try
                {
                    Comp component1
                        = theFactory.CreateComp(1);
                    Comp component2
                        = theFactory.CreateComp(2);

                    Console.WriteLine(component1.GetValue());
                    Console.WriteLine(component2.GetValue());

                    component1.SetValue(1);
                    component2.SetValue(-1);

                    Console.WriteLine(component1.GetValue());
                    Console.WriteLine(component2.GetValue());
                }
                catch(Exception ex)
                {
                    Console.WriteLine("Oops: " + ex.Message);
                }
            } // theFactory is Disposed here.
        }

        public static void Main()
        {
            try
            {
                Work();
            }
            catch(Exception ex)
            {
                Console.WriteLine("Error:" + ex.Message);
            }
        }
    }
}
```

Example 8-16. Using Transactions in Enterprise Services (VB.NET)

✗ VB.NET (ES)

```vb.net
' Factory.vb part of ESLib.dll
Imports System.EnterpriseServices

<Transaction(TransactionOption.Required), JustInTimeActivation()> _
Public Class Factory
    Inherits ServicedComponent

    Public Function CreateComp(ByVal key As Integer) As Comp
        ContextUtil.MyTransactionVote = TransactionVote.Abort

        Dim theComp As New Comp

        theComp.init(key)

        ContextUtil.MyTransactionVote = TransactionVote.Commit

        Return theCOmp
    End Function
    Protected Overloads Overrides Sub Dispose( _
            ByVal disposing As Boolean)
        If disposing Then
            ContextUtil.DeactivateOnReturn = True
        End If

        MyBase.Dispose(disposing)
    End Sub
End Class


' Comp.vb part of ESLib.dll
Imports System.EnterpriseServices

<Transaction(TransactionOption.Required), JustInTimeActivation()> _
Public Class Comp
    Inherits ServicedComponent

    Private theKey As Integer
    Private theVal As Integer

    Friend Sub init(ByVal key As Integer)
        ContextUtil.MyTransactionVote = TransactionVote.Abort

        theKey = key
        theVal = key * 10

        ContextUtil.MyTransactionVote = TransactionVote.Commit
    End Sub
```

```
    Public Function GetValue( ) As Integer
        Return theVal
    End Function

    Public Sub SetValue(ByVal val As Integer)
        ContextUtil.MyTransactionVote = TransactionVote.Abort

        theVal = val

        If val < 0 Then
            ContextUtil.DeactivateOnReturn = True
            Throw New ApplicationException("Invalid value")
        End If

        ContextUtil.MyTransactionVote = TransactionVote.Commit
    End Sub
End Class


'Test.vb part of ESUser.exe
Imports ESLib

Module Test
    Public Sub Work( )
        Dim theFactory As New Factory

        Try
            Dim component1 As Comp = theFactory.CreateComp(1)
            Dim component2 As Comp = theFactory.CreateComp(2)

            Console.WriteLine(component1.GetValue( ))
            Console.WriteLine(component2.GetValue( ))

            component1.SetValue(1)
            component2.SetValue(-1)

            Console.WriteLine(component1.GetValue( ))
            Console.WriteLine(component2.GetValue( ))
        Catch ex As Exception
            Console.WriteLine("Oops: " + ex.Message)
        Finally
            theFactory.Dispose( )
        End Try
    End Sub

    Public Sub Main( )
        Try
            Work( )
        Catch ex As Exception
```

Example 8-16. Using Transactions in Enterprise Services (VB.NET) (continued)

```
                Console.WriteLine("Error:" + ex.Message)
            End Try
        End Sub
End Module
```

`Comp` is a `ServicedComponent` with one method, `Method1( )`. This method throws an exception if the parameter `val` is less than 0. Note that `Comp` has its `Transaction` attribute set as `TransactionOption.Required`. `Factory` is a `ServicedComponent` that is used to create objects of `Comp`. In the `Main( )` method of `Test`, you create two instances of `Comp` by calling the `CreateComp( )` method of the `Factory`. You then invoke `Method1( )` on the two instances. The exception that is thrown by the second call to `Method1( )` is displayed in the catch handler block.

When you execute the code on Windows Server 2003, it runs as you would expect and produces the result shown in Figure 8-20.

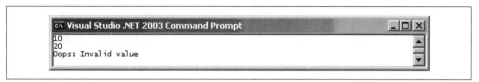

Figure 8-20. Output from Example 8-15 on Windows 2003 Server

But if you run the same code on Windows XP, you get the error shown in Figure 8-21.

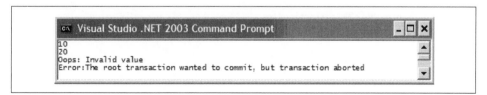

Figure 8-21. Output from Example 8-15 on Windows XP

The reason for this problem is that while one of the `Comp` components has voted to abort the transaction, the root object (the instance of the `Factory`) that created this object wants to commit it. Windows Server 2003 has no problem with that. But Windows XP does.

The solution is for the component `Comp` to tell the `Factory` that it is setting the transaction vote to `Abort`. The root object must then set its vote to `Abort` as well. This is not ideal because now the component needs to have a back pointer to the root object that created it. The code that does this is shown in Example 8-17 and Example 8-18. It uses an interface to break the cyclic dependency between the component and its factory.

Example 8-17. Communicating with the root object (C#)

```
// Factory.cs part of ESLib.dll
using System;
using System.EnterpriseServices;

namespace ESLib
{
    public interface ITransactionCoordinator
    {
        void SetVoteToAbort( );
    }

    [Transaction(TransactionOption.Required), JustInTimeActivation]
    public class Factory : ServicedComponent, ITransactionCoordinator
    {
        public Comp CreateComp(int key)
        {
            ContextUtil.MyTransactionVote
                = TransactionVote.Abort;

            Comp theComp = new Comp( );

            theComp.TheTransactionCoordinator = this;

            theComp.init(key);

            ContextUtil.MyTransactionVote
                = TransactionVote.Commit;

            return theComp;
        }

        protected override void Dispose(bool disposing)
        {
            if (disposing)
            {
                ContextUtil.DeactivateOnReturn = true;
            }
            base.Dispose (disposing);
        }

        #region ITransactionCoordinator Members

        public void SetVoteToAbort( )
        {
            ContextUtil.MyTransactionVote = TransactionVote.Abort;
        }
```

Example 8-17. Communicating with the root object (C#) (continued)

```
        #endregion
    }
}


// Comp.cs part of ESLib.dll
using System;
using System.EnterpriseServices;

namespace ESLib
{
    [Transaction(TransactionOption.Required), JustInTimeActivation]
    public class Comp : ServicedComponent
    {
        private int theKey;
        private int theVal;

        private ITransactionCoordinator theTXNCoordinator;

        internal ITransactionCoordinator TheTransactionCoordinator
        {
            get { return theTXNCoordinator; }
            set { theTXNCoordinator = value; }
        }

        internal void init(int key)
        {
            ContextUtil.MyTransactionVote
                = TransactionVote.Abort;

            theKey = key;
            theVal = key * 10;

            ContextUtil.MyTransactionVote
                = TransactionVote.Commit;
        }

        public int GetValue()
        {
            return theVal;
        }

        public void SetValue(int val)
        {
            ContextUtil.MyTransactionVote
                = TransactionVote.Abort;
```

Example 8-17. Communicating with the root object (C#) (continued)

```csharp
        theVal = val;

        if (val < 0)
        {
            ContextUtil.DeactivateOnReturn = true;
            if (theTXNCoordinator != null)
                theTXNCoordinator.SetVoteToAbort( );

            throw new ApplicationException(
                "Invalid value");
        }

        ContextUtil.MyTransactionVote
            = TransactionVote.Commit;
    }
  }
}
```

Example 8-18. Communicating with the root object (VB.NET)

✔ VB.NET (ES)

```vbnet
' Factory.vb part of ESLib.dll
Imports System.EnterpriseServices

Public Interface ITransactionCoordinator
    Sub SetVoteToAbort( )
End Interface

<Transaction(TransactionOption.Required), JustInTimeActivation( )> _
Public Class Factory
    Inherits ServicedComponent
    Implements ITransactionCoordinator

    Public Function CreateComp(ByVal key As Integer) As Comp
        ContextUtil.MyTransactionVote = TransactionVote.Abort

        Dim theComp As New Comp

        theComp.TheTransactionCoordinator = Me

        theCOmp.init(key)

        ContextUtil.MyTransactionVote = TransactionVote.Commit

        Return theCOmp
    End Function
```

Example 8-18. Communicating with the root object (VB.NET) (continued)

```
    Protected Overloads Overrides Sub Dispose( _
        ByVal disposing As Boolean)
        If disposing Then
            ContextUtil.DeactivateOnReturn = True
        End If

        MyBase.Dispose(disposing)
    End Sub

    Public Sub SetVoteToAbort( ) _
        Implements ITransactionCoordinator.SetVoteToAbort
        ContextUtil.MyTransactionVote( ) = TransactionVote.Abort
    End Sub
End Class


' Comp.vb part of ESLib.dll
Imports System.EnterpriseServices

<Transaction(TransactionOption.Required), JustInTimeActivation( )> _
Public Class Comp
    Inherits ServicedComponent

    Private theKey As Integer
    Private theVal As Integer

    Private theTXNCoordinator As ITransactionCoordinator

    Friend Property TheTransactionCoordinator( ) _
        As ITransactionCoordinator
        Get
            Return theTXNCoordinator
        End Get
        Set(ByVal Value As ITransactionCoordinator)
            theTXNCoordinator = Value
        End Set
    End Property

    Friend Sub init(ByVal key As Integer)
        ContextUtil.MyTransactionVote = TransactionVote.Abort

        theKey = key
        theVal = key * 10

        ContextUtil.MyTransactionVote = TransactionVote.Commit
    End Sub
```

Example 8-18. Communicating with the root object (VB.NET) (continued)

```
    Public Function GetValue() As Integer
        Return theVal
    End Function

    Public Sub SetValue(ByVal val As Integer)
        ContextUtil.MyTransactionVote = TransactionVote.Abort

        theVal = val

        If val < 0 Then
            ContextUtil.DeactivateOnReturn = True

            If Not theTXNCoordinator Is Nothing Then
                theTXNCoordinator.SetVoteToAbort()
            End If

            Throw New ApplicationException("Invalid value")
        End If

        ContextUtil.MyTransactionVote = TransactionVote.Commit
    End Sub
End Class
```

Note that `Method1()` informs the root object that it wants to abort the transaction. The root object then sets its transaction vote to `Abort`. After this modification, the program produces the same result on XP as on Windows Server 2003.

One moral from this story is to run unit tests not just on your machine but also on every supported platform. How practical is this? Well, it's not just practical, it's highly feasible with project automation and continuous integration tools like NAnt, NUnit and Cruise Control .NET.

 If you have hardware/cost limitations, you can use a product such as VirtualPC or VMWare to run these tests on different platforms on the same hardware.

 IN A NUTSHELL

ServicedComponents don't behave the same on all Windows platforms. Make sure you test early and often on all supported versions.

SEE ALSO

Gotcha #75, "AutoComplete comes with undesirable side effects ."

#75 AutoComplete comes with undesirable side effects

The AutoComplete attribute in Enterprise Services provides a very convenient way to communicate the intent to commit or abort a transaction. When a method marked with that attribute is invoked, the method automatically votes to commit the transaction if the method is successful. If the method fails, which is indicated by throwing an exception, the vote is automatically set to abort. This sounds pretty logical, so what's the concern? Let's examine the code in Example 8-19.

Example 8-19. Effect of AutoComplete

✗ C# (ESAutoComplete)

```
//MyComp.cs as part of ESLib.dll
using System;
using System.EnterpriseServices;

namespace ESLib
{
    [Transaction(TransactionOption.Required)]
    public class MyComp : ServicedComponent
    {
        private string theMessage = "UnSet";

        [AutoComplete]
        public void SetInfo(string msg)
        {
            theMessage = msg;
        }

        [AutoComplete]
        public string GetInfo( )
        {
            return theMessage;
        }
    }
}

//Test.cs as part of ESUser.exe
using System;
using ESLib;

namespace ESUser
{
    class Test
    {
        [STAThread]
```

Example 8-19. Effect of AutoComplete (continued)

```
        static void Main(string[] args)
        {
            MyComp theComp = new MyComp( );

            theComp.SetInfo("hello");

            Console.WriteLine(theComp.GetInfo( ));
        }
    }
}
```

✗ VB.NET (ESAutoComplete)

```
'MyComp.vb as part of ESLib.dll
Imports System.EnterpriseServices

<Transaction(TransactionOption.Required)> _
Public Class MyComp
    Inherits ServicedComponent

    Private theMessage As String = "UnSet"

    <AutoComplete( )> _
    Public Sub SetInfo(ByVal msg As String)
        theMessage = msg
    End Sub

    <AutoComplete( )> _
    Public Function GetInfo( ) As String
        Return theMessage
    End Function

End Class


'Test.vb as part of ESUser.exe

Imports ESLib

Module Test

    Sub Main( )
        Dim theComp As New MyComp

        theComp.SetInfo("hello")

        Console.WriteLine(theComp.GetInfo( ))
    End Sub

End Module
```

In this example, you create an instance of MyComp in the Main( ) method of the Test class. (The MyComp class stores a field named theMessage and initializes it to "UnSet.") You then call SetInfo( ) to set theMessage to "hello," then call GetInfo( ) to read it back. When the above code is executed you get the output shown in Figure 8-22.

Figure 8-22. Output from Example 8-19

What went wrong? Why didn't you get the expected result of "hello?"

The client is not dealing directly with the MyComp object, but with an invisible proxy. When the SetInfo( ) method is called, the method executes on the actual component. At the end of the method, due to the AutoComplete attribute, the transaction is committed by an internal call to SetComplete( ).

However, this call has a side effect. It not only sets the vote, it also sets the ContextUtil.DeactivateOnReturn property to true. As a result, the object is deactivated upon the return from the SetInfo( ) method. In other words, as soon as the method completes, the object is destroyed (kind of like working for the Mafia). When the GetInfo( ) method is invoked again using the proxy reference, another instance of the object is created automatically. theMessage is initialized to "UnSet" in this newer object, and that's what GetInfo( ) returns to you.

Let's consider the code changes in Example 8-20.

Example 8-20. Safely communicating intent to commit

✔ C# (ESAutoComplete)

```
//MyComp.cs as part of ESLib.dll
using System;
using System.EnterpriseServices;

namespace ESLib
{
    [Transaction(TransactionOption.Required)]
    public class MyComp : ServicedComponent
    {
        private string theMessage = "UnSet";

        //[AutoComplete]
        public void SetInfo(string msg)
        {
            ContextUtil.MyTransactionVote
                = TransactionVote.Abort;
```

Example 8-20. Safely communicating intent to commit (continued)

```
            theMessage = msg;

            // If something is wrong, throw exception
            // and the vote will remain in Abort.

            ContextUtil.MyTransactionVote
                = TransactionVote.Commit;
        }

        //[AutoComplete]
        public string GetInfo( )
        {
            ContextUtil.MyTransactionVote
                = TransactionVote.Abort;

            // If something is wrong, throw exception
            // and the vote will remain in Abort.

            ContextUtil.MyTransactionVote
                = TransactionVote.Commit;

            return theMessage;
        }
    }
}
```

✔ VB.NET (ESAutoComplete)

```
'MyComp.vb as part of ESLib.dll
Imports System.EnterpriseServices

<Transaction(TransactionOption.Required)> _
Public Class MyComp
    Inherits ServicedComponent

    Private theMessage As String = "UnSet"

    '<AutoComplete( )> _
    Public Sub SetInfo(ByVal msg As String)
        ContextUtil.MyTransactionVote _
            = TransactionVote.Abort

        theMessage = msg

        ' If something is wrong, throw exception
        ' and the vote will remain in Abort.

        ContextUtil.MyTransactionVote _
            = TransactionVote.Commit
    End Sub
```

Example 8-20. Safely communicating intent to commit (continued)

```
'<AutoComplete( )> _
Public Function GetInfo( ) As String
    ContextUtil.MyTransactionVote _
        = TransactionVote.Abort

    ' If something is wrong, throw exception
    ' and the vote will remain in Abort.

    ContextUtil.MyTransactionVote _
        = TransactionVote.Commit

    Return theMessage
End Function
```

```
End Class
```

In the methods of the component, you first set the transaction vote to Abort. If the method is successful, you change the vote to Commit. If the method is not successful, you throw an exception, leaving the transaction vote as Abort. You do not use the AutoComplete attribute on the methods. The advantage of this is that the object is not automatically deactivated without your explicit intent. The output after the above code change is shown in Figure 8-23.

Figure 8-23. Output after code change in Example 8-20

The AutoComplete attribute comes with a side effect. Understand its impact on an object's lifetime. It is better to explicitly set the transaction vote to Abort or Commit, rather than using the AutoComplete attribute. Use AutoComplete only if you really want the object to be discarded when the method completes.

 IN A NUTSHELL

Instead of using the AutoComplete attribute, directly set the transaction vote in your code. Avoid the side effect of AutoComplete that automatically deactivates the component.

SEE ALSO

Gotcha #74, "ServicedComponents implemented inconsistently on XP and 2003."

Resources

Bibliography

[Albahari02]   Ben Albahari, Peter Drayton, and Brad Merrill. *C# Essentials*, Second Edition. O'Reilly Media, Inc. , Sebastopol, CA, 2002.

[Ballinger03]   Keith Ballinger. *.NET Web Services : Architecture and Implementation.* Addison-Wesley, Boston, MA, 2003.

[Beck03]   Kent Beck. *Test-Driven Development : By Example.* Addison-Wesley, Boston, MA, 2003.

[Bloch01]   Joshua Bloch. *Effective Java : Programming Language Guide.* Addison-Wesley, Boston, MA, 2001.

[Box98]   Don Box, *Essential COM.* Addison-Wesley, Reading, MA, 1998.

[Box03]   Don Box with Chris Sells. *Essential .NET : The Common Language Runtime.* Addison-Wesley, Boston, MA, 2003.

[Cline99]   Marshall Cline, Greg Lomow, and Mike Girou. *C++ FAQs*, Second Edition. Addison-Wesley, Reading, MA, 1999.

[Drayton03] Peter Drayton, Ben Albahari, and Ted Neward. *C# in a Nutshell : A Desktop Quick Reference*, Second Edition. O'Reilly Media, Inc. , Sebastopol, CA, 2003.

[Evjen04]   Bill Evjen, et al., *Professional VB.NET 2003*, Third Edition. Wiley Pub., Indianapolis, IN, 2004.

[Ferrara02] Alex Ferrara and Matthew MacDonald. *Programming .NET Web Services.* O'Reilly Media, Inc. , Sebastopol, CA, 2002.

[Freeman04] Elisabeth Freeman. *Head First Design Patterns.* O'Reilly Media, Inc. , Sebastopol, CA, 2004.

[Gamma95]   Erich Gamma, et al. *Design Patterns : Elements of Reusable Object-Oriented Software.* Addison-Wesley, Reading, MA, 1995.

[Griffiths03]   Ian Griffiths and Matthew Adams. *.NET Windows Forms in a Nutshell.* O'Reilly Media, Inc. , Sebastopol, CA, 2003.

[Hamilton03]   J.P. Hamilton. *Object-Oriented Programming with Visual Basic .NET.* O'Reilly Media, Inc. , Sebastopol, CA, 2003.

[Hamilton04]   Bill Hamilton. *NUnit Pocket Reference.* O'Reilly Media, Inc. , Sebastopol, CA, 2004.

[Hunt00]   Andrew Hunt and David Thomas. *The Pragmatic Programmer : From Journeyman to Master.* Addison-Wesley, Reading, MA, 2000.

[Hunt03]   Andrew Hunt and David Thomas. *Pragmatic Unit Testing in C# with NUnit.* The Pragmatic Programmers, LLC, Raleigh, NC, 2003.

[Jeffries04]   Ron Jeffries. *Extreme Programming Adventures in C#.* Microsoft Press, Redmond, WA, 2004.

[Lea00]	Doug Lea. *Concurrent Programming in Java : Design Principles and Patterns*, Second Edition. Addison-Wesley, Reading, MA, 2000.
[Lowy03]	Juval Löwy. *Programming .NET components.* O'Reilly Media, Inc. , Sebastopol, CA, 2003.
[Martin03]	Robert C Martin. *Agile Software Development : Principles, Patterns, and Practices.* Pearson Education, Upper Saddle River, NJ, 2003.
[Meyers96]	Scott Meyers. *More Effective C++ : 35 New Ways to Improve Your Programs and Designs.* Addison-Wesley, Reading, MA, 1996.
[Meyers98]	Scott Meyers. *Effective C++ : 50 Specific Ways to Improve Your Programs and Designs*, Second Edition. Addison-Wesley, Reading, MA, 1998.
[Newkirk04]	James W. Newkirk and Alexei A. Vorontsov. *Test-Driven Development in Microsoft .NET.* Microsoft Press, Redmond, WA, 2004.
[Robinson04]	Simon Robinson, et al. *Professional C# (Programmer to Programmer)*, Third Edition. Wiley Pub., Indianapolis, IN, 2004.
[Stroustrup00]	Bjarne Stroustrup. *The C++ Programming Language*, Special Edition. Addison-Wesley, Reading, MA, 2000.
[Thai03]	Thuan Thai and Hoang Q. Lam. *.NET Framework Essentials.* O'Reilly Media, Inc. , Sebastopol, CA, 2003.

On the Web

Agile Developer

http://www.agiledeveloper.com/download.aspx. Here you'll find articles and discussions related to .NET and software development by Venkat Subramaniam.

CLR Profiler - Managed Code Performance Tool

http://www.gotdotnet.com/team/clr/about_clr_performance.aspx. In addition to the CLR Profiler tool, at this URL you will find articles and discussions related to performance of managed code.

Common Object Operations

http://www.developer.com/open/article.php/989091. This is Jeffrey Richter's article on how to properly implement the operations that all objects must exhibit. It talks about object equality, identity, hash codes, and cloning.

Cruise Control .NET

http://www.sourceforge.net/projects/ccnet. Cruise Control .NET is an open source automated continuous integration tool for Microsoft .NET. It uses tools such as NUnit and NAnt, and integrates with your source control system (e.g., CVS and Visual Source Safe) to automatically build and test your code as it is checked into the source control system.

C# FAQs

http://blogs.msdn.com/csharpfaq. This is a site where you can ask and get answers to many C# Frequently Asked Questions.

C# Language Specification

http://msdn.microsoft.com/library/en-us/csspec/html/CSharpSpecStart.asp. This site contains the actual C# Language Specification.

Design Guidelines for Class Library Developers

http://msdn.microsoft.com/library/en-us/cpgenref/html/cpconNETFrameworkDesignGuidelines.asp.

This site presents design guidelines for developing class libraries and components using the .NET framework.

Don't Lock Type Objects!

http://msdn.microsoft.com/archive/en-us/dnaraskdr/html/askgui06032003.asp. An article that discusses why locking the type metadata is a bad idea.

Draco.NET

http://draconet.sourceforge.net. Like Cruise Control .NET, Draco.NET is an easy to use Windows service application for continuous integration.

ECMA-CLI

http://www.ecma-international.org/publications/files/ECMA-ST/Ecma-335.pdf. Common Language Infrastructure (CLI)—Partitions I to V (Standard ECMA-335 2nd). Here you will find definitions and details on CLI, CLS, and CTS.

Equals vs. ==

http://blogs.msdn.com/csharpfaq/archive/2004/03/29/102224.aspx. Article titled "When should I use == and when should I use Equals?" discusses issues with the Equals( ) method and the == operator.

Exploring the Singleton Design Pattern

http://msdn.microsoft.com/library/default.asp?url=/library/en-us/dnbda/html/singletondespatt.asp. This article by Mark Townsend discusses the Singleton Design Pattern and its effective use in .NET.

FxCop

http://www.gotdotnet.com/team/fxcop. FxCop is a code analysis tool that checks .NET code for conformance to the Microsoft .NET Framework Design Guidelines.

Garbage Collection

http://msdn.microsoft.com/msdnmag/issues/1100/GCI/default.aspx. Jeffrey Richter's article titled "Garbage Collection: Automatic Memory Management in the Microsoft .NET Framework" presents in great detail the garbage collection heuristics in the .NET CLR.

Groups @ Google

http://groups.google.com. This is a great resource to search for just about any information you need. Most of the time you'll find answers here to what you are looking for. At other times, you can take comfort that others are having similar pain.

Gotdotnet

http://www.gotdotnet.com. This .NET framework community web site has resources, articles, and discussions on various topics related to .NET.

Hashcode

http://www.interact-sw.co.uk/iangblog/2004/06/21/gethashcode. In this article, titled "The Rules for GetHashCode," Ian Griffiths talks about the surprises of hash codes.

Implementing Finalize and Dispose to Clean Up Unmanaged Resources

http://msdn.microsoft.com/library/default.asp?url=/library/en-us/cpgenref/html/cpconFinalizeDispose.asp. Here you'll find Microsoft's description of the Dispose Design Pattern.

Implementing the Singleton Pattern in C#

http://www.yoda.arachsys.com/csharp/singleton.html. This interesting article delves deep into the issues with Singleton thread-safety.

Languages Available in .NET

http://www.gotdotnet.com/team/lang. This site has an up-to-date list of the available languages.

MSDN

http://msdn.microsoft.com. Here you can search and access online documentation and articles related to Microsoft products in general.

MSDN Magazine

http://msdn.microsoft.com/msdnmag. *MSDN Magazine* has a wealth of information. Here you will find several articles that are of interest to any .NET programmer.

NAnt

http://sourceforge.net/projects/nant. NAnt is an open source Ant-like build tool for .NET. This tool helps you automate the build of your code and exercise your unit tests.

NDoc

http://sourceforge.net/projects/ndoc. NDoc is a nice tool that allows you to generate HTML and MSDN like documentation. It uses reflection and XML comments in your code.

NUnit

http://sourceforge.net/projects/nunit. NUnit is an open source unit testing tool for Microsoft .NET. Even though this originated from JUnit (Java unit testing tool), it has been written in C# and uses a number of .NET features. It can test your .NET application, regardless of the .NET language used.

PInvoke.net

http://www.pinvoke.net. Avoid the trial-and-error approach to figuring out the VB.NET and C# managed code mapping to Win32 and other APIs; This site allows you to find, edit, and add C# and VB.NET PInvoke signatures.

Reflector

http://www.aisto.com/roeder/dotnet. Reflector is a class browser for .NET that allows you to view of your code and all its relationships.

ReleaseComObject( ) Issues

http://blogs.msdn.com/yvesdolc/archive/2004/04/17/115379.aspx. This is a short blog entry, titled "Discussion of Marshal.ReleaseComObject and its dangers," which talks about the problems with `ReleaseComObject( )`.

http://samgentile.com/blog/archive/2003/04/17/5797.aspx. This is a blog titled "ReleaseCOMObject revisited."

Test Driven Development

http://www.agiledeveloper.com/articles/TDDPartI.pdf. A hands-on tutorial on Test Driven Development (TDD) using NUnit.

Unexpected Errors in Managed Applications

http://msdn.microsoft.com/msdnmag/issues/04/06/NET. This is an article titled "Unexpected Errors in Managed Applications" by Jason Clark.

VB FAQs

http://blogs.msdn.com/vbfaq. This is a site where you can ask and get answers to many VB.NET frequently asked questions.

VS.NET Tips and Tricks

http://www.agiledeveloper.com/articles/VSDOTNETCodeEditingTipsAndTricks.pdf. This article shows 25 tricks in Visual Studio to improve your productivity.

Index

About the Author

Venkat Subramaniam is the founder of Agile Developer, Inc. and has been working with .NET since its pre-release Beta 2. He has used it extensively on commercial projects for his clients and has offered several courses on developing applications using .NET. He has trained and mentored more than 3,000 software developers in the United States and Europe. He speaks frequently at software development conferences. He is also an adjunct professor for the practice of computer science at University of Houston and teaches at Rice University's School for Continuing Studies. He holds a B.S. in computer engineering, an M.S. in electrical engineering and a Ph.D. in computer science. He is the recipient of the 2004 UH Computer Science Department Teaching Excellence award.

Colophon

Our look is the result of reader comments, our own experimentation, and feedback from distribution channels. Distinctive covers complement our distinctive approach to technical topics, breathing personality and life into potentially dry subjects.

The animal on the cover of *.NET Gotchas* is a hammerhead shark. This shark has a wide, thick head, which resembles a hammer. The hammerhead can grow up to 11.5 feet long and weighs as much as 500 pounds. It is usually brownish-gray in color, with an off-white underbelly. The unique shape of this shark's head offers increased bouyancy, which helps the hammerhead swim more effectively. The rounded shape also enhances the shark's vision; its eyes are placed nearly three feet apart apart and offer an extremely wide view.

Hammerheads swim in schools and are found throughout the oceans of the world. They prefer warm tropical waters, however, especially those with a high concentration of food—fish, stingrays, other sharks, squid, octopus, and crustaceans. They are also known to eat their own young, and, on occasion, humans. A highly developed sensor system makes hammerheads extremely effective predators because they can easily detect the weak electrical fields generated by all animals.

Philip Dangler was the production editor and proofreader, and Derek Di Matteo was the copyeditor for *.NET Gotchas*. Mary Anne Weeks Mayo and Claire Cloutier provided quality control. Julie Hawks wrote the index.

Ellie Volckhausen designed the cover of this book, based on a series design by Edie Freedman. The cover image is a 19th-century engraving from the Dover Pictorial Archive. Karen Montgomery produced the cover layout with Adobe InDesign CS using Adobe's ITC Garamond font.

Marcia Friedman designed the interior layout, based on a series design by David Futato. This book was converted by Andrew Savikas to FrameMaker 5.5.6 with a format conversion tool created by Erik Ray, Jason McIntosh, Neil Walls, and Mike Sierra that uses Perl and XML technologies. The text font is Linotype Birka; the heading fonts are Helvetica Neue and Adobe Myriad Condensed; and the code font is LucasFont's TheSans Mono Condensed. The illustrations that appear in the book were produced by Robert Romano, Jessamyn Read, and Lesley Borash using Macromedia FreeHand MX and Adobe Photoshop CS. The tip and warning icons were drawn by Christopher Bing. This colophon was written by Philip Dangler.

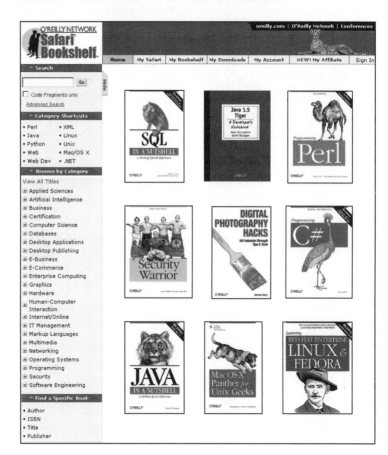

Related Titles Available from O'Reilly

.NET

.NET and XML

.NET Compact Framework Pocket Guide

.NET Framework Essentials, *3rd Edition*

.NET Windows Forms in a Nutshell

ADO.NET in a Nutshell

ADO.NET Cookbook

C# Essentials, *2nd Edition*

C# Cookbook

C# Language Pocket Guide

Learning C#

Learning Visual Basic.NET

Mastering Visual Studio.NET

Mono: A Developer's Notebook

Object Oriented Programming with Visual Basic .NET

Programming .NET Components

Programming .NET Security

Programming .NET Web Services

Programming ASP.NET, *2nd Edition*

Programming C#, *3rd Edition*

Programming Visual Basic .NET, *2nd Edition*

VB.NET Core Classes in a Nutshell

VB.NET Language in a Nutshell, *2nd Edition*

VB.NET Language Pocket Reference

Keep in touch with O'Reilly

1. Download examples from our books

To find example files for a book, go to:

www.oreilly.com/catalog

select the book, and follow the "Examples" link.

2. Register your O'Reilly books

Register your book at *register.oreilly.com*

Why register your books?
Once you've registered your O'Reilly books you can:

- Win O'Reilly books, T-shirts or discount coupons in our monthly drawing.
- Get special offers available only to registered O'Reilly customers.
- Get catalogs announcing new books (US and UK only).
- Get email notification of new editions of the O'Reilly books you own.

3. Join our email lists

Sign up to get topic-specific email announcements of new books and conferences, special offers, and O'Reilly Network technology newsletters at:

elists.oreilly.com

It's easy to customize your free elists subscription so you'll get exactly the O'Reilly news you want.

4. Get the latest news, tips, and tools

www.oreilly.com

- "Top 100 Sites on the Web"—PC Magazine
- CIO Magazine's Web Business 50 Awards

Our web site contains a library of comprehensive product information (including book excerpts and tables of contents), downloadable software, background articles, interviews with technology leaders, links to relevant sites, book cover art, and more.

5. Work for O'Reilly

Check out our web site for current employment opportunities:

jobs.oreilly.com

6. Contact us

O'Reilly & Associates
1005 Gravenstein Hwy North
Sebastopol, CA 95472 USA

TEL: 707-827-7000 or 800-998-9938
(6am to 5pm PST)

FAX: 707-829-0104

order@oreilly.com
For answers to problems regarding your order or our products. To place a book order online, visit:

www.oreilly.com/order_new

catalog@oreilly.com
To request a copy of our latest catalog.

booktech@oreilly.com
For book content technical questions or corrections.

corporate@oreilly.com
For educational, library, government, and corporate sales.

proposals@oreilly.com
To submit new book proposals to our editors and product managers.

international@oreilly.com
For information about our international distributors or translation queries. For a list of our distributors outside of North America check out:

international.oreilly.com/distributors.html

adoption@oreilly.com
For information about academic use of O'Reilly books, visit:

academic.oreilly.com

O'REILLY®

Our books are available at most retail and online bookstores.
To order direct: 1-800-998-9938 • *order@oreilly.com* • *www.oreilly.com*
Online editions of most O'Reilly titles are available by subscription at *safari.oreilly.com*